The euro

The euro

Edited by

Paul Temperton

The Independent Economic Research Company, UK

JOHN WILEY & SONS

Chichester • New York • Weinheim • Brisbane • Singapore • Toronto

Published by
John Wiley & Sons Ltd.
Baffins Lane, Chichester
West Sussex PO19 1UD, England

National 01243 779777
International (+44) 1243 779777
E-mail (for orders and customer service enquiries): cs-books@wiley.co.uk
Visit our home page on http://www.wiley.co.uk, or http://www.wiley.com

Other Wiley Editorial Offices
John Wiley & Sons, Inc. 605 Third Avenue,
New York, NY 10158-0012, USA

WILEY-VCH Verlag GmbH, Pappelallee 3
D-69469 Weinheim, Germany

John Wiley & Sons (Asia) Pte Ltd, 2 Clementi Loop #02-01,
Jin Xing Distripark, Singapore 0512

John Wiley & Sons (Canada) Lt, 22 Worcester Road,
Rexdale, Ontario M9W IL1, Canada

British Library Cataloguing in Publication Data

A catalogue record for this book is available from the British Library

ISBN 0-471-97955-4

Designed and typeset by Nick Battley, London
Cartoons by Peter Bugh
Printed and Bound in Great Britain by Biddles Ltd., Guildford and Kings Lynn
This book is printed on acid-free paper responsibly manufactured from sustainable forestation, for which at least two trees are planted for each one used for paper production.

Contents

III: INSTITUTIONAL AND LEGAL ISSUES

IV: THE FOREIGN EXCHANGE MARKET

 **Foreword**

John C. Corrigan

Chairman
EFFAS-European Bond Commission
National Treasury Management Agency

The full extent of the profound impact of the planned introduction of the euro on European financial markets continues to be the subject of intense debate. Many questions remain as to the precise consequences for banking, asset management, bond, equity and currency markets. In promoting the publication of this book the European Bond Commission of the European Federation of Financial Analysts' Societies (EFFAS) seeks to answer many of these questions or at least raise the debate to a more informed level.

EFFAS is a pan-European federation of some seventeen national societies of investment analysts and securities managers with over ten thousand members. The Federation's bond expert group—The EFFAS European Bond Commission—has a successful track record in providing information and sponsoring debate on the development of financial markets, notably through its publication programme. The Bond Commission's book *The European Bond Markets*, which recently had its sixth edition published, is widely acknowledged by market participants as one of the most authoritative guides to the bond markets across Europe. An earlier publication, *The European Currency Crisis*, dealt with the dark days of 1992/93 when it appeared to many that the plans for the single currency had been wrecked. It is fitting, therefore, that Paul Temperton, who was the editor of that book and who has been a steadfast supporter of the single currency project, should now be the editor of *The euro*.

In *The euro*, Paul has once again succeeded in assembling in one publication the views of authoritative commentators who focus clearly on the issues involved. I have no doubt that the book will make a signal contribution to the single currency process. Thanks are due to Paul for his enthusiasm and tireless energy, to my colleagues on the European Bond Commission for their support in promoting this project and last, but by no means least, to Nick Battley for his patient technical assistance.

J.C.C.

Dublin, September 1997

Preface

Paul Temperton

(Editor)

The Independent Economic Research Company (TIER)

As this book goes to print in September 1997, financial markets have never exhibited more optimism over the prospect of the euro arriving on schedule in January 1999. But that optimism is a recent phenomenon. The period from the summer of 1992 up until the start of 1996 saw a series of crises and marked volatility in Europe's currency, bond and equity markets. Confidence in the European Monetary Union (EMU) project was, throughout that period, at a low ebb. It would be unwise to view the tranquillity of the markets in the more recent past as an indication that the final run-up to the launch of the euro will be without problems. Expectations in financial markets themselves can change quickly and certainly renewed currency volatility could endanger the euro project. But the biggest problem that remains is that many issues surrounding the euro's introduction are still not clearly understood. This book is an attempt to shed light on these issues.

There are two clear impressions which can be drawn from the contributions to the book.

First, the practical issues surrounding the euro's introduction are well on the way to resolution. Legal uncertainties have been resolved; there is growing agreement on how to manage the changeover in bond markets; retailers are beginning to prepare for the switchover; the European Monetary Institute's work in preparing for the launch of the European Central Bank is on schedule; designs for notes and coin have been agreed; and so on.

Second, the euro's introduction is a story of short-term costs with longer-term benefits. Many *countries* have suffered as the fiscal tightening which has been necessary to prepare for the euro has slowed their recovery from recession. This has been especially painful during 1997. But the longer-term benefits of the introduction of the euro seem easily to outweigh these costs (as is demonstrated in Chapter 5). *Financial companies* are starting to experience the costs involved in introducing the euro. Job losses in dealing rooms have occurred as companies realize that fewer foreign exchange and bond market staff will be needed in the single currency environment. But the eventual benefit should be a larger, more transparent and efficient European financial market that will rival that of the United

States. Other *firms* are starting to experience the costs of management time involved in the planning process, investment in new systems, staff training, and so on. But again the prize will be a deeper and more firmly based single market; greater economies of scale; and more efficient use of resources.

There are dissenting views and it is right and proper to include them in this book. In particular, Tim Congdon discusses 'why the euro will fail' in Chapter 9.

However, the largest part of the book is taken up with a discussion of the economic and financial market implications of the euro. I hope that it will be a timely and useful contribution to general understanding of the subject.

P.T.

Buckinghamshire, September 1997

Section

I

The background to the euro

Paul Temperton
The Independent Economic Research Company (TIER)

Chapter
1

Introduction

The planned launch of the euro in January 1999 is, without doubt, one of the most significant events in the economic and political development of Europe. But, with little more than a year to go to that launch there are still may questions surrounding that new currency. In early 1998 the most crucial question will be : Which countries will be in the 'first wave' of those replacing their national currencies with the euro? Indeed, we could still be asking whether the launch will be delayed? And at the same time some of the more fundamental issues surrounding the new currency will continue to be raised. What are the benefits of using the euro? Why will it be better than sticking with national currencies? Will the benefits of the euro outweigh the costs? Will the euro be a strong currency? Can it really be an effective replacement for the Deutschemark? Could there be another financial market upheaval similar to the ERM crises of 1992 to 1993? And, if so, would this wreck the entire project?

These are just some of the frequently asked questions about Europe's new currency which we aim to answer in this book.

The first section of the book sets out the background to the euro, with the three chapters adopting a progressively shorter historical perspective. In Chapter 2, Graham Bishop describes how the 'march to euroland' is the culmination of developments over the course of the last fifty years, with the seeds of the current project being sown as early as 1946 by Winston Churchill. But it is important to remember that it is only a few years ago that recurrent ERM crises rocked Europe's financial stability. Indeed, the memory of this period is still acute in the minds of many policy makers. An example of how a country has successfully managed the transition from the 1992-1993 ERM crisis to being successfully prepared for EMU is given by Alfons Verplaetse, governor of the National Bank of Belgium in Chapter 3. Expectations about whether the euro will be launched on time and which countries will take place in EMU and form the 'euro area' have changed quite extensively since that crisis. As recently as early 1996, for example, financial markets thought it highly unlikely that Italy would be one of the initial members of EMU. Now, financial markets put a 60 per cent probability on Italy joining. Indeed, as discussed by Avinash Persaud in Chapter 4, financial markets have never exhibited more optimism over the prospect of a broad based EMU arriving on schedule than they do today.

Perspectives from different countries form the substance of the second section of the book. Crucially, we discuss the costs and benefits of the euro for Germany (Chapter 5). The story is one of short-term pain (particularly in the form of fiscal tightening) for longer-term gain. The gain eventually more than outweighs the cost, but it is significant that mid-1997—the period of greatest angst about the entire euro project—was the time at which the costs of preparation were at their greatest. Nevertheless, if this economic cost-benefit analysis is anywhere near correct, Chancellor Kohl is completely justified in forcing through the EMU project in the face of what has been, at times, tremendous opposition (see Figure 1.1).

A STRIDE TOWARDS MONETARY UNION

Figure 1.1

A slightly broader perspective on the costs and benefits of the euro is given from a UK perspective in Chapter 6. Ironically, the UK will probably satisfy the convergence conditions for joining the first wave of countries moving to EMU, but is unlikely to do so. In contrast, Italy and Spain are both extremely keen to join but further structural reform will be needed in both countries for EMU membership to be sustainable. Spain seems to be ahead of Italy in this respect, but as is noted by Federico Prades in Chapter 8, much more needs to be done in Spain after EMU goes ahead. For both Spain and Italy, a major concern is how well they will manage—assuming they are members of the euro area—once the ability to devalue their

The pattern of interest rates in Europe...

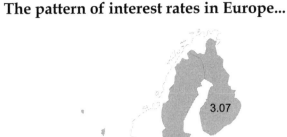

Figure 1.2   **Three-month interest rates, June 1997**

currencies is removed. As Mike Young points out in Chapter 16 this ability has been the key to generating economic growth and equity market returns in the early 1990s – without it Spanish and Italian equity markets can be expected to perform less well than the 'core' (particularly Germany).

A peculiar feature of the pattern of interest rates in the run-up to the euro's launch is that although there is a significant degree of convergence between long-term interest rates in likely euro area countries that is not the case for short-term rates. This pattern will change as soon as the euro is launched, when short-term interest rates in all of the euro area countries will be identical, being set by the European Central Bank (see Figures 1.2 and 1.3). There is still concern about whether the ECB will be an effective replacement for the Bundesbank, an issue is discussed in Chapter 10. Equally, there are also some remaining legal issues (see Chapter 11).

When the euro is launched it will be in financial markets that its impact is first felt and sections four and five deal, in turn, with the foreign exchange and capital market impacts.

...will change radically when the euro is launched

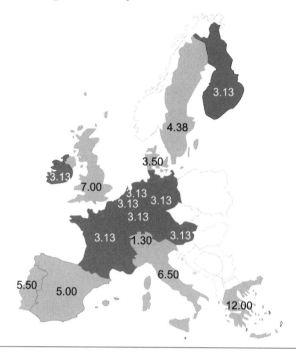

Figure 1.3   **Three-month interest rates after the euro is launched***

assuming Germany, France, Austria, Belgium, Netherlands, Luxembourg, Ireland and Finland are the initial countries joining the euro area, using TIER forecasts

Three aspects of the foreign exchange market are considered. First, the thorny issue of fixing the conversion rates between national currencies and the euro (Chapter 12). Second, the issue of whether the euro will be a strong or weak currency in the foreign exchange market (Chapter 13); and the impact which the euro will have on central European countries (Chapter 14).

Bond and equity market implications are discussed in Chapters 15 and 16.

Although it will be in the capital markets that the euro's impact is first felt, the period between 1999 and 2002 will see growing preparations for the euro's use by businesses and the consumer. Chapter 17 deals with the implications for accounting and Chapter 18 the impact on the consumer.

Various legal texts concerning the euro are included as Appendices.

Chapter 2

Graham Bishop
*Salomon Brothers
International Limited*[1]

The march to euroland

In less than 350 business days, Europe's financial markets will finish their long march and arrive in euroland. For analytical purposes, the purpose and mechanics of that long march can be split into four parts:

- European politics and EMU: A 50-year march
- Momentum towards the euro: Maas To Amsterdam
- Preparations: detail and vision
- The euro markets: possible investment characteristics

European politics and EMU: A 50-year march

There is no doubt that the case for monetary union should stand alone on economic grounds, and must do so. But there is a powerful political context. If the economists could prove that EMU will not work on economic grounds, then they would have a power of veto. Though some of them have tried, they have failed. Tremendous difficulties lie ahead, because the conversion to a single currency is an operation of unparalleled administrative magnitude. There has been nothing like it at all in the world before, so we should not underestimate the scale.

Political vision

This author was honoured to speak in Zurich on 19th September 1996. That was the fiftieth anniversary of Winston Churchill's speech which launched the drive after World War II towards a united Europe. It is worth quoting some extracts from Churchill's speech to give a flavour of why Europe is where it is today:

---

[1]
The views expressed are the author's own and not necessarily shared by Salomon Brothers International Ltd., or any of its affiliates.

'I am now going to say something which will astonish you. The first step in the re-creation of the European family must be a partnership between France and Germany.'

'In all this urgent work, France and Germany must take the lead together'

'Great Britain, the British Commonwealth of Nations, mighty America and, I trust, Soviet Russia must be friends and sponsors of the new Europe'.

That speech was the starting point for the European Union and was given just a year after the end of the Second World War. But, even at the beginning, when Churchill was setting out how he saw Europe developing, there was a different, separate path for Britain and its Empire. Britain has yet to bridge that initial divide.

The Single European Act

Preamble:
'....to continue the work .... and to transform relations as a whole among their States into a European Union'

Article 1:
'The European Communities ... shall have as their objective ... making concrete progress towards European unity'.

Figure 2.1

No-one who reads the Single European Act and sees these statements (see Figure 2.1) about European Union, and progress towards European Unity can be in any real doubt as to what was intended by those who signed and ratified these Treaties. The relevant part, in relation to the single currency and the financial markets, is encapsulated within the famous 'Four Freedoms'; the free movement of goods, persons, services and capital. The last two are the key to why a single currency now has an air of inevitability.

The EU already has a substantial degree of financial market integration, which is happening for very powerful reasons quite apart from EMU. This single financial market reflects global market trends — technology-based communications and computing power, which are part of global 'cyber society' rather than the politics of European Union.

Consider some of the implications:

- Payments for rising trade: the single market was intended to remove the barriers for goods. It succeeded. The Customs Union succeeded first and the single market is on the way to its natural result: A barrier-free market right across Europe. This needs payments systems across borders, because the goods have to be paid for.

- Retirement savings: the populations of Europe are getting older. Increasingly, European citizens are obliged to save for themselves, because of the inadequacy of public pension systems. Some of that money is going to go abroad.

- When it does go abroad, some of the savers will put their money into Government bonds to fund deficits. If they fund a particular government's deficit but subsequently become concerned about their investment, then they will take their money home again, creating a huge crisis.

For example, on Black Wednesday in September 1992, the game was up for the UK because those who managed these retirement savings — the major pension funds and life assurance companies — realized the existing economic policy would not work. They started to send some of their money, a small proportion, abroad. But a small proportion of those savings was a very large sum. Once some of the foreigners wanted to take their money home, the Bank of England's reserves were run out.

That type of problem is likely to recur. Where there is a build up of liquid savings and a foreign diversification by investors who subsequently become nervous, then such flows will happen again because the market systems exist, and they are unlikely to be abolished. This is likely to result in unstable capital flows so unless there is a single currency there may continue to be intermittent, but major, crises. Either Europe will go forward to a single currency or, in today's world, there will be crises regularly punctuating our tranquillity. Eventually, the EU would go back to controls because there is not a stable situation in the middle. The post-war political

Evolving to a common structure

	Full yield curve	Repo market	Futures	Swaps	Deposit futures
Austria	✓	✓	✓	✓	-
Belgium	✓	✓	thin	✓	thin
Denmark	✓	✓	thin	✓	thin
Ecu	✓	✓	thin	✓	✓
Finland	✓	✓	thin	✓	✓
France	✓	✓	✓	✓	✓
Germany	✓	✓	✓	✓	✓
Greece	-	-	--	-	-
Ireland	✓	unofficial	thin	thin	-
Italy	✓	✓	✓	✓	✓
Netherlands	✓	✓	thin	✓	-
Portugal	✓	✓	soon	✓	-
Spain	✓	✓	✓	✓	thin
Sweden	✓	✓	✓	✓	✓
UK	✓	✓	✓	✓	✓

Figure 2.2   Financial market structure

drive has created the Single Market, with its technological and financial systems – but the movement is incomplete, and the system is not yet in equilibrium.

Markets have evolved to a common structure in the last decade. All have most of the attributes of a modern capital market: a full yield curve, repos, futures and swaps. These components can be welded rapidly into a single capital market once the final component – the single currency – exists.

Birth of the euro – A 15-year gestation

1988	Hanover Summit appoints Delors Committee
1989	Delors report accepted
1990	IGC starts
1991	IGC concludes: Maastricht Treaty signed
1993	Maastricht ratified
1995	Commission's Green Paper
	EMI Report
	Madrid Summit sets conversion timetable
1998	Spring: decide EMU entrants
1999	Lock exchange rates
	Convert financial markets
2002	Euro is single currency

Figure 2.3

Momentum towards the euro: Maas to Amsterdam

The political drive unleashed 50 years ago has already taken us a long way. Is EMU something which was just dreamt up at Maastricht and will go away again? The answer has to be 'No'. The fifteen-year gestation does not account for the preceding events. When the Treaty of Rome was written, they did not need to discuss a single currency because the Bretton Woods system of fixed exchange rates already existed. Bretton Woods came to an end in 1972, but Europe still yearned for currency stability. So the Hanover Summit in 1988 appointed Jacques Delors to produce a report. The Delors Committee Report was actually a report on 'How should we do it?', not 'whether it should be done'. But, rather than ask the question 'Do we want to do it?', it was obvious to the heads of government, or at least to those on the Continent that the answer was 'Accept the Report' and write a treaty to implement it.

This is really a very short space of time for such a profound change in the affairs of nations. For financial markets the process may seem interminable but, in the historical scale, it is very quick. The build-up of momentum is striking: The Commission's Committee of Independent Experts – the Maas Committee – met in Brussels in February 1995, and held 'Hearings'. A large number of questionnaires were sent out to all sorts of banks, industries, associations for the blind, vending machine manufacturers, retailers — anyone who had an interest in the single currency and how to convert to it. Many people turned up in Brussels to comment and it was striking that few had any idea of how they were going to do it. This was only two years ago; with four years to go to the event — the biggest practical event in post-war economic history and no-one had any idea how they were going to do it.

However, the momentum had begun. The Maas Committee Report was an input to the Commission's Green Paper in the summer of 1995. Many institutions, banks, representative organizations etc. suddenly realized that the politicians meant to do it. The Commission sent out its Green Paper and asked for comments. There was a huge response. As a result, at the Cannes Summit the Heads of Governments decided that they would agree on the timetable in December 1995 in Madrid. The Madrid Summit set the conversion timetable and the momentum began to build.

The recent Summit of the EU Heads of Government in Amsterdam made further good progress on key building blocks for EMU, even if the Treaty agreed at the same time lacked the bold vision necessary for enlarging the EU.

- ERM II was formally enacted, and that will represent a helping hand to those states that wish to accept it, prior to entry into EMU later.

- The Stability and Growth Pact was finally agreed. This was a key political step, because the prospect of an EMU member allowing its finances to deteriorate to the point where it needs to be bailed out is grave. Such a bail-out would be unacceptable to the people of Europe and therefore would have catastrophic political consequences.

- A key weakness in the Stability Pact is that it makes no provision for a framework to ensure that the financial markets remain stable if severe penalties have to be imposed on a State.

- The Legal Framework for the euro was accepted.

The EMI fulfilled its goal of preparing the blueprint for the European Central Bank and published that in January 1997. Many people will be very surprised to find that the political preparations for EMU are virtually complete now. The driving forces have upped the momentum another notch.

The detail and the vision

The detail

The process is under way. In the Spring of '98 the heads of government will decide which states are 'in'. At the beginning of '99, exchange rates will be locked and the financial markets converted. This statement often comes as a great shock to many people: in less than 350 London business days, much of the activity on City trading floors will be denominated in euros. Is everyone prepared for that? The honest answer can only be that the process is 'just starting'.

Financial and commercial companies are now thinking about—though hardly preparing for—the conversion. A flood of paper is being created, even in the City. Despite the uncertainty about UK membership, this thinking process is accelerating and the Bank of England is 'encouraging' the wholesale markets to be totally ready via a series of working parties and the introduction of its excellent Quarterly *Practical Issues Arising from the Introduction of the Euro*.[1]

Many professional associations have put forward their views, after intensive discussions, and the European Commission recently published a consultation document—the 'Giovannini Report' on the steps necessary to create the framework for a standardized euro capital market.

The vision

As Figure 2.4 shows, the EU population is significantly bigger than the United States, even before enlargement takes place. The GDP and foreign trade data indicates the financial and economic scale of the EU relative to the trading partners.

However, investors are aware of public debt and, as a percentage of GDP, that started at about 35 per cent of GDP at the onset of the oil crisis and has virtually doubled during the intervening 20 years. The cost of servicing that debt—the simplest credit test—is the proportion of income that goes on interest payments. That has tripled over these two decades. The credit markets are aware of this build up of debt and are beginning to price it in. There is a perceived risk.

Interestingly, while public debt has risen dramatically the unemployment rate has multiplied by five. Unemployment has moved

---

1
  Contact Bank of England Public Enquiries Group on 0171 601 4878

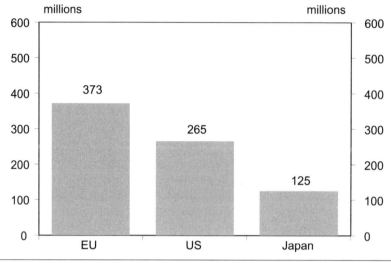

Figure 2.4   **Population**

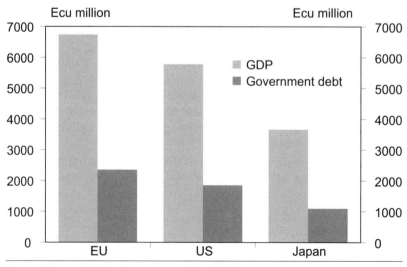

Figure 2.5   **GDP and government 'bond' debt**

almost in lockstep with public debt (see Figure 2.6) so perhaps the Treaty
of Amsterdam's Employment Chapter is finally sending the right message:
Unemployment will be reduced by creating a skilled and adaptable labour
force – not increased public debt.

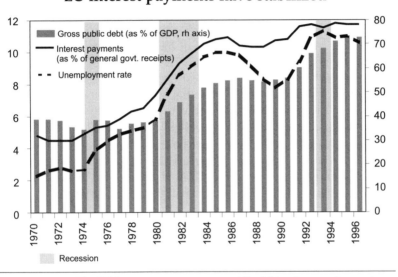

EU interest payments have stabilized

Figure 2.6   The EU: interest expense, gross public debt and unemployment

Can the EU use its economic clout to turn these huge public liabilities
into a benefit and make a virtue out of necessity? Implicitly, the
Community is aiming to maximize capital inflows and, bearing in mind
that the Community will be the largest capital market, the largest foreign
trader etc., then the chances of the euro becoming a world 'reserve
currency' should be quite high. Therefore attracting inflows – as well as
reducing outflows from the Community – should be one way of benefiting,
by minimizing interest costs.

What policies should be undertaken to achieve this objective? In its own
interest, the public sector has already moved significantly. For example,
the French Treasury states its debt management objectives: Improve
liquidity with simplicity and transparency, subject to achieving minimum
borrowing costs in the long term, but balancing prudence with interest
costs.

Stimulating private credit innovations may not be a direct objective of
public policy makers but they may not be indifferent to the possibilities.

Once there are public benchmarks – that base of highly liquid government bonds – then items such as asset-backed securities can be regarded as layered on top. Those assets could be mortgages, residential or commercial, or credit cards from banks, retailers or manufacturers. Corporate bonds and higher yielding bonds from other countries can be considered and that could include Eastern and Central Europe – with the candidate members of the Community borrowing in this market.

All these innovations will offer somewhat higher yields – a hierarchy of yields above the public sector benchmarks. Investors will be looking to replace the currency games they may have played and may well be attracted to such innovations. They may be only prepared to put a modest proportion of their assets into such securities but, considering the scale of assets, sizeable sums could flow into the bonds of, for example, Central and Eastern European countries. That would be a private sector voluntary financing of the next building block of the European political vision.

The relative scale of the future euro market is readily apparent but the immediate feature is the much larger number of issues compared to the US. The average issue size of the US is 11 billion Ecu, whereas for the Europeans it is 5.5 billion Ecu – or one half the size (see Figure 2.7).

EU bond market: larger than the US or Japan

	EU	US	Japan
Market value (Ecu billions)	2353	1854	1096
Issues	425	171	147
Average issue size	5.5	10.8	7.5

Figure 2.7   Central government 'bond' debt
'Bond' = fixed rate, over 1-year life, constituent of World Government Bond Index as at July 97

This is a key issue affecting the liquidity sought by investors. From the perspective of a market-maker, the size of the issue is the basis of liquidity. Time and again this is where Europe loses out in relative liquidity, showing a large number of issues and therefore a small average size.

If the euro-bond market is to be a competitor for the US Treasury market, what issue size are investors looking for?. The euro market needs issues of 10 or 11 billion Ecu at the long end or 15 billion Ecu at the short end to match US Treasury issues on-the-run. With benchmark bonds of that scale in Europe then, in the fullness of time, they should be seen by global investors as directly comparable to the liquidity offered by the US Treasury market—if all the other conditions are in place. What are the chances of achieving that?

Figure 2.8 shows the maturities that will happen in each year after monetary union for each of the member states which are in the Salomon Brothers' Index. It is evident that, of the major issuers (Germany and France), there are enough bonds maturing in each year to produce easily benchmarks which would compete directly with the Treasury market. A number of EU countries could do the same. It is clear from the chart that if Europe as a whole were to think about its collective good it would be possible to produce benchmark yield curves from quite a few countries. If there were single issues for each year—or perhaps, even two or three in a year. It seems conceivable that globally liquid benchmarks *could* be created. This would be to the collective good of Euroland, but it does not solve all

Large amount of debt to be redeemed between 1999 and 2005

Maturity year	1999	2000	2001	2002	2003	2004	2005
Belgium	13	15	14	10	11	16	8
Denmark	10	11	9	4	11	13	2
Germany	60	64	66	72	61	37	32
Spain	18	17	14	21	16	6	8
France	37	37	39	31	35	39	38
Ireland	3	2	3	-	2	2	-
Italy	73	38	45	39	27	26	22
Netherlands	17	19	19	15	11	16	17
Austria	7	8	6	8	4	4	4
Portugal	3	3	1	1	2	1	2
Finland	6	-	8	-	-	10	-
Sweden	12	12	12	5	16	-	11
UK	23	29	28	22	18	19	29

Figure 2.8   **Central government 'bond' maturities**
Note: Maturities are in billions of Ecu

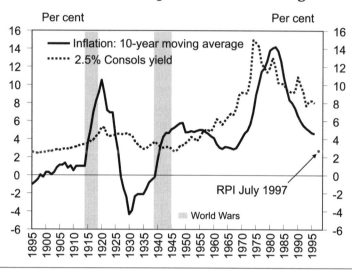

Figure 2.9   A century of UK inflation expectations

the problems, because the issuers will be in competition with each other to minimize spreads. It must be recognized that the competition will always be there but the first task is to get the lowest possible 'benchmark yield' level. The remaining question is how the credit spread above that is minimized.

The logical conclusion is straightforward:

- Redenominate the entire stock of tradable public debt into euro at the earliest moment. Several states have already committed to do that.

- Issue all new tradable debt in euro. That was a specific agreement by the heads of government at Madrid in December 1995.

- While undertaking the redenomination, use the opportunity to offer investors the chance to transform their holdings into new global-scale, and therefore highly liquid, bonds. Though everyone wishes it were smaller, the existing size of Italy's debt, paradoxically, offers Italy the chance to be at the forefront of this new market.

- Review the technical functioning of each market to ensure that it is consistent with the European standards that have emerged from the detailed work done in the last few months (see comments above).

With these steps, the bonds of EU governments that participate in EMU should command the lowest interest rates in the world consistent with Europe's economic fundamentals on the usual questions of inflation, public finance etc.

The euro markets: possible investment characteristics

The future euro markets will be different in nature to today's markets. Two features are worth highlighting:

If the ECB succeeds in maintaining the price stability that Europe seems to have within its grasp today, then long term interest rates may well be under 5 per cent. The history of the UK long-term interest rates — which mirrors that of the US and, say, the Netherlands — demonstrates that this would bring those rates back to the 'normal level' seen before the 1960s..

The no bail-out rule is embedded in the Treaty of Maastricht (as Article 104b). It may have enormous significance though hopefully it will never be tested. If it is tested, investors will need to be aware of credit risk in the euro bonds issued by European governments in a way that has not been known since our grandparents went off the Gold Standard after the First World War. Profound implications flow from that new credit risk.

Chapter
3

Alfons Verplaetse
Governor, National Bank of Belgium

From currency crisis
to single currency

In this chapter we look at the way in which one country — Belgium — has prepared to become a member of the euro area. It acts as a case study of how a currency which was unable to avoid the intense pressures of the ERM crisis of 1993 has, however, successfully prepared for the euro.

Belgium was well on the way to establishing currency stability against the Deutschemark before the currency crises in the ERM in 1992 and 1993. This reflected a long tradition of currency stability in Belgium — after the break up of the Bretton Woods system Belgium joined the snake and was a founder member of the EMS. This currency stability has been important given the very open nature of the Belgian economy. And currency stability against the Deutschemark has been an important element in ensuring the maintenance of low inflation. It is in the area of public finances that Belgium has had the greatest difficulties in preparing for the euro. But the country started to tackle the problems at an early stage and is now confident of being one of the first wave of countries to move to EMU.

Developments in the years to 1992

Belgium has a long history of exchange rate stability...

The Belgian monetary authorities always considered that, in a small, open economy, setting a target exchange rate was the best way of achieving price stability. Thus, Belgium has never opted for a system of flexible exchange rates. Immediately after the collapse of the Bretton Woods fixed exchange rate system, the Belgian franc joined the 'monetary snake'. It subsequently the became integrated into the EMS exchange rate mechanism at its inception. Apart from the determination to play an active part in the construction of Europe, this choice was based on:

- the small size of the Belgian economy;

- its very open character;
- the general use of mechanisms for index-linking incomes.

These features mean that any depreciation in the franc is liable to push up the cost of imports and start an inflationary spiral.

Despite this general approach, the Belgian economy's adverse reaction to oil shocks meant that the government had to devalue the franc by 8.5 per cent in 1982 and, at the same time, it adopted a series of measures intended to limit the inflationary effects of the devaluation and safeguard the thus restored competitiveness of businesses. Since then, however, the objective in terms of exchange rates as formulated at the time of general realignments of the central rates in the EMS had been gradually reinforced: from maintaining the stable franc in relation to the average of partner country currencies, it turned increasingly towards a stable rate against the Deutschemark. In June 1990, the government confirmed this development, made possible by the good performance of the Belgian economy in terms of external accounts and inflation, by the public decision to link the franc to the Deutschemark. This decision comprised two commitments: first, not to alter the rate of the franc against the mark in the event of a general EMS realignment; and second, to ensure that the fluctuation margins of the franc against the mark were narrower than the ± 2.25 per cent applicable at that time in the EMS. With competitiveness restored by the 1982 devaluation and subsequently safeguarded, this objective was attained without difficulty until 1992, so that Belgium more than satisfied the exchange rate stability criteria of the Maastricht Treaty.

..and of low inflation...

This stability in the Belgian franc exchange rate was accompanied by greater convergence in the EU countries in terms of inflation, with Belgium producing a highly satisfactory performance. The Belgian inflation rate has always been among the lowest in the European Union. Even the devaluation of the Belgian franc in 1982 had only a modest impact of inflation, and that was rapidly absorbed. By 1992, the inflation rate of 2.4 per cent was well below the EU average (4.3 per cent) and the convergence criterion threshold (4 per cent).

Finally, in consequence of these trends in exchange rates and inflation, Belgium had gained a favourable position in the process of interest rate convergence. In 1992, long-term interest rates in Belgium were 8.7 per cent, which was well below both the EU average (9.6 per cent) and the convergence criterion threshold (10.7 per cent).

Thus, as regards these three criteria, right from the start of the formal convergence process Belgium was among the leaders comprising Germany, France, Denmark, Ireland and the Benelux countries.

...but has had less favourable public sector developments

On the other hand, Belgium's position was far less favourable as regards public finances: in 1992 the public deficit and the public debt stood at 6.9 and 129 per cent of GDP respectively, which not only exceeded the reference values set by the convergence criteria (3 per cent and 60 per cent) but were also higher than the European average (5.1 per cent and 60 per cent).

Belgiums's public finances

	1981	1988	1992	1993	1994	1995	1996	1997e
Net balance	-12.7	-6.8	-6.9	-7.1	-4.9	-3.9	-3.2	-2.8
Structural balance	*-12.3*	*-6.8*	*-8.3*	*-6.4*	*-4.5*	*-3.5*	*-2.5*	*-2.3*
Primary balance	-4.9	+3.1	+3.8	+3.6	+5.1	+5.1	+5.3	+5.2
Gross debt	91	129	129	135	133	131	127	125

Figure 3.1
Sources: National Accounts Institute, European Commission

At first sight, this performance looks mediocre, but it must be seen in context. First, by 1992, the level of the public deficit had fallen well below the record figures of the early eighties: in 1981 it had peaked at nearly 13 per cent, practically double the 1992 figure. The subsequent improvement had been achieved by a large-scale policy of rehabilitating public finances, implemented in a particularly difficult context, namely that of the 'snowball effect' produced by the burden of interest on the public debt. On the other hand, the deficit of the EU countries as a whole had hardly diminished at all in relation to the 1981 level. Second, this rehabilitation had allowed a large surplus to emerge on the primary balance i.e. excluding interest charges: from a primary deficit of 5.1 per cent in 1981, to a surplus of 3.8 per cent in 1992 (one of the highest figures in the European Union). This situation favoured the subsequent rapid process of budgetary consolidation. Third, public debt, which had continued to grow extremely fast up to 1988, in spite of the reduction in the total deficit, began to stabilize.

Thus, well before the Treaty of Maastricht, Belgium had begun a vigorous process of budgetary rehabilitation, which meant that in some respects it was better placed than other countries to carry on the process.

Policies implemented from 1992 to 1996 to achieve convergence

As long ago as 1992, the government introduced the convergence programme to formalize the medium-term goal of meeting the Maastricht criteria. The plan set annual targets which would progressively reduce the deficit to 3 per cent of GDP in 1996. It also introduced three general norms that, given reasonable macroeconomic assumptions, would ensure the 1996 target was achieved: the social security system must be in equilibrium, tax revenue must increase with nominal GDP, and primary expenditure of the federal authorities must not increase in real terms.

These various norms have been broadly respected and the medium-term fiscal goal has been largely achieved, despite a sharp deterioration of the economic situation in 1992/1993 and a less pronounced one in 1996. However, to offset the negative impact on the budget of macroeconomic conditions and keep the deficit reduction on track, the government had to introduce unexpectedly difficult packages of corrective measures. The budget savings achieved by the packages included new direct and indirect taxes and employee's social contributions, cuts in primary expenditure and various savings resulting for better debt management and improved tax collection.

Belgium withstood the 1992 ERM crisis

Throughout the period in question, the monetary policy objective remained as before: a stable exchange rate between the Belgian franc and the German mark. Belgium's determination to maintain a close link between the two currencies was nevertheless severely tested during various periods of turbulence in the EMS exchange rate mechanism.

Developments in the first eight months of 1992 were very similar to those in the previous two years. By small interest rate adjustments, the monetary authorities generated a net outflow of short-term funds broadly matching the typical current account surplus and the net inflow of long term capital. Short-term interest rates were quite stable, and the differential *vis-à-vis* Germany, which had uninterruptedly narrowed since the mid-eighties, became negative. The Belgian franc remained in the upper half of the EMS narrow band, and slightly above its German mark central rate, without needing outright intervention.

The situation changed drastically during the first stage of the EMS crisis which started in September 1992 and continued virtually to the end of the year. In contrast to the episodes of foreign exchange unrest of the eighties, the Belgian franc was never seriously threatened during the period, but on the contrary, together with the German mark and the Dutch guilder, served as refuge currency. This is evidenced by the radical shifts which took place in the balance of payments of the BLEU: a very substantial net demand for francs developed on the foreign exchange markets, chiefly owing to a dramatic reversal in short-term capital flows. In this market conditions, it would probably have required sizeable interest rate changes to affect capital flows, and the monetary authorities considered that a major, unilateral cut in rates could have jeopardized the credibility of its hard currency policy. During this period, the exchange rate for the Belgian franc against the German mark remained unchanged, and interest rates declined markedly, but remained broadly in line with German rates, contrary to the experience of most other ERM currencies. Hence, the purpose of the Bank's interventions in the foreign exchange market was to support other currencies. Part of the foreign exchange acquired were used to repay public debt denominated in foreign currencies, in order to avoid disrupting of monetary conditions and hampering monetary policy.

...but strains emerged in 1993

In the first half of 1993, conditions were similar to what they had been before the crisis, with short-term capital outflows again producing overall balance of payments equilibrium. There were two short spells of downward pressure on the Belgian franc in early February and late March, when uncertain domestic political situation and cashing in of government bonds by foreign investors combined with the normal closure of positions in Belgian francs opened in previous months. In both episodes, the prompt increase in official interest rates was however very effective and the National Bank was able to reverse quickly this movement. While German interest rates halted their decline for most of the spring, rates continued to fall in Belgium and short-term differentials became negative again.

Major strains reappeared in July, and this time pressure to sell included the Belgian franc. Through a combination of rate increases and modest intervention in foreign exchange markets, the National Bank was nevertheless able to maintain the close link between its currency and the German mark until nearly the end of the month.

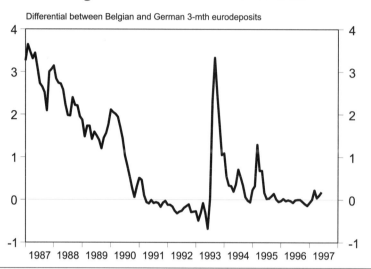

Figure 3.2

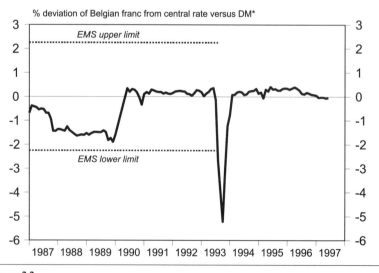

Figure 3.3
* On 2 August 1993, the bands were widened to +/- 15 per cent; only the 'old' limits are shown

Pressure to sell the Belgian franc intensified after the loosening of the ERM at the beginning of August 1993. The commitment to a firm exchange rate link with the fundamentally strongest currencies of this mechanism was then reasserted, but the widening of the fluctuation margins did necessitate greater flexibility in the actual conduct of foreign exchange policy. This tactical adjustment combined with the readiness of the National Bank to raise interest rates whenever required by foreign exchange market conditions has worked well.

After a temporary dip in the second half of 1993 to around 6.5 per cent below its central rate *vis-à-vis* the German mark the Belgian franc recovered as rapidly as it had weakened, and by the end of January 1994 was back at its par value with this currency. Several factors contributed to this sharp reversal in international capital flows and the Belgian franc's position on exchange markets. The vigorous increase in short-term rates by the National Bank in the summer of 1993 underlined the authorities' total determination to maintain the close link with the German mark, in accordance with the official line. Later, the global plan with its emphasis on fiscal consolidation and safeguarding international competitiveness greatly increased the credibility, especially in the international financial centres, of the economic policy pursued by Belgium. Restoration of confidence in the Belgian franc was then consolidated by the large and growing current account surplus, the improvement in the economic situation and progress in reducing the public sector deficit. Moreover, as the pressure eased, the monetary authorities cut money market rates, but only gradually and without jeopardizing the newfound strength of the Belgian franc. The central rate fell back to the level of the Bundesbank 'repo' rate in May 1994, and then declined in line with it until July. At the end of 1994, as short-term differentials with Germany became negative, the National Bank reduced domestic liquidity to reverse this tendency.

The Belgian franc and interest differentials with Germany remained relatively stable early in early 1995. At the beginning of March, however, after the depreciation of the Spanish peseta and the Portuguese escudo within the ERM, the franc came under some pressure, prompting the National Bank to raise interest rates and tighten liquidity conditions. This was quickly followed by an easing, which led to the disappearance of the interest rate differential towards the middle of the year.

The period since mid-1995 has been rather uneventful, with a reduction in the volatility of key monetary variables. The National Bank has repeatedly reduced its interest rates, generally in line with the Bundesbank, but occasionally ahead of it in view of the strength of the Belgian franc in foreign exchange markets. Money market rates have thus remained very close to German rates, falling by 134 basis points from June 1995 to June 1997.

With money rates as low as German rates, and sometimes slightly lower, the National Bank has relied on intervention in foreign exchange markets to curb the appreciation of the Belgian franc *vis-à-vis* the Deutschemark. To prevent these purchases from unduly affecting domestic liquidity, they were almost fully sterilized through the repayment of Belgian public debt denominated in foreign currencies and by swaps between the National Bank and commercial banks.

Current situation and prospects

So far, Belgium has certainly satisfied the criterion regarding exchange rate stability set out in the Maastricht Treaty. The same applies to the criterion of stable prices. At the end of 1996, inflation in Belgium had fallen to 2.1 per cent, which was well below the reference value used to measure fulfilment of this criterion.

As we saw at the start of this chapter, the durability of the convergence achieved by Belgium is also reflected in the level of its long-term interest rates. These are also well below the reference value used for checking whether a member state meets the convergence criterion on interest rates.

Since the adoption of the initial convergence programme in 1992, Belgium has continuously maintained the degree of convergence required by the treaty as regards stable prices, stable exchange rates and the convergence of long-term interest rates. It is accepted that this highly favourable situation can be sustained throughout 1997, which will form the basis for the joint report on convergence to be drawn up by the EMI and the Commission. Belgium's sustained performance in this matter reflects important structural factors, which include the credibility of the monetary policy applied by the National Bank but also the importance accorded by the authorities to safeguarding the competitiveness of the Belgian economy, in particular by pursuing a policy of wage moderation and budgetary rehabilitation.

In this last respect Belgium still did not comply fully with the Treaty criteria in 1996. The net deficit came to 3.2 per cent of GDP, or just over the set limit. However, when evaluating this figure it is necessary to take account both of developments since the start of the formal convergence process and of the situation in other European countries. Thus, Belgium's public deficit has been cut by some 4 points of GDP, i.e. over half in relation to the 1992 figure, while the corresponding reduction in the EU as a whole has been very small, namely 0.7 points of GDP. At 3.2 per cent, Belgium's deficit was lower than the figure for the EU as a whole in 1996, which stood at 4.3 per cent, while the opposite applied in 1992. Finally, if we take account of the effect of macroeconomic activity on the budget, i.e. if we exclude cyclical influences, the improvement has been even more marked and the 'structural' Belgian deficit can be estimated at around 2.5 per cent of GDP in 1996.

As for the gross public debt, this was 127.4 per cent of GDP or 1.5 lower than in 1992, but here, too, the situation must be seen in context. First, its evolution was far more favourable than that of other UE countries, whose debt rose from 60 to 73 per cent of GDP over the same period. Next, the situation was strongly influenced by the sharp recession in 1993; if we take that year for comparison, the public debt has fallen by some 8 points of GDP in Belgium while increasing by the same extent in EU countries as a whole. Finally, the level of the primary government surplus, which at 5.3 per cent is by far the largest of any EU country, meant that the reverse snowball effect which resumed since 1993 can continue and accelerate.

The budgetary rehabilitation will continue subsequently so that Belgium will be among the first to qualify for EMU and then to comply with the stability pact.

Thus, on the basis of realistic assumptions regarding growth and inflation, the spending cuts and increased revenue incorporated in the 1997 budget will make it possible to reduce the public deficit to 2.8 per cent of GDP this year, fully satisfying the Treaty criteria. According to forecasts made by the European Commission in April 1997, the deficit should actually fall even lower. The public debt will drop to some 125 per cent of GDP, or nearby 10 percentage points lower than in 1993, which will certainly represent a reduction in the public debt which is 'sufficient and approaching the reference value at a satisfactory pace'. In the medium term, i.e. from 1998 to 2000, the Belgian authorities have expressed in their new convergence programme their intention to maintain a large primary surplus which will make it possible to reduce the overall deficit to 1.4 per cent of GDP in 2000, accelerating the automatic reduction in the ratio of the debt to GDP. After 2000, the Superior Finance Council has proposed a long-term scenario to reduce the ratio of debt to GDP on the assumption of a nominal growth of GDP of 4.3 per cent per annum and stabilization of the effective rate of interest on the public debt at its current level. It also assumes that the primary surplus will be maintained until the overall deficit is cut to zero, and that it will subsequently be reduced in line with interest payments in order to maintain the equilibrium of the overall budget while satisfying part of the demand for additional public spending associated with the ageing population. In this scenario, the ratio of the debt to GDP will be around 60 per cent in about twenty years' time.

Belgium's membership of European monetary union will be the culmination of policies which have long been steadfastly pursued by the Belgian authorities. The goals which they set themselves well before the Treaty of Maastricht was signed were both ambitious and precisely formulated: the budget was to achieve a permanent reversal of the snowball effect, notably on the basis of a high and growing primary surplus; for monetary and foreign exchange policy, the goal was to link the Belgian franc closely to the Deutschemark. This policy mix, which was incidentally recommended by the Treaty, was also highly consistent and able to generate considerable synergy: exchange rate stability made it possible to reduce the interest rate differential of the Belgian franc and thereby ease the interest burden borne by the government, and budgetary rehabilitation contributed to the credibility of the monetary and foreign exchange policy. Finally, during the crucial period from 1992 to 1996, these policies were applied with great tactical flexibility when the conditions for implementing them proved difficult, and with steadfast adherence to the medium-term strategic objectives. At no time was there any doubt about the authorities determination to carry through the process of convergence to completion, and market players made no mistake about that.

Avinash Persaud
J.P. Morgan Europe[1]

Chapter
4

The euro: broad-based and on time?

The financial markets have never exhibited more optimism over the prospect of a broad EMU arriving on schedule than they do today. That is the verdict of the J.P. Morgan EMU Calculator™. The Calculator is an analytical tool for revealing the market's probability of individual countries joining Germany in a monetary union. The Calculator has become very popular, gracing the desks of many central bankers, investors and corporates. Its principal innovation is that it estimates expectations *real time*. Users can see how political and economic events impact market expectations, blow by blow. Further, being real time means the Calculator has generated a wealth of data which enables us to analyse the EMU process in ways not previously possible. Indeed, shifts in market expectations towards a broad EMU and a weak euro were first identified by the Calculator in the autumn of 1996, long before this view became fashionable among commentators. We explain briefly what the Calculator tells us about market expectations, how it works, how markets respond to the ebb and flow of EMU expectations and where the main risks lie for corporates and investors on the road to EMU.

Expectations can be measured by the EMU Calculator

The EMU Calculator derives market probabilities from the forward interest rate swaps market where investors swap future floating rate interest payments for fixed rate ones. The market's current probability of Italy participating in EMU in 1999, for instance, can be derived by comparing today's level of the spread between lira and Deutschemark post-1999 swap rates, the zero level implied by EMU and the level we might expect to see

[1] *With assistance from Mark Goddard*

Narrow EMU is virtually certain; broad-based is likely

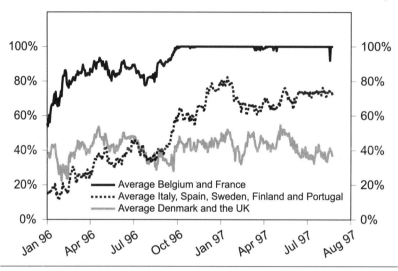

Figure 4.1   **Market probability of countries joining EMU**

if Italy were not to participate in EMU. We estimate the non-EMU spread using the current level of Italian and German short-term interest rates and the past correlation between the lira-Deutschemark swap spread with similar spreads outside of Europe. The error in these calculations can be estimated. Their impact is to bias our estimate of market probabilities by a modest +/-5.0 per cent.

The EMU Calculator tells a story of rising EMU optimism over the past two years, ebbing every now and then, only to flow strongly again later (see Figure 4.1). In the summer of 1996 the market adopted the view that a narrow EMU would arrive in 1999 with some certainty. Expectations that Germany, France, Belgium-Luxembourg, Netherlands and Austria would be in EMU rose to nearly 100 per cent. Despite worries over the size of fiscal deficits in Germany and France, market conviction that these six countries will be in EMU has hardly been shaken.

Expectations have shifted from a narrow to a broad EMU

Once the market had fully priced-in a narrow EMU, the focus of attention turned away from whether EMU would arrive or not, to whether it would be narrow or broad. Since September 1996, EMU expectations in Spain,

Portugal, Finland and Italy have climbed substantially. However, expectations that these countries will join EMU have been volatile. Between September 1996 to December 1996 expectations rallied strongly, reaching a peak on 14 December 1996 when Europe's Leaders signed the principles of a 'Stability Pact' in Dublin. The Stability Pact was designed to ensure fiscal probity after EMU-day with a complex process of heavy fines for those countries which exceed a deficit to GDP ratio of 3.0 per cent. The market concluded that if there was an agreement to keep deficits low after EMU day, there was less need to be strict about convergence prior to EMU-day. That meant it would be easier for Europe's formerly high-yield periphery to participate in EMU on Day One. The Stability Pact has been critical to market expectations surrounding the size of EMU.

No sooner was the ink dry on the Stability Pact; EMU expectations in the periphery began to soften. Between January and May 1997 EMU expectations in the periphery fell from 65-75 per cent to 50-60 per cent. Two factors contributed to this. First, the Bundesbank became concerned that the haste of some governments to bend their deficits down to the 3.0 per cent reference rate of the Maastricht convergence criteria was undermining the credibility of the putative euro. The Bundesbank began to introduce the 'fifth convergence criteria', arguing that hitting the Maastricht reference rates was not enough, countries had to show they could 'sustain' low deficits. The need for sustainability was seen then to reduce the chances of Europe's periphery making it to EMU on time.

At the beginning of 1997, the public debate on the euro in Germany started to turn nasty. Germany reported a record high unemployment rate in January 1997 and economic nationalism began to flower. Some politicians began to pander to the public's new euroscepticism. When asked in an opinion poll in early June whether they backed Chancellor Kohl's stand that EU countries should stick to the 1999 deadline, 82 per cent of respondents said 'No'. The strength of this opinion began to undermine EMU optimism in Italy, Spain, Portugal and Finland.

By the summer of 1997, optimism surrounding a broad EMU returned. This was largely triggered by very positive developments on the fiscal front in Europe's so-called periphery. Courtesy of an economic recovery and deficit reduction measures taken earlier, Spain, Portugal and perhaps Italy are likely to turn in fiscal deficit to GDP ratios within a whisker of 3.0 per cent and possibly below levels in Germany and France. It will be increasingly difficult for Germany, or any other country, to deny Italy, Spain, Portugal and Finland a place at the party.

Will a broad EMU mean a weak euro?

Every rise in EMU expectations in 'periphery' currencies has dragged the Deutschemark lower. Initially, rising EMU expectations were felt most strongly within Europe via a rapid narrowing of yield spreads and a sharply higher Italian lira and Spanish peseta. Between September 1995 and September 1996 the Italian lira rallied 15 per cent versus the Deutschemark. However, as EMU expectations continued to grow, 'convergence' became more priced-in and a broad EMU appeared more likely , the currency impact shifted out of the ERM. Today the U.S. dollar and sterling are the most sensitive currencies to changing EMU

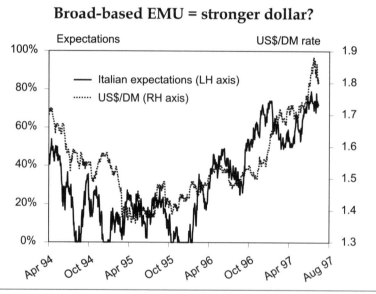

Broad-based EMU = stronger dollar?

Figure 4.2   **Probability of Italy joining EMU vs. the US$/DM exchange rate**

expectations. In part this is because there is little remaining value in European currencies. The lira and peseta, so close to their ERM central parities, probably have less than 1.0 per cent to rally if their participation in EMU became a certainty. (The market believes the existing ERM central parities will be chosen as EMU conversion exchange rates.)

Another reason why the dollar and sterling have profited from rising EMU expectations is that the market equates a broad EMU with a soft euro. There is a widespread conviction that a motley collection of European central bankers, unaided by a strong fiscal centre, overseeing an area with

France and Belgium almost certain; Italy...

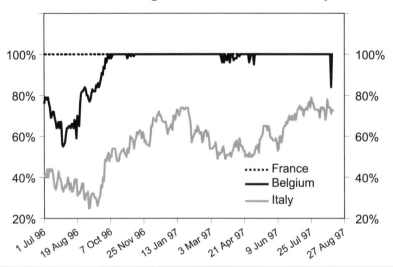

Figure 4.3   Probability of France, Belgium and Italy joining EMU

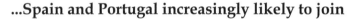

...Spain and Portugal increasingly likely to join

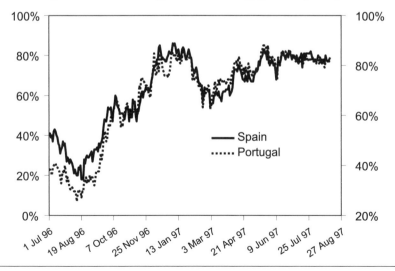

Figure 4.4   Probability of Spain and Portugal joining EMU

...with Finland the leading Nordic contender...

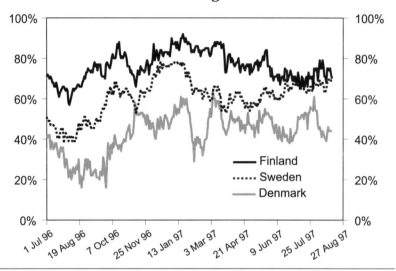

Figure 4.5   Probability of Finland, Sweden and Denmark joining EMU

...and the UK likely to be 'out'

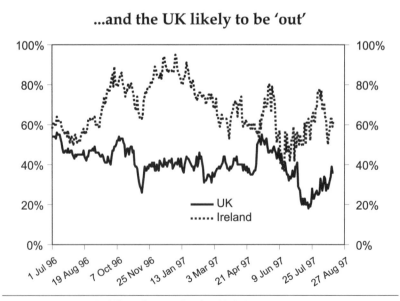

Figure 4.6   Probability of UK and Ireland joining EMU

strong economic disparities and high unemployment will be biased to an easy monetary policy.

The principal risks to the market are that EMU does not arrive or that it arrives and the euro is strong. The risks of an EMU delay are not insignificant, especially given the tumultuous market implications, and lie somewhere between 15-25 per cent. The German public is so far not warming to the idea of giving up the Deutschemark for a euro shared with Italy. However, the risk of a strong euro is a bigger risk. If the euro arrives it will be the currency of the world's largest economic bloc, largest exporter and largest importer. It will rapidly become an invoicing currency for trade and investment. This is the principal ingredient for any currency to become a major reserve currency. As the euro is bestowed reserve currency status, the euro could strengthen sharply. Ecu/dollar is currently in the region of $1.10. By 2002, when national currencies are removed and euro notes and coins are circulated, euro/dollar will be closer to $1.50 than $1.00.

The euro is expected to strengthen against the dollar

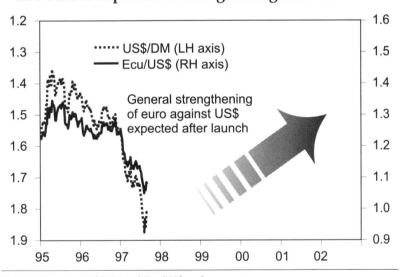

Figure 4.7   US$/DM and Ecu/US$ exchange rates

The economics of
the euro

Nikolaus Keis

Bayerische Vereinsbank, Munich

Chapter 5

The euro and Germany

In this chapter we look at the effects on the German economy of the introduction of the euro. The framework used is to identify the economic costs and benefits, both in the run-up to the euro's introduction and after it has been implemented.

The main costs in the run-up to the introduction of the euro are that:

- *fiscal policy* has to be tightened not only in Germany but also in other European countries; and that

- *short and long-term interest rates* in Europe will be higher as a result of an EMU 'risk premium'.

Such an EMU 'risk premium' is also likely to lead to European currencies being weaker against the US dollar and the yen than would otherwise have been the case. In the short-term this will tend to push up inflation, but it may also help boost European exports. The euro's introduction also requires additional investment spending on the part of business to 'gear up for the euro'. Such stronger exports and investment, however, do not offset the effect of the tighter fiscal policy and higher interest rates so, in the run up to the euro's introduction, German economic activity will be lower than would otherwise have been the case. The main costs are borne in 1997.

After the euro is introduced, however, benefits in the form of the elimination of foreign currency transactions costs and the elimination of exchange rate risk in the euro area will begin to benefit growth. Further gains will result from additional supply-side effects—i.e. higher fiscal discipline and lower wage growth—and structural improvements in the capital markets, which will become more liquid, deeper and more diverse. All these factors will bring down interest rates, thus fuelling investment spending.

On balance, compared with the path the economy would have taken without the euro's introduction, growth will be depressed in 1997, 1998 and 1999. By the year 2002, the losses seen in the run-up to EMU will have been just offset by the post-EMU gains. By 2005, however, the accumulated gains to the German economy are expected to be substantial. In a nutshell, the story is one of short-term pain for long-term gain.

German growth — with and without the euro

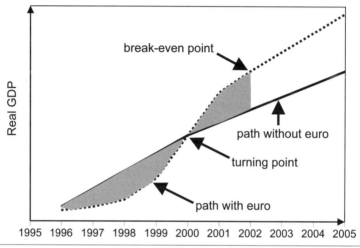

Figure 5.1

Before the introduction of the euro

Working assumptions

The following working assumptions are used:

1. The euro is introduced in January 1999;

2. EMU takes off with a core-group of six to seven countries (Germany, France, the Netherlands, Belgium, Luxembourg, Austria and possibly Ireland)[1];

3. These countries will broadly meet the economic convergence criteria contained in the Maastricht Treaty.

---

[1] *Assuming that Italy, Spain and Portugal will also participate in the first round would not change our main results significantly.*

Fiscal tightening in Germany

Germany's public sector deficit was 3.8 per cent of GDP in 1996. In early 1997 it was generally though that without any tightening of fiscal policy the budget deficit would probably have amounted to about 3.5 per cent of GDP. In an attempt to meet the 3 per cent target a package of measures was introduced early in 1997, cutting government spending by DM40bn. Even so, it looked likely by mid-1997 that the 3 per cent target would still be exceeded. This led to a proposal by the finance ministry to use the profit from revaluing the gold reserves to reduce the budget deficit; the plan was, however, dropped following Bundesbank opposition. Further tax increases and/or reductions in government spending may still therefore be implemented in the second half of 1997.

The direct effect of this fiscal tightening, according to our estimates, is to cut GDP growth in 1997 by around 0.7 per cent. It would not be correct, however, to ascribe all of this reduction in output to the introduction of the euro. Even without the euro, preparations the deficit would also have been tackled in 1997. On balance, we assume an EMU-induced real GDP loss in 1997 of DM15bn, representing 0.4 per cent of GDP.

Fiscal tightening in other countries

With the exception of Luxembourg, all prospective EMU members were in the position in early 1997 of having to reduce their public deficits, sometimes considerably, in order to meet the deficit and debt criteria contained in the Maastricht treaty

In our simulations we have applied the Maastricht criteria rather strictly. All EMU core members must have reduced their public sector deficit to 3 per cent of GDP in 1997. In addition, the debt ratio—in as far as it exceeds 60 per cent—must be moving downwards. These requirements also apply in subsequent years. The other EU countries are projected to fulfil the criteria by 2000 to a large extent. Fiscal retrenchment is generally assumed to take place via a reduction of government expenditures, but in France and Belgium income tax is also increased. The effects on the various countries are strongly contradictory. In several countries real government spending has to be reduced by more than 3 per cent. The losses in GDP for the core countries amount to some 1.5 per cent of GDP in 1997. For some non-core countries the effects are even larger.

Lower growth in other EU countries reduces the demand for German exports. According to our simulations, the reduction in GDP from this effect also amounts to around 0.4 per cent of GDP in 1997.

Costs & benefits of the euro for Germany

1. Before the euro

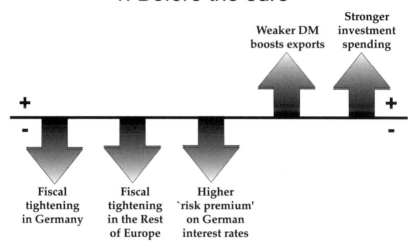

2. After the euro

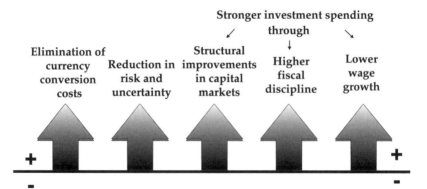

Figure 5.2

The EMU risk premium: higher bond yields

It is clear that in the run-up to EMU the bond market has at times set a 'risk premium' on German long-term interest rates. It is difficult to measure this precisely, but one indication is given by the yield differential between Germany and the USA, adjusted for inflation. This shows that 'real' interest rates in Germany were as much as 100 basis points higher than in the USA at times during 1995 and 1996. We estimate the EMU-induced risk premium to have been 50 basis points on average during 1996 and we forecast it to average 75 basis points in 1997 and 25 basis points in 1998.

The EMU risk premium: a weaker Deutschemark

We assume that EMU leads to a 10-15 pfennig weakening of the Deutschemark against the dollar.

A mild weakening of the Deutschemark against the French franc is also likely, but no specific change *vis-à-vis* the hard European currencies is taken into account in our analysis. Similarly, we assume that pressure to meet the Maastricht criteria will prevent any significant change in the value of the traditionally weaker European currencies versus the Deutschemark in the run-up to EMU.

Real German-US interest rate differential

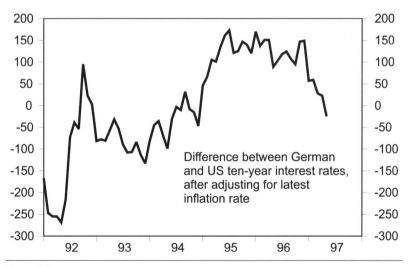

Figure 5.3

Even so, the resulting improvement of price competitiveness should lead to stronger exports (and weaker imports). This improvement in exports takes some time to work through, however (the well-known 'J-curve effect').

Will consumer spending be affected?

Higher import prices as a result of a weaker Deutschemark will act to depress consumer spending. Apart from this, however, there are no obvious reasons why households should change their consumption behaviour either in anticipation of, or after, the introduction of the euro.

Investment spending: a boost for growth in the run-up to EMU

In the run-up to the introduction of the euro many sectors of the economy will have to carry out additional investment spending. The financial sector will be particularly affected. It will be necessary to put into place a dual or multi-currency accounting system; staff training for the euro will be required and additional information will have to be provided to consumers.

Reliable cost estimates are not available. According to a survey of the European Bank Union in spring 1994, the outlays of banks in all 15 EU countries during the three years up to 1999 would amount to ECU 20bn (around DM38bn). Corresponding to its share in the EU economy (23 per cent), German banks would have to spend almost DM9bn. However, the same survey mentions a figure of 2 per cent of current costs of banks, which would imply a cost of DM2bn for German banks. On the other hand, if one uses some of the bank-specific estimates (Bayerische Vereinsbank: DM120m, Deutsche Bank: DM250m) and project a total figure — assuming a greater than proportional cost for smaller organizations, who will not be able to take advantage of economies of scale — the cost would work out to be almost DM4bn. We also need to take into account that the costs of large projects are often underestimated initially.

Bearing in mind these considerations, we assume the costs to be DM5bn for the banking sector and DM10bn for the total financial sector (including insurance and social insurance).

We see the adjustment expenditures for most of the goods producing firms as relatively modest. The *Middelstand* (small businesses) will adjust its accounting system later, when the costs of doing so will probably be lower; while large, internationally orientated companies already have to transform transactions in several currencies, making then more easily adaptable to the introduction of the euro.

On balance, we assume that the additional DM10bn of investment spending is undertaken over the three years — 1996 to 1998 inclusive — up to the euro's introduction. The maximum effect on GDP is reached in 1999, when GDP is 0.14 per cent higher than would otherwise have been the case.

Aggregate effect

We can add together the effects of fiscal tightening in Germany and other European countries, a higher risk premium on interest rates and on the currency as well as the effect of higher investment spending, to obtain an estimate of the overall effect on German GDP.

On this basis, the greatest 'cost' to German GDP growth is in 1997, when GDP is 0.8 per cent lower than would have been the case if the country had not been preparing for the euro.

These calculations, of necessity do not take into account, any effect that the preparations for EMU have on general business and consumer confidence. It is certainly the case at times that many European countries have been caught in a 'vicious circle' whereby fiscal tightening and the dampening effect on economic growth leads to even slower growth, leading to a bigger budget deficit and so on. Such effects, which would increase the costs of preparing for the euro, are not specifically taken into account.

Before the euro: a vicious circle

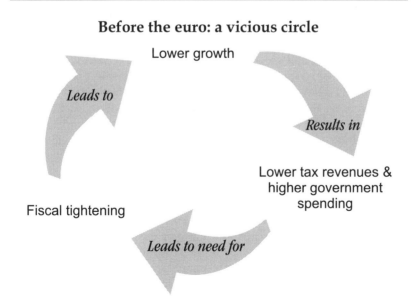

Figure 5.4

After the introduction of the euro

In assessing the benefits to the German economy after the introduction of the euro, we have—as a first step—based our work on the estimates produced by the European Commission in 1990. That is, the real output gains from the euro are assumed to be 5 per cent over a time span of 10-15 years, or about 0.4 per cent per annum.

The main gains stem from:

- the disappearance of exchange rate related transaction and information costs and

- the disappearance of exchange rate risks and the related reduction of investment risks

These changes lead to a better allocation of resources and a more efficient market. They are also likely to stimulate stronger investment spending, giving a further boost to growth.

However, there are four reasons for thinking that the actual gains from the euro may be somewhat higher than these estimates:

- **First,** there may be greater structural consequences. For example, the European capital market will become more liquid, deeper in many segments and more diverse in terms of the range of instruments available. For companies issuing debt and equity this implies lower capital costs. For the financial sector in general there will be increased competition and greater 'pressure to perform'. Even with a small number of countries in the euro area, the European bond market would become the second largest in the world—behind the USA, but before Japan. It could therefore become more independent from US interest rate movements. The financial infrastructure will be modernized and thus more productive. All these factors will help to bring lower European interest rates.

- **Second,** the 'shareholder value' concept—familiar in the US—may become a more prominent feature of German business.

- **Third**, the introduction of the euro will make differences in wages throughout the euro area much clearer. Just as the euro illustrates quickly to the Portuguese worker how much one can earn in Germany, it helps clarify to German employers and employees how much hourly wage costs are in Portugal. Real wage growth could be more modest, which should lead to more employment and growth.

- **Finally**, we also expect a medium-term gain from improvements in supply conditions triggered by the euro. The Maastricht criteria and the stability pact require a change in fiscal policy. Countries will find it much more difficult to run up government debt s, which should lead to lower real interest rates. According to an IMF estimate, the rise in the debt ratio in industrial countries from 40 per cent to 70 per cent in the last 15 years has led to an increase in real interest rates of 100 to 250 basis points. The corollary is that real interest rates will fall as the stock of debt in relation to GDP tends to fall. This may allow lower taxes and greater freedom for the private sector of the economy.

The growth effects arising from the improvement in the supply-side of the economy and structural improvements are very difficult to quantify, not least because they may generate a 'virtuous circle' of stronger growth. We see, however, no reason why they should be any lower than those identified in the European Commission's earlier study. Nevertheless, we err on the side of caution and thus assume that they will add one half of the effects identified by the European Commission (i.e. to boost GDP growth by 0.2 per cent p.a.).

After the euro: a virtuous circle

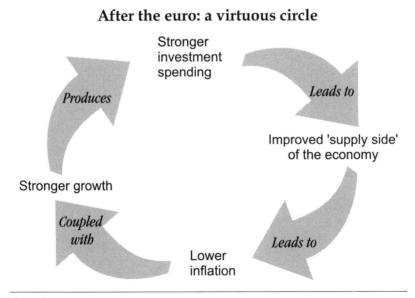

Figure 5.5

Overall effects & conclusion for the German economy

Taking into account the costs incurred in preparing for the euro and the subsequent benefits the following picture emerges for the German economy.

- The preparation for the euro implies an initial reduction in German economic growth.

- The highest 'cost' is in 1997 when we estimate that real GDP will be around 0.8 per cent lower than would otherwise have been the case.

- With the introduction of the euro in 1999 the expansionary effect on the economy begins to come through.

- By the year 2000 the level of GDP is back to the level it would have been in the absence of the costs of preparing for the euro.

- By the year 2002, the pre-euro losses have been made good by the post-euro gains.

- The net GDP gain amounts to almost DM120bn (in 1997 prices).

- In 2005, real economic activity will be higher by almost DM100bn (in 1991 prices).

- Over 10 years. net wealth gain (aggregated real GDP discounted by an assumed 5 per cent p. a. amounts to DM140bn

Chapter
6

David Miles

Centre for Economic Policy Research &
Imperial College, London

The UK and the euro

This chapter[1] analyses the policy implications for the UK of the euro. It does not say whether it is right or wrong for the UK to join EMU, but emphasizes that whatever decision is taken there will be big changes in the economic environment which will require policy responses. The aim of the chapter is: to analyse the changes in microeconomic and macroeconomic policies that will make the euro work better if the UK does join; and to investigate how policies might need to change so as to reduce any costs, and increase and benefits, of not joining.

Issues if the UK does join the euro area

If the UK joins the euro area, then:

- it will lose the power to set national interest rates. Short-term interest rates for countries participating in EMU will be set by the European Central bank;

- longer-term interest rates will differ only marginally from those in other countries in the euro area, mainly reflecting differences in risk premiums

- it will be unable to change its exchange rate against other countries participating in the euro.

1

This chapter is an abridged version of The Ostrich and the EMU: Policy Choices Facing the UK published by the Centre for Economic Policy Research (telephone 0171 878 2900), London, in June 1997 with support from the Esmee Fairbairn Charitable Trust.

The significance of these changes depends on several factors: the size of economic shocks that are specific to the UK; the degree of flexibility in labour markets; and differences in the way that a common European monetary policy would affect countries in the euro area.

Clearly, the UK's economic cycle has recently been out of line with the cycle on the Continent. This partly reflects differences in monetary policy, and to that extent joining EMU would make the UK cycle more like that of other members. But even EMU would not eliminate some distinguishing features of the UK economy. The obvious structural differences include:

–   **Oil production:** The UK is a sizeable net exporter of oil an the only EU country that is a net exporter of all primary energy. This will continue for some time. (Figures 6.1 and 6.2)

–   **Personal debt:** The UK's stock of household debt is, and is likely to remain, substantially higher than the EU average (see Figure 6.3)

–   **Company borrowing:** Corporate use of the bond market is relatively low in the UK, and reliance on short-term bank loans has been above the EU average (see Figure 6.4).

–   **Public expenditure:** As a proportion of GDP, government expenditure and taxes are lower in the UK than in most EU countries (see Figure 6.5)

–   **Trade:** The proportion of UK trade that is currently with other EU members is below average (see Figure 6.6).

Of course, most countries are unusual in some respect and it is useful to use a wider measure of how far countries are subject to specific shocks. One simple guide is the correlation of national GDP with growth in the EU as a whole (see Figure 6.7). On this measure, the UK, is indeed in the group of economies which have not been highly correlated with the EU cycle. Some studies using more sophisticated econometric techniques have come up with similar findings. For example, Figure 6.8 shows correlations between aggregate supply and demand shocks estimated by Bayoumi and Eichengreen.[1] They found that the UK had a relatively low correlation of both demand and supply shocks, though Finland and Ireland were even more out of line with the EU norm.

[1]
Bayoumi, T. and Eichengreen, B. 'Operationalizing the Theory of Optimum Currency Areas' *CEPR Discussion paper No. 1484, October 1996. Aggregate demand shocks are those which affect demand conditions in the economy and it is assumed that their only long-run effect is on prices. Supply shocks can also affect output in the long run.*

The UK is a net exporter of oil...

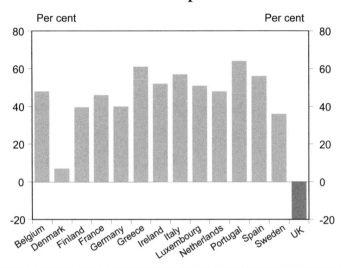

Figure 6.1   1995 imports of crude oil & petroleum (% of domestic energy consumption)

...and of primary energy in general

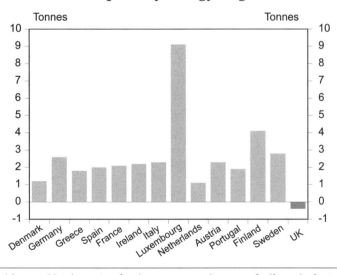

Figure 6.2   Net imports of primary energy (tonnes of oil equivalent per person)

UK households are highly indebted...

	% of GDP	Year
UK	79	1995
Norway	70	1993
Spain	58	1995
Germany	56	1995
Sweden	54	1994
France	50	1995
Finland	41	1994
Italy	24	1994

Figure 6.3   Financial liabilities of the household sector (% of GDP)
Source: OECD balance sheets of non-financial sector

...and UK companies make little use of the bond market

Sweden	69.5
Germany	31.2
Belgium	55.5
Austria	36.5
Switzerland	35.8
Norway	19.2
Finland	19.2
Italy	13.7
France	11.6
Iceland	9.6
Netherlands	7.6
Spain	6.1
Ireland	3.2
UK	2.9

Figure 6.4   Corporate bonds outstanding in 1995 (% of GDP)
Source: Merrill Lynch 'The Size & Structure of World Bond Markets', October 1996

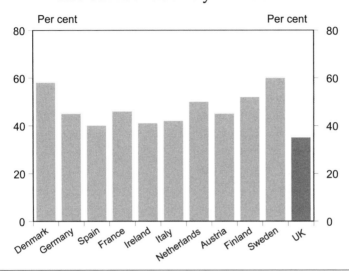

Figure 6.5   Total tax receipts of general government (% of GDP in 1994)

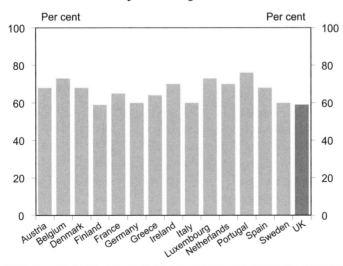

Figure 6.6   Average % of exports & imports to EU in 1995 (% of total)

UK growth is not strongly linked with the rest of the EU...

France	0.91
Belgium	0.87
Germany	0.85
Italy	0.79
Spain	0.79
Austria	0.78
Portugal	0.76
Netherlands	0.75
Denmark	0.69
Sweden	0.67
Greece	0.66
Luxembourg	0.64
UK	0.63
Finland	0.59
Ireland	0.20

Figure 6.7   **Correlation of the annual growth of national GDP with EU GDP, 1961-1993**

...and the UK does not respond like Germany to shocks

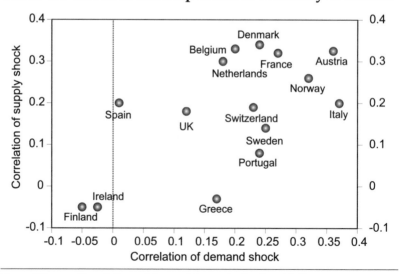

Figure 6.8   **Correlations of demand & supply shocks with Germany**
Source: Bayoumi and Eichengreen (1996)

Any such conclusions are based on the past and the more important question is whether the idiosyncrasies of the UK economy will persist into the future, especially if the UK joined EMU. One of the likely benefits would be increased trade and integration, which would affect the structure of economies, probably making them more synchronized. But even that is not certain. It is conceivable that the lower costs of cross-border trade would encourage more specialization, so that individual EMU member countries became more dependent on particular industries. Even if shocks were uniform across the euro area, individual countries would still have different degrees of labour mobility and would have different responses to interest rate changes.

This analysis has major implications for fiscal policy, an issue to which we now turn.

Fiscal policy

Could fiscal policy mimic monetary policy?
If the UK lost control over short-term interest rates then fiscal policy would have to play a larger role in counter-cyclical policy. One way of thinking about this is to ask whether fiscal policy could mimic the effects which changes in interest rates would have had on the economy. It is possible to think of several such methods, but all have inherent difficulties.

First, tax deductibility of interest could be reduced — thereby raising the post-tax interest rate — when it was desired to slow economic growth, and vice versa. Unfortunately, this approach would require frequent changes in tax rates, which is difficult and undesirable.

Second, sales taxes (VAT and excise duties) could be varied. If macroeconomic policy needs to be tightened, a temporary increase in sales tax may persuade consumers to postpone spending. The one major weakness of this approach is that in an overheating economy, raising indirect taxes adds to inflationary pressure at just the wrong time.

Third, government expenditure could be varied but it is not desirable (nor politically feasible) to reverse decisions on big items of government expenditure at short notice.

Other schemes could be developed. For example, taxpayers could receive income tax refunds if GDP falls or they could hold back some tax payments in a downswing. But to run through all of these options is to highlight their inherent weaknesses. There are no simple and non-distortionary ways of boosting fiscal flexibility to offset the loss of monetary policy autonomy.

What about the Stability Pact?

At the EU Dublin summit in December 1996, governments agreed on penalties for running excessive deficits (see Figure 6.9). It is hard to know whether these rules will be applied in practice, but in principle the fines for exceeding a budget deficit of 3 per cent of GDP could be very large. For example, over the last thirty years the average UK budget deficit has been 3 per cent of GDP. The deficit was less than 3 per cent of GDP in fewer than half the years.

Stability Pact fines

DEFICIT	FINE	
3%	0.2%	
4%	0.3%	
5%	0.4%	
6%	0.5%	*(maximum)*

Country is not fined if GDP falls by 2% or more

For falls in GDP of 0.75% to 2.0%, fines are discretionary

Figure 6.9   Stability Pact fines for exceeding budget deficits*
all figures as a percentage of GDP

Faced with such fines, the strategy of aiming for a small surplus could be sensible. This would allow, in a downturn, greater scope for loosening fiscal policy without hitting the 3 per cent limit.

Would fiscal policy still be autonomous?

The autonomy of fiscal policy could be affected at two levels.

First, a national government's ability to raise revenue to finance national spending could be reduced. If people can easily move to countries where taxes are low, then some of the better off may opt out of a redistributive tax and spending system. In principle, labour mobility is likely to be enhanced by EMU; in practice, the effect is unlikely to be great as language and cultural differences (for example) probably have much more influence on migration.

In fact, more problems are likely to arise from labour immobility. If some countries have high and rising unemployment, they may seek greater fiscal transfers from the EU.

Second, the freedom of governments to have their own tax and benefit systems may be affected. The Maastricht Treaty has no direct implications for the harmonization of tax structures and welfare programmes but a single currency would probably affect the substitutability of goods, services and financial assets. We consider these implications under four headings: indirect taxes; income taxes and benefits; taxes on companies; and capital taxes.

Indirect taxes

There are currently EU restrictions on the VAT rates that EU governments may set: the standard rate cannot be under 15 per cent and no more than two reduced rates are allowed.[1] Despite these restrictions, VAT rates still vary widely across the EU and neither rates nor exemptions have converged much over the last ten years. Would the introduction of the euro require rapid and complete harmonization of taxes? The experience of the United States suggest not. There, individual states have rates of sales tax that differ as much as in EU countries. It seems that non-currency factors ensure that such differences persist. Cross border tax-driven shopping is already important in many EU member countries and will probably increase when the euro is introduced, but it seems unlikely that this will attain sufficient importance to necessitate harmonization of indirect taxes. The European Commission has recently published proposals for a much greater harmonization of VAT systems but such an introduction is not formally linked to the introduction of the euro.

Income taxes and benefits.

In or out of EMU, countries are less likely to harmonize their income taxes and welfare systems than their indirect taxes. Mobility of labour within Europe is low and people are unlikely to migrate in large numbers for tax reasons alone. The same goes for welfare payments and public services which already vary widely across the EU and have not prompted much migration. It is not obvious that any of this inertia would change simply because the euro came into existence.

---

[1] *There are some other minor exceptions*

Taxes on companies

In contrast, once currency risk is eliminated companies may well pay more attention to differences in the costs of doing business in different countries. As an 'in', the UK (with relatively low employment and corporate taxes) would become more attractive for businesses wishing to sell in Europe. Precisely for that reasons, other euro area members may try to harmonize company taxes. Pressure to harmonize corporate taxes would probably be just as strong if the UK were 'out'. If its corporate tax system were thought to be attracting companies form the Continent, EMU members would probably complain that the UK was making the whole project more difficult.

Capital taxes

If companies are more footloose than people, financial capital is positively nomadic. With currency risk eliminated, all euro-denominated assets will become closer substitutes for one another, no matter where they are issued. The implication is that, for investors facing a particular set of tax rules, the expected post-tax returns on assets should be closer than is now the case, when currency risk still matters. It is not clear, however, that national rules on capital taxes therefore need to be closer. Currently, double tax agreements mean that holdings of many classes of foreign assets are taxed as if they were domestic assets. Although this heightens incentives to live and be taxed in a particular country, tax exiles are unlikely to become much more numerous purely because of a single currency.

The transmission mechanism

The balance sheets of UK households, companies, banks and building societies are significantly different from those in the main Continental economies. Personal debt is proportionately higher, and more of it is at variable interest rates. UK companies are similarly more dependent on floating-rate debt. And banks and building societies rely heavily of retail deposits paying variable rates that are closely linked to those set by the Bank of England.

In the UK, only 15 per cent of the outstanding mortgage debt is at fixed rates, which anyway tend to be fixed for less than four years. In Germany, just over 50 per cent of mortgage debt is at rates that are completely fixed; in France, the figure is as much as 90 per cent. The implications is clear: unless UK balance sheets become more European, inside EMU the UK would be more sensitive to changes in short-term interest rates than other countries.

Of course, policy could be framed so as to encourage a move to more European-style balance sheets? A switch from variable to fixed rate debt could be encouraged, maybe by setting differential capital adequacy requirements for banks and building societies, favouring fixed-rate loans. Policies to help reduce gearing could also be implemented, say through various tax changes which would make debt more expensive. The current tax breaks for mortgages (MIRAS) and companies (full deductibility of interest payments from taxable income, but less generous treatment for equity funding) encourage debt financing.

The labour market

The seriousness of the loss of policy flexibility inside EMU depends to a large extent on the structure of the labour market. If nominal wages are inflexible, then exogenous shocks will change real variables (employment and output). In a single currency area, a given degree of labour market inflexibility will become more costly in terms of lost jobs and output. But having flexible labour markets is desirable anyway. Low marginal tax rates and a benefits system that does not discourage job creation are good things for every country. It is not obvious that EMU *per se* raises new policy issues for the UK labour market.

The UK as an 'out': longer term macroeconomic issues

The changing environment

As an 'out' the UK could continue to use all its existing policy instruments. In itself, this may seem an advantage; though the macroeconomic record of the past thirty years provides numerous examples of those instruments being misused. What is certain is that the wider context for macroeconomic management would change: living next door to an EMU with which the bulk of the UK's trade was conducted would have major ramifications.

If EMU works well, the euro would become the key currency for UK business and a large proportion of its trade would be priced and paid for in euro. Similarly, UK investors (and overseas investors holding UK financial assets) would view euro-denominated assets as a natural part of their portfolios. Any perception that the UK would have higher and more variable inflation than the EMU countries, or generally looser fiscal policy, would cause the demand for sterling assets to fall.

Even if EMU works badly, the UK could suffer. EMU members would probably be particularly sensitive to the sterling-euro rate, and prone to accuse the UK of stealing an unfair competitive advantage within the Single Market by devaluing the pound. The 'common concern' clause of the Maastricht Treaty means that EU countries that do not adopt the single currency are obliged to consider the knock-on effects for EMU members of any change in exchange rates. In a sense there is nothing new in this (EU countries outside the ERM re under a similar obligation) but the context will have changed. If EMU members no longer have their own national monetary policy, they will be even more alert to the behaviour of others.

Perceptions of motive would count for a lot. It would be far better for the UK to be seen as a sympathetic 'out'; 'out' because of its concern over its structural economic idiosyncrasies, but nonetheless committed to greater economic integration in Europe. If the UK were seen as a carper and a blocker, wanting the benefits of the Single Market without the obligations of the single currency, it would surely suffer increasing discrimination from EMU members.

Policy instruments and targets

As an 'out' the key policy issues will be:

- If an inflation target is to be retained, how tight should it be?

- Does it make sense to assign instruments to targets: having the Bank of England set interest rates to hit the inflation target, and setting tax and spending plans in a long-term context to control debt and deficits (and perhaps using intervention to influence the value of sterling)?

- Should there be a target for the sterling-euro exchange rate?

The ECB will aim to achieve price stability. If this means that there is an explicit inflation target in EMU, it would have implications for the UK. For example, it would be difficult for the UK's inflation target to be higher than the ECB's without some loss of credibility.

Although the precise level of the UK inflation target would matter, the credibility of the means to achieve it would count for much more. The recent move to give the Bank of England operational independence will help in this respect.

We mentioned above the danger of sharp movements in the sterling-euro exchange rate so some kind of exchange rate stability would certainly be welcome. But if the UK were to adopt and exchange rate target against the euro would this replace, or be combined with, the inflation target? If the latter then these two targets would need two policy instruments. For all the reasons demonstrated by ERM experience, the interest rate needed to keep inflation low would not necessarily be consistent with the exchange rate target.

Fiscal policy

As an 'out' the UK would not be subject to the Stability Pact, and so would not be subject to fines if its budget deficit exceeded 3 per cent of GDP. As the 3 per cent limit is arbitrary, it is hard to see that not sticking to this limit would seriously endanger credibility.. Nonetheless, it already has some symbolic significance. As a result, if any UK government did want to exceed the 3 per cent limit it would need to explain why; it would also probably need to stress that the move was temporary; and it would also need a longer-term framework of policies to ensure that the ratio of its total debt to GDP remained on a sustainable path.

The ways ahead

The UK has four possible strategies for EMU:

- Join at the start
- Decide to join at a later date
- Wait and see
- Decide in principle not to join

Join at the start

Joining at the start would require:

- A fully independent central bank by the end of 1998. The government would therefore have to attach high priority to drafting and passing a new Bank of England Act that was in important respects, different from that outlined by Gordon Brown when he gave the Bank of England operational independence.

- A significant tightening in macro-economic policy before the UK was subject to an interest rate that was would probably be much lower than it needs for its current cyclical state. Interest rates in EMU's first wave candidates are now 3 per cent below UK rates, and the gap might be wider in a year's time.

- A lower exchange rate.

- Enhancing automatic fiscal stabilizers to compensate for the loss of autonomy over monetary policy.

–   Reducing the tax incentive to use debt. This will help make the transmission mechanism of UK monetary policy more like that in other EMU candidates.

Delayed entry

A decision to delay entry by, say, three or four years would ease or eliminate the practical problems of trying to achieve these things in time for the start of EMU. It will not be imperative to make the Bank of England fully independent by the end of 1998, though legislation should not be delayed for long. It will also be desirable to bring in legislative measures to enhance the fiscal stabilizers; they will then have a chance to start working. But the bigger advantages of delay relate to conjunctural and exchange rate considerations. By 2001 or 2002 the euro interest rate may well be broadly what the UK economy needs in the cyclical circumstances it will then find itself.

Wait and see

A wait-and-see strategy has the obvious advantage that some of the uncertainty about EMU – on the operation of monetary policy, on the demand for, and value of, the euro, on the strains generated by a single short tem interest rate for all the 'ins' – will be reduced. But in order to keep open the option of joining EMU some way down the road it would still be desirable to reduce the fiscal deficit and remove tax incentives to use debt. It would also be sensible to draft the amendments to the Bank of England Act in a way which allowed it to operate as part of the European Central Bank.

Staying out

If the UK was to stay out of EMU, the euro-sterling exchange rate would be of great significance: it would be more important for UK business than any bilateral rate now is. Sharp fluctuations could be damaging and because countries inside the single currency area could not independently do much to alter their exchange rate against the UK, the UK could risk discrimination in certain respects. The surest way of avoiding this is to participate actively in the development of the single market. Much will depend on attitude. If the UK is seen as a constructive agnostic, it will be listened to on such subjects as competition policy. If it comes across as a whingeing outsider, it will not.

Chapter 7

The euro

Rosanna Maddalena
Senior Economist
San Paolo Bank

Italy's road towards the euro

Italy's road towards European Monetary Union (EMU) is perhaps the longest and most hard fought in Europe. A history of undisciplined public spending and the frequent use of currency devaluation to revitalise the economy still represents an obstacle for Italy's EMU participation in the first wave despite recent achievements. Since June 1996, when the Prodi government was elected, Italy has rejoined the ERM, has introduced strict budget measures to tackle its borrowing requirements, and has reduced inflation to 1.5 per cent. The road ahead, however, remains uncertain, with the primary focus being Italy's ability to sustain its recent trend towards economic convergence to average EU levels. Failure to deliver significant structural reform in social spending and a convincing 1998 budget could foil Italy's chances for early EMU participation.

The Italian economic convergence trend has been clear and drastic since mid 1996 year. Inflation is very low and the 1997 budget deficit figures should reach a respectable 3.0-3.2 per cent of GDP, despite lower tax revenues as a result of sluggish economic growth in the first half 1997.

Fiscal discipline: structural vs. transitory measures

Italy has recently abandoned the long wave of undisciplined budget spending, entering a new age of fiscal rigour. Concrete measures to tackle transfers and government purchases have led to a state sector borrowing requirement (SSBR) of 29.5 trillion lira in the first half of 1997, approximately half the level of 1996. As a result, the 1997 public deficit/GDP target of 3.0 per cent required by the Maastricht criteria is well within reach.

A supplementary mini budget had to be released early in 1997 after slower than expected GDP growth brought into question the government's forecast of 2.0 per cent growth in the year. The supplementary 1997 Budget, however, focused on few permanent changes. Structural measures, instead, are expected in the coming 1998 Budget, which will focus on

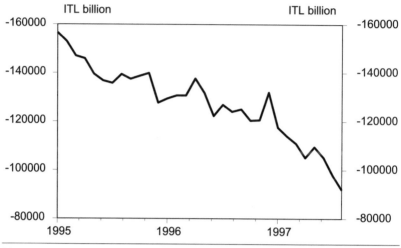

The SSBR has shrunk dramatically...

Figure 7.1   Italy's state sector borrowing requirement (12-month accumulated values)

...and is planned to be under 3% of GDP from 1997

	1996	1997	1998	1999	2000
Primary expenditure	38.4	38.1	38.8	38.4	38.0
- *Social protection*	*19.3*	*19.5*	*19.9*	*19.9*	*19.8*
- *Other expenses*	*13.2*	*12.7*	*12.9*	*12.6*	*12.2*
Capital accounts	4.0	3.3	3.7	3.8	3.9
Interest payments	10.8	9.7	8.6	8.5	8.0
Total payments	**53.2**	**51.2**	**51.1**	**50.7**	**49.9**
Total revenue	**46.4**	**48.2**	**47.0**	**46.3**	**45.8**
Primary surplus	4.0	6.7	4.5	4.1	4.0
Deficit	**6.7**	**3.0**	**4.1**	**4.4**	**4.1**
Target deficit			2.8	2.4	1.8
Planned budget correction			*1.2*	*2.0*	*2.3*

Figure 7.2   Public administration accounting trends (as % of GDP)
Source: Treasury Ministry

Inflation has plummeted...

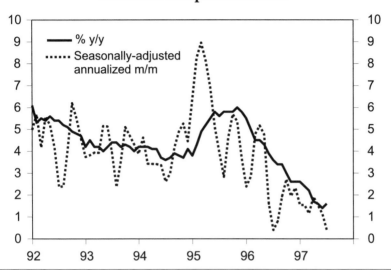

Figure 7.3   CPI year-on-year percentage change vs. seasonally-adjusted annualized month-on-month CPI

...and inflation expectations have continued to fall

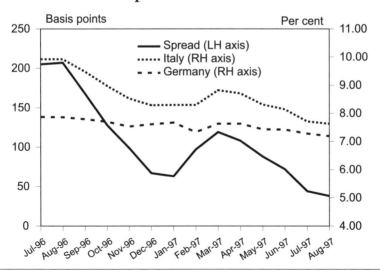

Figure 7.4   Implied one-year BTP/Bund spread (taken at the longest end of the curve)

Yields have carried on falling...

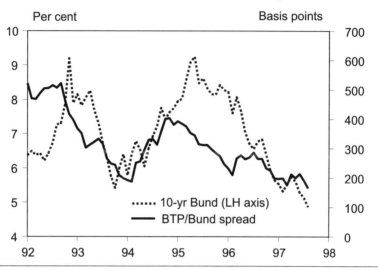

Figure 7.5   German 10-year yield and BTP/Bund spread

...as the lira has remained stable

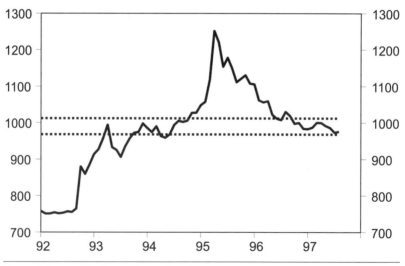

Figure 7.6   Lira/Deutschemark exchange rate

changes in the welfare system, and in particular on pension expenditure. The 3-year economic plan, known as DPEF, contains the main guidelines in terms of government budget policy. The government, unions and employers' association representatives began negotiations on welfare reforms in June 1997 to formulate a plan for the achievement of the DPEF guidelines. It is expected that these measures will consolidate 'temporary' achievements in tackling fiscal spending into permanent, and hence sustainable, ones in the long run.

Inflation at European standards...will it be sustainable in a fixed exchange rate regime?

After the November 1995 peak of 6.0 per cent, inflation has been decreasing, reaching a 30-year low of 1.4 per cent in June 1997. As shown in Figure 7.3, the seasonally-adjusted annualised inflation rate, which is the measure thought to be closely monitored by the Bank of Italy, has been below the unofficial 2 per cent target since the beginning of the year.

Despite the recent Consumer Price Index (CPI) dynamics, doubts may still arise about whether Italy will be able to maintain its current CPI performance once exchange rates are fixed irrevocably. The EMU environment itself, however, could be considered a 'guarantor' for the long run sustainability of low inflation. EMU's participation will in fact provide further stimuli for Italy to liberalize and deregulate industrial sectors that have been, thus far, sheltered from foreign competition (i.e. utilities, services, etc.). Competitiveness gains in these sectors, coupled with increases in flexibility in the labour market, will provide the necessary conditions for Italy to comfortably stay in the new low inflationary world and avoid the need for competitive devaluation.The financial markets seem to share the view that the past history of accelerating price dynamics is old news. In fact, the dramatic trend reversion in the annual rate of inflation has been well imbedded in market long term expectations, as extrapolated by the 10 year BTP/Bund forward rate spread taken at the longest end of the curve (i.e. from year 9 to year 10).

As a result of the favourable fundamentals and the acceptance of the Convergence Plan presented to the European Commission in July 1997, the 10 year BTP/Bund spread has broken the psychological 100 basis point barrier. In addition, despite a generalized foreign exchange market turbulence in the summer of 1997, the lira has maintained its level within +/- 2.25 per cent of its central ERM parity.

Conclusion

Italy's road towards EMU economic convergence has been a hard one. Significant progress has been made in the past year, starting with hard line fiscal policies, declining inflation and currency stability. Nonetheless, a past history of unrestrained fiscal policy has resulted in a public debt to GDP ratio in excess of 120 per cent, way beyond the 60 per cent Maastricht requirement. The latter, however, can be overridden if long term sustainability of the most recent economic trends can be demonstrated. As such, Italy's call for structural reforms will be the focal point of the assessment of its bid for EMU participation in the first wave.

Chapter 8 — The euro

Federico Prades
Economic Adviser
Spanish Banking Association

Spain and the euro

In the last ten years, the Spanish economy has faced a number of important challenges. Spain joined the EEC (as it was then termed) in January 1986. Since then, the Single Market project has been completed, the EU has been further expanded and the EMU project has been launched.

In this environment, Spain's integration into the EU has required extensive restructuring, liberalization and adaptation of the institutional, productive and financial sectors of the economy. Spain has successfully met these challenges and it is nowadays a more open, modern and integrated economy with good performance prospects. Further challenges face Spain, however, when the euro is introduced.

Growth remains strong...

Spain differs from many European economies in that growth has remained strong during the mid-1990s. In the first quarter of 1997, real GDP was around 3 per cent higher than a year earlier, a rate of growth well above the European average. Strong investment spending, exports and, more recently, consumer spending have been the main areas of growth.

This growth has also produced job creation, with employment growing by over 2 per cent year-on-year.

...and there has been significant improvement in correcting basic imbalances

In May 1997, the annual inflation rate reached a historic low of 1.5 per cent. This reflected an across-the-board decline in all of the components of the consumer price index.

Public sector finances are also running according to plan. In the first five months of 1997, the accumulated public sector deficit was 1.2 per cent of GDP, implying (on a straightforward arithmetical basis) that the deficit will be slightly less than 3 per cent of GDP in the full year, and hence that Spain will meet this Maastricht criterion.

Thanks to the sharp fall in interest rates, the subsequent impact on debt servicing costs and GDP growth running somewhat faster than predicted, the eventual result may be a deficit even lower than that 3 per cent target. Furthermore, the percentage of public deficit to GDP has fallen some 2.5 points since 1995. Spain looks well placed to meet the EMU budget deficit criteria for 1997.

The situation of the foreign sector is comfortable. In 1996, the current account balance was in surplus equal to 0.7 per cent of GDP; and this trend has continued into 1997. Exports are strong with growth of 10 per cent in real terms — and Spain has increased its share of world exports — while imports, although increasing rapidly, have limited their growth to 6-7 per cent. In April 1997, Spain's foreign exchange reserves stood at $62 billion dollars, an increase of 35 per cent over a year earlier.

Interest rates have fallen sharply

The improvements in inflation and the public sector deficits have led to a sharp decrease in Spanish interest rates and their differential with other European countries. Since the beginning of 1996, the Bank of Spain's intervention rate has dropped by 400 basis points from 9.25 per cent to 5.25 per cent and other short term interest rates and bond yields have also fallen. Interest rates have also fallen relative to Germany, with the yield differential between ten-year Spanish and German bonds down to 70 basis points by mid-1997.

After the upheaval of March 1995, the peseta exchange rate has been broadly stable against the main currencies in the ERM. In fact, the exchange rate for the Deutschemark has been within the (pre-1993) 2.25 per cent bands since early 1996.

Estimates of purchasing power parity for the peseta show the currency to be fairly valued at around its current exchange rate of peseta 84-85/DM (see Figure 8.1)[1]

1
  For example, the PPP estimates shown in Figure 8.2 show the peseta's PPP value on the basis that the peseta was at its PPP level in the first quarter of 1987. Relative cost and price changes in Spain and Germany since that time are then used to calculate the PPP path. This is the path the exchange rate would have followed if it had followed the trend in relative prices in Spain and Germany. It shows that Spain entered the ERM at an exchange rate which was slightly overvalued against the DM; that the fall In the peseta during the ERM crises in 1992/93 was excessive; and that the exchange rate is now close to its PPP level.

The peseta is stable in the ERM...

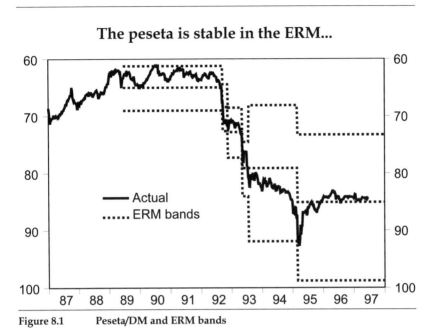

Figure 8.1   Peseta/DM and ERM bands

...and fairly valued on a PPP basis

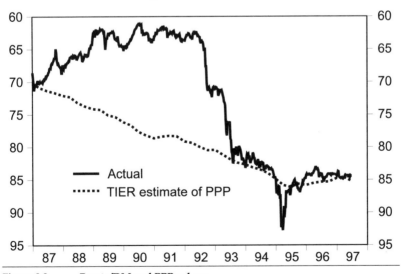

Figure 8.2   Peseta/DM and PPP values

Interest rates are falling sharply...

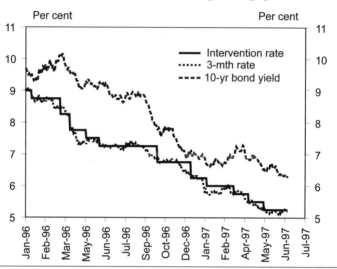

Figure 8.3   Spanish interest rates

...and getting closer to Germany

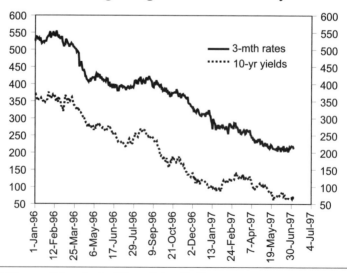

Figure 8.4   Interest rate differentials with Germany

Figure 8.5

Spain will join EMU

On balance, Spain is well placed to achieve the convergence criteria included in the Maastrict Treaty. The economy satisfies the exchange rate stability and the interest rate criteria; and there will be no problem in fulfilling the inflation and the public sector borrowing requirement criteria. Gross public debt, though slightly above the required 60 per cent of GDP, is expected to diminish in 1997. On balance, Spain will join EMU from the start.

Post-EMU priorities: deepening structural reforms

The government and most economic agents are convinced that Spain's membership of EMU is not in itself a solution to the problems of growth and job creation: further structural reform is needed. These reforms are aimed at three areas:

- overhauling the hard core of public debt;
- flexibility of the labour market; and
- the introduction of more competition within the services sector.

Up to now, reduction of the public sector deficit has been based on freezing government employees' salaries, reduced capital spending and the action of automatic stabilizers. The privatization policy is extensive and has been a success, although it has concentrated on profit-making companies.

Recently, employers and union representatives have agreed to certain reforms in the labour field such as lower termination costs for new contracts, incentives for open-ended contracts and better definitions of causes for dismissal. These measures are expected to have a positive effect on employment creation.

However, to take advantage of the potential available growth and the opportunities offered by the euro, it's necessary to continue deepening and widening these structural reforms.

Professor Tim Congdon
Lombard Street Research

Why the euro will fail

The argument of this chapter is controversial: it is that neither the EU, nor a subset of its members, will have a single currency on 1 January 1999, 1 January 2002, 1 January 2003 or, indeed, at any date in the relevant future. The coming failure—like the previous failures to reach the 1997 EMU deadline and indeed to meet a previous 1980 target set by the Werner Committee in the early 1970s—is already inevitable. The explanation is that Europe's political leaders have not understood the essential nature of the project on which they have embarked.

For most of these leaders, the unification of currencies consists, primarily, in the redenomination of units. They think that currency unification is similar to decimalization or metrication, and they correctly believe that these processes of redenomination—although expensive and a nuisance—change nothing fundamental in a nation's political system. While often urging currency unification as a step on the path to eventual political union at a later date, the leading supporters of EMU have not recognized that currency unification is impractical—indeed, impractical to the point of impossibility—without the prior or simultaneous establishment of political union. Further, they have not seen that the requisite political union must include a centralization of fiscal powers far more comprehensive than envisaged in the Maastricht Treaty.

Many people involved in EMU have focused on the convergence criteria specified in the Maastricht Treaty, as if it would be an easy step from the fulfilment of these criteria to currency unification itself. Fulfilment of the criteria would greatly facilitate unification, but they are only necessary conditions for the process to start. They in no sense define, or describe, the actual mechanics of moving from the present situation to the intended goal of a shared single currency. In fact, the convergence criteria are best interpreted as being necessary and (perhaps) sufficient conditions for the success of a fixed-exchange-rate area. They are most certainly not sufficient for the completion of a monetary union. The focus on the convergence criteria in the political debate is a serious misdirection of emphasis.

The prediction of EMU's failure made here may seem surprisingly bold and unequivocal. But it is important to remember one key point: there is no example in history of significant sovereign nation states sharing a single currency.

The three functions of money

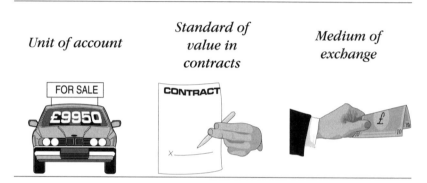

| Unit of account | Standard of value in contracts | Medium of exchange |

Figure 6.1

As is well known from the textbooks, money has at least three functions—to serve as a unit of account in price displays; to provide a standard of deferred value in contracts; and to act as a medium of exchange in transactions. The view that redenomination is the heart of currency unification stems from a misconception about the nature and relative importance of these three functions. The core of this misconception is to take the unit-of-account function as the crucial one in moving towards EMU. Many advocates of EMU seem not to have understood that they must also specify—at all stages of the process—how a money, or a number of monies, are to fulfil the two other functions.

In fact, the two other functions of money are not only vital for everyone who uses money, but also create most of the serious practical difficulties in currency unification. In particular, money can act as a medium of exchange only if it has *value*. The fact that money possesses value has a number of vital implications. In all modern societies, where money's original link with a commodity base has been broken, the conferment of value on money is a highly political matter. The note liabilities of the central bank (which is banker both to the government and the banking system) are 'legal tender'. So their nominal value depends on the force of law, not on their intrinsic value. Bank deposits can also be used to make payments and are therefore money, but they have this property only because of a general belief that they can be converted back into notes. In short, the nominal value of money, and hence its ability to act as a medium of exchange, depends on the force of law or, to put it another way, on the power of the state.

But the state's power to fix the nominal value of money does not mean that it can also, by mere proclamation, stabilize the real value of money. The value of money relative to goods and services in the aggregate depends, like the value of individual goods and services to each other, on supply and demand. If too much of a money relative to the quantity of goods and services is created, its value in terms of goods and services declines. Similarly, if too much of one money, *A*, is created relative to the quantity of another money, *B*, the price of money *A* in terms of money *B* ('the exchange rate') falls. This vulnerability of the exchange rate — while separate national currencies are still legal tender and have value — is crucial and needs to be strongly emphasized.

The state has the power to fix weights and measures; it undoubtedly also has the power to fix, within its own borders, the nominal value of the notes issued by its banker. But these are merely powers of denomination. It cannot guarantee the real value of its banker's note liabilities, even within its own borders; and it cannot give a totally safe guarantee about the value of these notes in terms of another currency. Of course, it may organize monetary policy in order to attempt to stabilize either the real value of a currency (i.e., the domestic price level) or a currency's international exchange rate. But its scope to organize monetary policy in this way must not be confused with its much simpler power of legal-tender denomination.

Much of the conceptual trouble in European currency unification stems from this confusion. It will be argued later in the chapter that the confusion is at its most grotesque in the proposals made by the European Commission and the European Monetary Institute for the change-over from the existing national currencies to the new single currency. The practical results of the proposals, as they currently stand, are likely to be at best bureaucratic muddle and, at worst, complete chaos. As the citizens (and policy-makers) of the EU begin to experience the muddle, the project will be abandoned. (Or, at any rate, it will be suspended, probably for another decade or two.)

The confusion between the unit-of-account and medium-of-exchange functions of money is fundamental. But it is the source of only some of the practical difficulties of EMU. The chapter will start with a review of the practical difficulties that Europe's monies will face, because of the EU's attempt to replace them with a new single currency, in fulfilling their functions as units of account and standards of deferred value.

Unit of account: the impact of EMU

The advantage of money, as a social institution, is that it constitutes a single unit of account within a defined area, which nowadays is invariably a nation state. As all domestic transactions and contracts are expressed in terms of this single unit of account, 'transactions costs' are drastically lower than if agents have to choose between several units of account. Of course, this advantage is lost in external transactions between agents in different countries, when conversion between currencies becomes necessary. A central aim of EMU is to reduce the transactions costs in such external transactions within Europe.

EMU would accomplish this end most neatly if the existing national currencies were abolished and replaced by the euro on a single day. However, the European Commission's Green Paper[1] on the subject rejects the 'Big Bang' approach of a sudden and total change, on the grounds that it would pose 'insurmountable difficulties'. Instead, the Commission proposes that Stage Three — when the exchange rate mechanism gives way to the single currency — is to consist of three periods, with a total length not exceeding four years. The three periods are:

Phase A   - when nothing much happens, apart from the formal establishment of the European Central Bank;

Phase B   - when exchange rates are 'irrevocably' fixed and the euro is created 'in its own right', so that transactions can be increasingly denominated in euro rather than national currency; and

Phase C   - when the euro becomes legal tender and the entire issue of national currency notes is to be exchanged, over a period of months, into euro notes.

While the official documents are not altogether clear:

1
 European Commission, "One Currency for Europe", Green Paper on the practical arrangements for the introduction of the single currency, 31 May 1995.

- *Phase A* appears to be the run-up to the start of Phase B on 1 January 1999;
- *Phase B* is to have a maximum length of three years (i.e., until 31 December 2001); and

- *Phase C* is to start (at the latest) on 1 January 2002 and to be completed quite quickly thereafter. Phase C is to last six months, according to the EMI Report[1], but only 'a few weeks', according to the Green Paper.[2]

Despite the ambiguities, the intention is evidently to have a period of dual pricing in Phase B and of parallel currency circulation in Phase C. In order to convert the national currencies into a single currency, there is to be a period in the relevant countries when the national currency and the euro are to coexist. There are to be two monies, or at least two units of account, at the same time. Clearly, one of the main advantages of money — that it reduces transactions costs because it constitutes a unique unit of account — is lost during the period of coexistence.

The increase in transaction costs during this period will depend partly on its duration. Retailers and banks are only now beginning to consider

Dual pricing

Cost for Marks & Spencer	£100m
Cost for all UK retailers	£2000m?
Cost for all EU retailers	£10,000m?

Figure 6.2

1 European Monetary Institute, 'The change-over to the single currency', November 1995, page 3.

2 European Commission, op. cit., page 17

this question, and to recognize a whole host of new and awkward problems. The evidence given to the Treasury Committee from retailers is clear-cut. The cost of change will be heavy and dual pricing is unacceptable if it is to last for any length of time. In evidence to the Treasury Committee of the House of Commons in 1996, Marks & Spencer put the cost of installing all the new systems and technology at £100 million, which implies a much larger figure (perhaps over £2000 million) for the retail sector as a whole. According to Mr. Bogg, 'There is a significant cost to systems if you are going to take dual currency at the point of sale because the software has to be adapted to do that.' Mr. Geldard, representing the British Chambers of Commerce, said frankly in his evidence that small businesses were short of information about the transition. On material prepared by the European Commission, he said, '...it is not information, it is a selling document. It has no practical information in it at all.' When pressed, his verdict became 'it is propaganda'.

In view of the problems of dual pricing and parallel circulation of legal tenders, many people believe that Phase B of Stage Three should be as short as possible. This conclusion was drawn by the Maas Committee, after it had conducted a survey of the relevant trade associations and took hearings on the subject in early 1995. However, there is considerable nervousness — particularly in the banking industry — about the feasibility of a short Phase B, unless the whole operation is expertly and meticulously planned in advance. Joint evidence from the British Bankers' Association and the Association for Payment Clearing Systems — also to the Treasury Committee of the House of Commons — agreed that, 'The proposed one-year duration of Phase A is too short to prepare and implement changes for the start of Phase B.' In a fascinating note, the former secretary to the UK's Committee of Inquiry on decimalization remarked that a critical path had to be mapped out for the mechanical task of manufacturing, distributing and storing all the banknotes and coins needed. In his words, 'It seems obvious that, even if all the specifications and designs were agreed now (and plainly they are not), then it would be well after the year 2000 before [the common designation of all prices across the EU in euro] could be attained.'

The banks may be particularly worried that, in Phase B, their own operations, including operations with the European Central Bank, are to be wholly in euro — whereas their customers remain free to use the national currencies. One aspect of this dichotomy needs to be highlighted. People leave money in banks because they believe that deposits can always, after the due period of notice, be converted into legal-tender notes. In order to meet this obligation, banks keep part of their assets in the form of 'vault cash' (i.e., notes in banks' tills) and another part in balances at the central bank. If their vault cash runs low, they convert some of their central bank balances into notes and withdraw them from the central bank. In that way, they have enough cash to meet their customers' requirements. But—if the Commission and EMI documents mean what they say—this standard set of operations will no longer be possible. (The operations have sometimes been characterized in the UK as the Bank of England acting as 'lender of first resort'.) If banks can deal with the ECB and national central banks only in euro, they presumably cannot convert their central bank balances into national notes. And, if they cannot extract national notes from the central bank, how can they meet customers' cash withdrawals?

In general, dual pricing and the concurrent circulation of distinct legal-tender notes are impractical. Economic agents converge on one money precisely because money confers its great benefits (in terms of cutting transactions costs) if it takes the form of only one unit of account. Most of the evidence submitted to official inquiries across Europe has suggested that—when the new currency was introduced—there would be rapid convergence towards it. If so, the intended three-year length of Phase B would become unnecessary.

However, there is an alternative view that, in Phase B, very few people and companies would adopt the new currency. The Commission and EMI policy documents are not entirely clear about the status of the euro in Phase B. Euro bank notes would not be legal tender, since no euro-denominated notes would be in circulation, whereas the national currencies would retain legal-tender status. The standard formula is that national currencies would nevertheless merely be 'expressions of the euro', which would be Europe's currency. Ostensibly, the everyday problems that arise from the separate identities of the national currencies would become a thing of the past. But would that really be so?

Since national-currency-denominated notes are only 'expressions of the euro', the question arises of their validity during Phase B for payment (i.e., as media of exchange) outside their country of issue. To be more specific, during the year 2000, would franc-denominated notes issued by the Banque de France be legal tender in Germany and would Deutschemark-denominated notes issued by the Bundesbank be legal tender in France? The answer to these questions seems to be 'no' (an official answer would be welcome!), but then it would be necessary to convert from francs into Deutschemarks when moving from France into Germany with the intention of making purchases in Germany (and vice versa when moving from Germany into France). Of course, there would be conversion costs in exchanging the currencies. So, francs and Deutschemarks would retain their separate identities and would not be mere 'expressions of the euro'.

A further question is the exact legal status of payments in euro during Phase B. It would continue to be illegal to refuse payments in national-currency notes in their countries of issue. But — as there are no legal-tender notes denominated in euro — would it be illegal to refuse cheque payments and other transfers in euro? Since, in most countries, any agent can refuse cheque payments and other transfers — even when denominated in the national currency — there would presumably be nothing illegal in refusing cheque payments and other transfers denominated in euros. In such circumstances, there would surely be a marked reluctance to hold euro deposits. However, if there were such reluctance, why should any significant transactions be in euro? The Green Paper talks hopefully of 'the immediate creation of a critical mass of activities in Ecu' from the outset of Phase B, with the usage of the euro trickling down smoothly from central bank operations, to wholesale money markets, to banking, to financial markets, and finally, to retail transactions. While this trickling-down is supposed to be voluntary, it is nowhere explained why, during Phase B, it should be rational for any individual company or institution to operate in euro rather than the national currencies. (Phase C — in which the euro is legal tender — would be a quite different matter.)

The claim that, during Phase B, the usage of euro will increase steadily, by the process of trickling-down, is pure conjecture. No one can say in advance whether this claim would be right or wrong. Because the adoption of the euro is voluntary, it is almost impossible to predict the speed at which the new currency would spread or, indeed, whether it would spread at all. The mere announcement of a new, allegedly superior unit of account is not enough to ensure that agents will want to use it, as has been clearly demonstrated by the almost 18 years of the Ecu's own existence. But, if hardly any agents start to use the euro in Phase B, the demand to hold it will be very limited. The small demand to hold euro implies that its supply must be also restricted if it is to keep its value, putting clear limits on the growth of the euro-denominated part of the banking system. This point — which is very important — will be picked up in the later discussion. (It has to be conceded to the EMU-optimists that some companies, such as Siemens and Phillips, have said that they intend to do all their internal accounting, including invoicing, in euro from 1 January 1999. But managers in these companies seem to be very uncertain about how they will proceed if their suppliers and customers continue to work in national currencies.)

The analysis in the last paragraphs contains a key message: EMU would be feasible — or, anyhow, closer to feasibility — if Phase B and Phase C were collapsed into a single Phase, ideally a very short one. That view is almost certainly correct. But the European Commission and the EMI, taking a cue from their political masters, have rejected the 'Big Bang' approach. They intend that, in Phase B, the euro will be a unit of account, but not that it should be a legal-tender liability of a particular institution with the value to qualify it as a medium of exchange. But—if a so-called 'money' is not legal tender and therefore has no value—it would be irrational for agents to use it as a unit of account in preference to existing national currencies. In effect, the official description of the euro's monetary status in Phase B (that the national currencies 'are expressions of the euro') is a contradiction in terms. The root of the error—as in other areas of this subject—is confusion between the unit-of-account and medium-of-exchange functions of money.

The three-year timetable envisaged for Phase B and the six-month timetable foreseen for Phase C is too long. They would, if ever attempted, lead to logistical difficulties quite as severe as those that the Commission fears would come from a 'Big Bang'.

Standard value in contracts: the impact of EMU

So, the strains of dual pricing and parallel currency circulation, and more generally of trying to run two units of account in harness, argue for a short—but very well-planned—period of change-over from the national currencies to the new single currency. Unhappily, the effect of a short change-over on the second function of money—to provide a standard for deferred payments—would be harmful. If the governments of Europe want to give their citizens money that is reliable and trustworthy in framing contracts, the change-over must last several years. Indeed, it may be that the dominant reason for the rather protracted duration of Phases B and C is that, when certain contractual problems are explained to them, these governments shrink from the consequences of a short change-over.

If all price terms related to a single point in time, money would not need to be used as a standard of deferred payment. However, in practice, the price terms in many contracts relate to extended periods of time. These terms are usually expressed as a rate of interest, although fixed nominal sums and indexation clauses are also common. (For example, insurance policies—which may last 30 years or more—often include obligations to pay claims to policy-holders up to a certain sum of money, expressed in nominal terms or in nominal terms adjusted by a price index.) These rates of interest, fixed nominal sums and indexation clauses are specific to a particular currency. As the substitution of one currency by another disrupts contracts with such terms, it impairs money's effectiveness as a standard of deferred payment. The extent of the disruption depends partly on the length of the contracts and partly on the extent to which the new currency differs from the old one. The disruption—in sharp contrast to the simple redenomination of current prices—can have major distributive effects on the contractual parties. (Examples of the affected contractual parties are insurance companies and their policy-holders, bondholders and the issuers of bonds, and the borrowers, depositors and shareholders of banks and housing finance intermediaries.)

Here lies the rationale for certain well-known features of the Maastricht Treaty. First, the disruption of contracts is most manageable if the change-over from the national currencies to the single currency takes several years. (During the change-over—i.e., in Phases B and C of Stage Three when both currencies are supposedly 'in being'—existing contracts can be run off in the old currency and painlessly replaced by contracts in the new currency.) Secondly, because a large gap in interest rates between the currencies due to be unified is likely to cause greater redistributive upheaval than a small gap, the Maastricht Treaty says that currencies can qualify only if the interest rate differentials between them are sustained at a low level over a period of some years.

The Maastricht Treaty's insistence on narrow interest rate differentials as a condition for participation is sensible. Indeed, the problem of contract discontinuity is now well known, and has been exercising many people. Banks are particularly concerned. As noted by an Italian banker, 'There is an important trade-off between ensuring the sanctity of contract and limiting (by some conventional solution) the extent of redistribution from debtors to creditors. The banking system is, of course, not extraneous to that difficulty, as it also has some portions of its balance sheet represented by medium- or long-term assets or liabilities.'[1]

However, to say that the problem of contract discontinuity is now well-known is not to accept that Europe's policy-makers know what to do about it. It is not sufficient to propose—as in the Commission's Green Paper and the communication from the Madrid summit—that the terms in existing contracts are to be redenominated, regardless of their distributive consequences. (So, if 'the rate of interest' in a 20-year fixed-rate franc contract maturing in 2005 was 9 per cent, it will remain 9 per cent in a 20-year fixed rate contract with interest and servicing payments in francs or euros during Phases B and C, and eventual repayment in euros.) The

---

1
Mario Sarcinelli, 'Bets off for '99', The Banker, March 1996, p.15

official recommendation, as it currently stands, is inadequate in at least two ways.

First, the reference interest rates and price indices in contracts relate to particular currencies and jurisdictions. (For example, in the UK interest rates can be expressed in terms of base rate, interbank rate, a finance house rate or whatever, whereas other countries have different types of interest rate. Further, the UK has a national retail price index, prepared every month with certain characteristics in terms of coverage, methods of compilation, and so on. Germany has regional consumer price indices. as well as a national index—again with each having its own characteristics. Ireland, meanwhile, calculates its consumer price index only once a quarter. In fact, every country has indices which are peculiar to itself.) The reference rates and indices may sometimes have a natural successor in the brave new world of EMU, but sometimes they will not. In all cases the choice of the successor rates and indices will have redistributive consequences. The contractual upheaval involved will undoubtedly lead to legal disputes and extra costs for business.

In one particular case—the market in interest rate and currency swaps—the impact of contract discontinuity could be devastating. The decisions to embark on certain types of swaps product often depend on the appearance of extremely small interest rate differentials, which may be technical in nature. Where swaps in the candidate EU currencies mature after 1 January 1999 or 1 January 2002, severe redistributional consequences are likely whatever happens, while the choice of the successor references rates is of vital importance to the parties involved. In its evidence to the Treasury Committee of the House of Commons, Barclays Bank noted that 'considerable legal uncertainty faces the financial community but there appears to be little indication of what, if anything, the authorities contemplate doing about it.'

Secondly, it cannot be a matter of indifference to the parties in financial contracts whether, during Phases B and C, they make or receive payments in the national currencies or euros. In Phase B, euro notes are not to be legal tender, and so the euro will not be much used (possibly not used at all) in retail transactions. Many customers of financial institutions (for example, people drawing on their bank deposits or receiving redemption money on the maturity of a life insurance policy) will be most unhappy if they receive euros and then are forced, at significant cost in terms of bank charges, to convert back into national currencies. The rigid, allegedly 'irrevocable', locking of exchange rates in Phase B will not be much comfort to these people, if they are constantly having to incur heavy commission and bank charges on small conversions between euros and the national currencies.

None of the discussion in this section should be taken to deny the theoretical feasibility of EMU. It is, of course, possible for Europe's leaders to pass laws that ride roughshod over the original intentions of contractual parties. (They appear to have decided on this course already.) It is also possible — although it would be very expensive — for dozens of committees to be formed to determine the correct successor rates of interest, price indices and so on, and for statistical agencies to be charged with the task of preparing the necessary data. (In fact, the EMI's attempts to harmonize the compilation of banking data across Europe are well advanced, although causing considerable inconvenience to national central banks and banking systems.) Finally, it is imaginable that Europe's governments might find a way of compensating their citizens, bankers and retailers for the cost of the millions of small currency conversions that would be needed in Phases B and C. It is imaginable, but surely very unlikely.

This discussion shows that, even in Phase B — when exchange rates are (in principle) irrevocably fixed, people would continue to worry about whether they took or made payments in euros instead of the national currencies. Costs of converting between them would remain. Further, and more damagingly, the demand to hold euros would depend on the relative ease of transacting in euros and national currencies. (Traders in certain markets might post wider differences between buying and selling prices when these prices are expressed in euros rather than national currencies.) It has become timely to consider how the problems of transition might affect the usage of the euro as a medium of exchange.

Medium of exchange: the impact of EMU

 Earlier in this chapter, a strong distinction was drawn between money as a unit of account and money as a medium of exchange. Contracts and prices can be stated in terms of a particular unit of account, or 'money', but a unit of account has no value in itself. On the other hand, when payments are made in 'money' as a medium of exchange, the money involved must have value. In modern circumstances, it has value because it is a claim on the central bank, either directly in the form of notes or indirectly via a bank deposit. In other words, money acts as a medium of exchange only if it is a liability of the banking system. The ultimate basis of the value of the central bank's note liabilities is their legal-tender status. (Coins — which have become trivial — are a minor exception.)

Units of account can be determined by administrative fiat (governments can add or subtract zeros to all prices, without changing any relative value);

the real value of money as a medium of exchange, by contrast, depends on the demand for it relative to the supply. The real value of money as a medium of exchange can be influenced by policies to control its supply, but—unless the state is to provide a formal guarantee of some sort—it cannot be determined by administrative fiat.

A defining feature of Phase B of Stage Three is that exchange rates are to be irrevocably fixed, so that—in the words of the Green Paper—'The Ecu ceases to be defined as a basket of currencies and becomes a currency in its own right, for which the national currencies are perfect substitutes, i.e., different denominations of the single currency'. As a result, '[o]fficial foreign exchange markets for the participating national currencies will disappear completely' (p. 15). The phrase 'a currency in its own right' appears decisive. But it is, in fact, hopelessly ambiguous and uncertain. Crucially, it begs the very fundamental question of whether, in Phase B, the Ecu/euro is to be merely a unit of account or is to become a fully-fledged medium of exchange with value in transactions. However, there is one consideration—already much emphasized in this analysis—which makes it most unlikely that the euro would become a fully-fledged medium of exchange during Phase B. This is that bank notes denominated in it are not designated as legal tender until Phase C.

Advocates of EMU may dismiss the objection as irrelevant, because everyone would know that the euro equivalent of their national currencies would be legal tender on 1 January 2002—but people would still have to use money between 1 January 1999 and 1 January 2002! In Phase B, euro-denominated deposits and transactions would have to compete with continuing deposits and transactions denominated in national currencies, even though the euro versions would suffer from the disadvantages of unfamiliarity, the inconvenience of conversion costs in small transactions and the extra computational burden. Whatever officialdom may say, people would still fear that the central rate between the euro and their national currencies might change. It was suggested earlier in this chapter that the demand to hold euros might be quite small in Phase B. If the ECB were to try to expand euro usage by issuing many euro-denominated liabilities, the value of such liabilities would fall relative to national currency notes.

As the euro could act as a medium of exchange only if it were a liability of banking systems, the questions arise of whether banks would also convert their assets into euros and how this process of conversion would be conducted. Even for the asset counterpart to the notes issued by the ECB, such questions are awkward. The official documents from the Commission and the EMI say that public debt should be redenominated into euro 'from the start of Phase B to the extent that it is technically possible'. So, public debt held by central banks should be straightforward to handle. But what about all the other assets held by central banks, including commercial bills and loans to banks? The problems become much greater for commercial banks, where the bulk of the assets are loans to the private sector. There is a clear risk that, because of their customers' actions, a large net currency exposure (either short or long of the national currency against the euro) would emerge.

The Green Paper makes a blithe conjecture about the disappearance of 'official foreign exchange markets' in Phase B. However, the national currencies would still be very much in existence — as media of exchange, which are liabilities of banking systems. (The documents say that the euro comes into being 'in its own right', not that the Deutschemark, franc and so on cease to exist in their own right.) Just as banks could become exposed to large net currency exposure between the euro and national currencies, so they could become exposed to large net currency exposures between the Deutschemark and the franc, the French franc and the Belgian franc, and so on. In contrast to the present situation, wherein a speculator can lose money because the rate can move against him (or her), in Phase B he or she could lose nothing except transactions costs. Far from abolishing speculative uncertainties, the scope for taking speculative positions would expand almost without limit.

The authors of the Green Paper might reply that these fears are groundless because eventual conversion into the euro at the fixed exchange rates is certain. But it is not certain. To repeat, politicians and bureaucrats can fix units of account, but they cannot — by sheer announcement — fix the relative values of distinct media of exchange. (And, of course, in Phase B the various national currencies would remain distinct media of exchange!) If governments were 100 per cent confident that, at the start of Phase C on 1 January 2002, the conversion rates of banks' assets and liabilities would be exactly as agreed at some date in 1998, they could give a guarantee to the banks to compensate them for any devaluations or revaluations that actually occurred. However — despite being pressed by London Investment Banking Association on the need for such a guarantee — the relevant authorities have refused to give one. (Information on this comes to the author from Mr. Graham Bishop — who does not, however, agree with the conclusions drawn here or elsewhere in this chapter. Note that the granting of a government guarantee to compensate for the foreign exchange losses would be much simpler to arrange if there were only one government instead of several.)

The Green Paper gives the game away by stating on p. 17 that, in Phase C, 'The old national currencies may be exchanged free of charge at the national central banks during the statutory [change-over] period laid down in each country.' A clear implication is that the same option—of free-of-charge conversion at the central bank—is not to be available in Phase B. However, if this is so, how can the national currencies and the euro be the 'perfect substitutes' envisaged on p. 15? And how are the whole panoply of monetary policy actions to be effective in Phase B, as the Green Paper pretends on p. 15 and p. 16, if banks are to be charged conversion costs whenever they try to convert national notes into euro notes? How can open market operations work, and lender-of-last-resort services be provided, if all conversion transactions between banks and central banks are subject to a charge? The very notion of 'monetary policy' becomes unmanageable.

The various points made in the last few paragraphs—about the costs of conversions between the national currencies and the euro, and the resulting lack of equivalence between the currencies and the euro—could be overcome if it were illegal during Phase B to carry out any exchange between the national currencies and the euro, except at the officially-determined 'irrevocably-fixed' exchange rates, precise to six decimal places. But that is preposterous. To be effective, not only would all exchanges between the existing and continuing national currency notes have to be at the fixed rate, precise to six decimal places (!), but so also would all transactions where an exchange of currencies was implicit. The computational burden would be absurdly high.

The argument in the last few paragraphs is profoundly damaging to the whole project of EMU. An analogy with building a house may be evocative, if a little overdrawn. The earlier analysis of the function of money as a unit of account suggested that the architects of EMU were proposing, during the construction Phase, to use bricks of different shapes and sizes (dual pricing, parallel circulation of legal tenders). The analysis of the function of money as a standard of deferred payment showed that they were designing a house without a roof (i.e., without the necessary legal and institutional framework for the clear redenomination of contracts). But the analysis of the function of money as a medium of exchange is even more destructive. The key planning documents are so incoherent about concepts and definitions that the house is being built on a verbal bog. In effect, such is their confusion between the roles of money as a unit of account and a medium of exchange that the authors of the Commission's Green Paper and the EMI Report do not seem really to understand what the term 'money' means.

Further practical problems—assuming that EMU is, somehow, completed

The point of this chapter is not to assert that the EU can never have a single currency. German monetary unification demonstrated both that currency unification is possible and how it ought to be done. It happened on a single day, 1 July 1990. (Or, perhaps, two days, i.e., 30 June and 1 July.) Thereafter, the ostmark was no longer legal tender anywhere in Germany; all the key monetary policy levers were centralized in the Bundesbank and all the essential fiscal powers were concentrated in the hands of the government of the former West Germany. The West German government—via the social security system, the Bundesbank and other agencies—had to spend large amounts of money on the process, and continues to do so. A large majority of the citizens of East Germany were eager for full political union with West Germany. Even so, their acceptance of currency unification was secured by a bribe—conversion of their money balances into Deutschemarks at a favourable exchange rate. The result was a huge cost to the taxpayers of West Germany. In effect, German monetary unification took place via the 'Big Bang' route, with the costs underwritten by a single government. This single government amalgamated the powers of two previously separate governments.

The message from this example—and, in fact, from previous examples of currency unification—is simple. The EU can have a single currency if:

1. it is prepared to make the change-over from a multiplicity of national legal tenders to a single European-wide legal tender on a single day, with (nearly) all prices and contracts redenominated immediately, and all redenominations complete within a few weeks;

2. all monetary policy levers are concentrated in the central bank, which is the sole issuer of the new legal tender;

3. the nations of the EU surrender ultimate control of taxation and government expenditure to a new central government which has fiscal sovereignty over all of them, and

4. this new central government has the power and the resources—with expenditure probably running into many billions of Ecus/euros—to compensate the private sector for losses from contractual upheaval and the costs in carrying out the currency changeover.

The Commission's Green Paper is wrong to claim that the Big Bang method would encounter 'insurmountable obstacles'. On the contrary, the only way to overcome the technical difficulties in currency unification is to pursue the Big Bang option, with all that means in terms of the formation of a federal European superstate. Many people may disagree with this verdict. They may insist that — despite the impracticalities identified in the analysis — a single currency will nevertheless emerge by the middle of 2002. Assume, charitably, that they are right. With the problems of transition overcome, would EMU work?

As noted earlier, there is no example in history of significant sovereign nation states sharing a single currency. Why? The answer may lie in the risk of serious 'free rider' problems. In essence, when there is one government, one state-sponsored central bank and one money, it is obvious where the responsibility for inflation lies. In the final analysis, it rests with the government. (Even if central bank incompetence has been the immediate cause of inflation, the central bank's behaviour is heavily conditioned by its relationship with government, which is its ultimate master.) By contrast, when there are several governments, a system of national central banks subordinate to a single European central bank and one money, who is to blame for inflation? The answer is 'not any one of the governments individually, but either the central bank or the central bank plus the governments taken collectively'. No single government remains under the same pressure to behave in a financially responsible manner, as at present.

Worse, they have every incentive to misbehave, in two ways. First, the larger the budget deficit, the higher the proportion of Europe's resources they can capture for the benefit of their own citizens without paying for it by taxation — but the larger the budget deficit collectively for all governments, the higher the risk of inflation. As is well known, the Maastricht Treaty and the Stability Pact have correctly tried to anticipate this danger by spelling out limits on budget deficits and the size of the total public debt. However, it remains unclear whether these limits would work in practice, as their effect can be evaded by definitional tricks of one kind or another. Moreover, the limits contained in the Maastricht Treaty and the Stability Pact clearly erode national fiscal sovereignty.

Secondly, the higher the proportion of short-term monetary financing of the budget deficit to non-monetary financing, the cheaper the cost of debt service to governments. (The shape of the yield curve, which traditionally slopes upward to the right, explains the relative cheapness of short-term financing.) But, again, the greater the amount of monetary financing by all governments collectively, the higher the risk of inflation.

The Maastricht Treaty recognizes this by prohibiting overdraft finance for governments at the ECB.

This second 'free rider' problem has not been much discussed in the literature of currency unification. It may be very important. If Europe's governments all want to borrow at the short end (to save interest costs), monetary control would break down. The ECB must therefore have some means of managing the maturity profile of the various governments' debt. But that would infringe the governments' current prerogative to fix the maturity profile. Governments and the ECB would be at loggerheads. The most vivid illustration is provided by a wartime emergency. If the UK went to war, its government would probably want to borrow from the Bank of England. At present it can do so without any restriction. (Of course, inflation would follow.) However, under EMU, the government would have to seek the ECB's permission to borrow at the short end. Plainly, the government's ability to finance and fight a war would be undermined. The UK would suffer a drastic erosion of sovereignty.

In its inquiry in 1996, the Treasury Committee of the House of Commons sought only limited evidence on this aspect of the subject. Mr. Martin Wolf of the *Financial Times* suggested that a complicated process of negotiation and compromise between national governments and the ECB would be needed. As the details (of Treasury bill issuance, of central bank and commercial bank transactions in public debt in the secondary market, of debt management tactics and so on) would inevitably be very political, Europe's finance ministers and central bankers would be foolish to postpone them until late in Phase A. Mr. Wolf is quite right to have characterized the ECB as 'a constitutional monstrosity', since it is not clear whether ultimate power over a range of monetary policy matters would rest with its officials or with democratically-elected governments. (A similar problem arises with foreign exchange intervention. Foreign exchange reserves are owned by governments, but decisions to intervene have monetary effects.)

Of course, the free rider problems would disappear if there were only one central government and one central bank. The tensions under EMU arise because several purportedly-sovereign governments attempt to share a single currency.

EMU, as envisaged in the Maastricht Treaty, will not work

The analysis in this chapter does not say that EMU is impossible. It claims rather that EMU is impractical to the point of impossibility if, one, it is attempted in the manner proposed by the Maastricht Treaty and, two, it is introduced before—rather in conjunction with—political union. In this context, political union must include a thorough-going centralization of fiscal and debt management powers.

There is no escape from the interdependence of political and monetary union. German politicians and Bundesbank officials have correctly emphasized that the two ideas are inseparable. Indeed, for many of Europe's leaders, the great merit of EMU is that it is a building-block—perhaps the most important building-block—in the construction of political union. In view of the proliferation of official statements associating political and monetary union, Mr. Kenneth Clarke's view that 'I do not believe EMU is any threat to the continued existence of the nation state' is puzzling.

At any rate, the EU will fail to create a single currency unless it simultaneously establishes a political union. Although the Maastricht Treaty is the most ambitious attempt yet to press for both monetary and political union in Europe, it does not go far enough in the centralization of fiscal powers to make currency unification practical. From a broader perspective, the coming collapse of the EMU process matters little. Life across the EU will go much as before, with governments instead concentrating on important and tractable policy issues. But—because of the absurd over-investment of political credibility in the EMU project—the failure to introduce the single currency will be widely regarded as the worst setback to European integration since the signing of the Treaty of Rome in 1957.

Section

III

The euro

Institutional and legal issues

Chapter 10

Darren Williams
& Richard Reid
UBS Limited

A central bank for Europe

The European Central Bank is due to assume control of European monetary policy in 1999. On paper, it is a strong replacement for the Bundesbank. In practice, it could be handicapped if the German central bank's low inflation constituency is not mirrored elsewhere in Europe. The statute of the European Central Bank attempts to create an independent central bank with a firm mandate for low inflation. The ECB's primary goal is to ensure price stability, it is prohibited from financing government deficits and is protected from political influence and interference. Indeed, on most relevant factors, the ECB scores as well as, if not higher than, the Bundesbank. But the Bundesbank's position amongst the world's most credible central banks is not due simply to the statute book. Rather, it reflects a domestic consensus in favour of low inflation which might not be shared by Europe as a whole. Without such a constituency, the ECB's ability to resist political pressure — which would surely arise should Europe fail to answer its unemployment problems — might be greatly reduced. Some European governments have already expressed their reservations about the blue-print for monetary union signed at Maastricht. The French government's insistence on a 'clarification' of exchange rate policy, an upgrading of the commitment to growth and employment, and a downgrading of the commitment to budgetary discipline, all represent potential threats to the independence of the central bank. The ECB will be a new central bank operating in a new monetary area and, as such, it is impossible to know exactly how it will perform. It is clear that, on paper, it is a fitting replacement for the German central bank. But if the current institutional setting is changed, especially to allow for the creation of a political counter-weight to the central bank, there might come a day when the passing of the Bundesbank is widely lamented.

The Bundesbank will be subsumed by the ECB

In eighteen months time, the face of European monetary policy is set to change. If, as is widely expected, EMU goes ahead on schedule, the Bundesbank will cease to be the dominant force in European monetary affairs.

Instead, as a constituent member of the European System of Central Banks (ESCB) which will govern European monetary policy during stage 3, the Bundesbank will be just one voice amongst many, and its influence will be much reduced. Despite an almost-impeccable track-record in the forty years since it came into existence, the German central bank is likely to have little more say over the course of European monetary policy than its less-credible counterparts from Southern Europe.

Fortunately, this is not the whole story. Although we will lose the Bundesbank as we currently know it, the central bank's work has not been in vain. Throughout the 1980s and 1990s, the Germanic model of central banking has been exported to most other European countries. So much so, that it is hard to believe that the Bundesbank could have been any tougher on inflation than the Bank of France or Bank of Italy have been in recent years.

But the Bundesbank's greatest legacy is that the future guardian of European monetary stability, the European Central Bank (ECB), has been designed along German central banking lines. Indeed, on paper, the ECB might even represent an improvement on the Bundesbank. Where there are ambiguities in the division of responsibilities between the central bank and the government in the Bundesbank Act, the Maastricht Treaty makes these explicit, mainly to the advantage of the central bank. In theory, the ECB is a form of 'super-Bundesbank'.

Theory is, of course, very different from practice. The Bundesbank's reputation for hard-nosed anti-inflation policies was not bestowed upon it by the Bundesbank Act. Rather, it was earned over a period of time, and through a series of tough battles with the federal government, some of which the Bundesbank lost, but most of which it won.

In this respect, the recent gold revaluation dispute between the Bundesbank and the government is instructive. When the central bank decided that Mr Waigel's plans posed a threat to its independence, it objected in a very public manner, and popular support for the Bundesbank caused the government to abandon its plans. It has been suggested that this represents an early victory for the ECB, although we are more sceptical. The Bundesbank's ability to successfully confront its own government owes much to the special position it holds within German society. Would the ECB be able to rely on such support?

Bundesbank Council

ECB Council?

Figure 10.1   Will the ECB be a good replacement for the Bundesbank?

If the ECB is to successfully take the place of the Bundesbank, it will have to earn its spurs. Unfortunately, it is impossible to know today precisely how the ECB will perform in practice. But there are several important clues and, in this article, we would like to explore these. We start by taking a closer look at issues related to central bank independence, move on to consider how these are likely to apply to the ECB, before finally drawing some conclusions.

Assessing central bank independence

The benefits of independence

Central bank independence has been the subject of considerable debate in recent years. Although many different methods have been used to quantify the degree of independence, most point to an inverse relationship between independence and inflation (see Figure 10.2). In other words, the more independent a central bank, the lower inflation tends to be. In addition, there has been little conclusive evidence of any relationship between the independence of a central bank and either the strength or volatility of economic growth.

It is the evidence suggesting that central bank independence delivers lower rates of inflation without any identifiable cost in terms of growth which lies behind the move towards greater independence in recent years. However, some caution is necessary, as there is little evidence to suggest a causal link between independence and low inflation. Rather, it can be argued that independent central banks are more likely to be established in countries where there is an existing consensus in favour of low inflation. Germany is a case in point.

Central bank independence in the European Union

Historically, the European countries have had very different approaches to central bank independence. Figure 10.3 suggests that the northern European countries such as Germany, Switzerland and, to a lesser extent, the Netherlands, have histories of strongly-independent central banks, but that countries such as France, Italy, Spain and the UK do not. (Note: while Figure 10.4 shows the results of just one study, the findings of alternative approaches are very similar.)

Of course, the last few years have seen significant changes in this latter group of countries, with even the Bank of England now 'operationally' independent of government control (this is not the same as full independence as the government retains the right to set the key inflation target). Meanwhile, the central banks in France, Italy and Spain have all

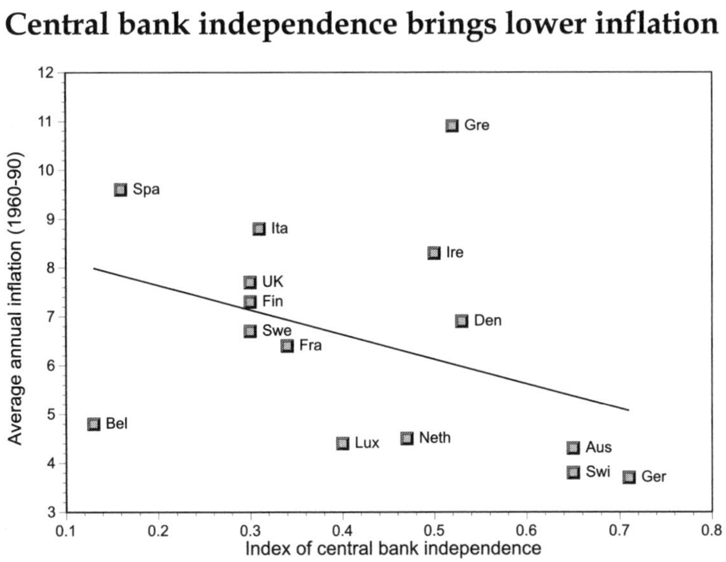

Central bank independence brings lower inflation

Figure 10.2   Central bank independence and inflation performance
Source: Bank of England, drawing on data in Cukierman, 1992. The index is a weighted average of data from 1950-89 of legal provisions regarding; (1) appointment and dismissal of the governor; (2) procedures for the formation of monetary policy; (3) objectives of central bank policy; (4) limitations on lending by the central bank. The minimum score (least independent) is zero and the maximum score (most independent) is 1.00. Note that independence has recently improved in many European countries.

been granted independence during the 1990s. It is, however, instructive that in none of these cases did the granting of independence pre-date the signing of the Maastricht Treaty (which committed EU governments to independent central banks).

Hence, it is not clear that France's move to grant independence to its central bank means that society has been fully converted to the concept of Germanic central banking. Rather, as recent arguments in favour of a political counter-weight to the ECB might suggest, the move might simply have been seen as a necessity for France to qualify for monetary union. Put another way, it is still not clear that the low-inflation consensus which allows the Bundesbank to conduct a strong anti-inflation policy in Germany exists on a wider European scale.

Functional independence

We shall return to the political dimension of EMU later. For now we shall focus on the ECB as proposed in the Maastricht Treaty. As mentioned earlier, the need to soothe German concerns about giving up the Deutschemark were critical to the success of the Maastricht negotiations and, consequently, the ECB has been constructed largely upon German central banking lines. Indeed, in some respects, one might argue that the ECB has been given an even stronger mandate than the Bundesbank:

- According to the Maastricht Treaty, the main responsibility of the ECB 'shall be to maintain price stability'. This is more explicit than the Bundesbank Act which states that the main function of the central bank is 'safeguarding the currency'. It is the Bundesbank, reacting to the deep-rooted fear of inflation in Germany, which has interpreted this clause in the strictest of fashions.

- The Maastricht Treaty forbids the ECB from granting 'overdrafts or any other type of credit facility' to EU or national government bodies. The Bundesbank Act was recently changed to bring it into line with this, having previously allowed the government to have minor credit facilities with the central bank.

In reality these are relatively minor differences. However, that the ECB compares favourably with a central bank which is widely regarded as being amongst the most independent and inflation-averse in the world must count as a strong point in its favour.

Institutional independence

Although the economic literature differs in the methods used to quantify central bank independence, there is considerable agreement over the importance of the institutional setting. How central bank officials are appointed, the length of their mandates, the security of their tenure and the government's ability to influence or interfere in central bank decisions are all regarded as important determinants of a central bank's independence.

Monetary policy decisions of the ECB will be made by the Governing Council, which comprises the Executive Board together with the Governors of the National Central Banks (NCBs) in the single currency area. This is a mirror image of the Bundesbank, where interest rate decisions are made by the Central Bank Council, which comprises the Directorate of the Bundesbank and the presidents of the Land Central Banks.

The ECB: an anatomical view

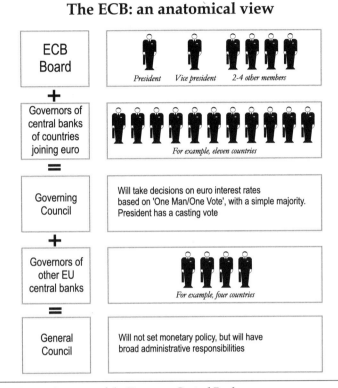

ECB Board	President Vice president 2-4 other members
+	
Governors of central banks of countries joining euro	For example, eleven countries
=	
Governing Council	Will take decisions on euro interest rates based on 'One Man/One Vote', with a simple majority. President has a casting vote
+	
Governors of other EU central banks	For example, four countries
=	
General Council	Will not set monetary policy, but will have broad administrative responsibilities

Figure 10.3   Structure of the European Central Bank

The appointment of members to the Executive Board has been the cause of some consternation, as they will be made 'by common accord of the member states'. In other words, they will be appointed by politicians. This alone, however, is not sufficient reason for alarm. After all, the members of the Bundesbank Directorate are also appointed by the government. In addition, some comfort can be drawn from the fact that all appointees to the Executive Board must be experts in either monetary or banking matters.

Once nominated to these positions, members of the Executive Board will have a mandate of eight years and this will not be renewable. Such a period compares favourably with existing central bank practice (it is the same as for the Bundesbank). Moreover, single terms are thought to remove at least some of the incentives for central bank members to bow to political pressure. Finally, while members of the Executive Board can be removed or dismissed, this is only possible in exceptional circumstances and only at the request of either the Executive Board itself, or of the Governing Council of the ECB.

The Executive Board will probably comprise six members (strictly speaking there can be between four and six members). In a broad monetary union this means they would be outweighed on the General Council by the Governors of the NCBs. This has led to concerns, not least on the part of the EMI, that the independence of the ECB could be put at risk if the statutes of the NCBs are not brought more closely into line with those of the ECB itself. Unfortunately, while the EMI has made a series of recommendations for NCB independence, the Maastricht Treaty is actually rather vague.

Voting behaviour of the ECB

On the assumption that the EMI's concerns over NCB statutes are addressed before EMU starts, the overall institutional setting of the ECB can be said to be on a par with, if not superior to, that of the Bundesbank. One area where the ECB is perhaps at a disadvantage, however, is that the Executive Board is likely to have a weaker weighting in Governing Council interest rate decisions than its counterpart, the Directorate, currently has in Bundesbank decisions.

There have been several attempts to determine the likely voting behaviour of the ECB. A useful starting point is to assume that the six members of the Executive Board are professional central bankers, and that they will thus adopt conservative voting habits. The unanimity required to elect members to the Executive Board, the length and security of their tenure and the requirement of technical expertise, all suggest this is a reasonable assumption.

Although this might be a reasonable assumption, it is also quite clearly a best-case scenario. This can be at least partially offset by assuming that the NCB members of the Governing Council vote according to their own government's preferences. This is clearly a worst-case scenario. Providing the euro members are restricted to a core grouping of just six countries (which seemed the most likely scenario last year) this would not represent a problem. The six members of the Executive Board, plus the Bundesbank representative, would give conservative central bankers a majority on a twelve-member Governing Council. This helps explain the Bundesbank's preference for a narrow EMU.

Today, the most likely scenario is that EMU will go ahead on a wide basis, probably including eleven countries. Even under this scenario, it would require only two other NCBs to join the Bundesbank for the conservative central bankers to hold a majority on the Governing Council. As Figure 10.6 highlights, longer-term track-records suggest that three

The ECB: Bundesbank Mark II?

ECB	Bundesbank

Primary goal/function

'The primary objective of the ESCB shall be to maintain price stability'

'The Deutsche Bundesbank regulates the amount of money in the economy ... with the aim of safeguarding the currency'

Relationship with government

'Without prejudice to the objective of price stability, the ESCB shall support the general economic policies of the Community.'
'When exercising the powers and carrying out the tasks and duties conferred upon them by this Treaty, neither the ECB, nor a national central bank, nor any members of their decision-making bodies shall seek or take instructions from Community institutions or bodies, from any government of a Member State or from any other body.'

'Without prejudice to the performance of its functions, the Deutsche Bundesbank is required to support the general economic policy of the Federal Cabinet. In exercising the powers conferred upon it by this Act, the Bank is independent of instructions from the Federal Cabinet.'

Decision-making body

The Governing Council, which comprises the members of the Executive Board (president, vice-president and between 2 and 4 other members) and the governors of the National Central Banks of the euro area (up to 15 at present, depending on the number of initial members of the single currency).

The Central Bank Council, which comprises the members of the Directorate (president, vice-president and up to 6 other members) and the presidents of the 9 Land Central Banks.

Cont.

ECB	Bundesbank

(cont.)

How members are chosen

'Members of the Executive Board shall be appointed from among persons of recognised standing and professional experience in monetary and banking matters and by common accord of the member states at the level of the heads of state or of government, on a recommendation from the Council after it has consulted the European Parliament and the Governing Council (of the ECB).'

National Central Bank governors are appointed according to relevant domestic procedures.

'Members of the Directorate must have special professional qualifications.'

'The president and vice-president and the other members of the Directorate are nominated by the Federal Cabinet and appointed by the president of the Federal Republic. When making such nominations, the Federal Cabinet shall consult the Central Bank Council.'

The above also applies to presidents of the Land Central Banks, except that they are nominated by the Bundesrat.

Term of office

For the Executive Board, this is normally for eight years and is non-renewable. (Note that some of the initial appointments will be for shorter periods to allow for continuity.)

Members can only be removed if they no longer fulfil the conditions required to carry out their duties, or for gross misconduct, and then only on application from the Governing Council or Executive Board.

The Treaty requires that NCB governors have a mandate of at least five years and that similar provisions as above apply for removal.

Directorate members and the presidents of the Land Central Banks are normally appointed for a period of eight years. These are renewable.

There are no provisions in the Bundesbank Act for removing a member of the Directorate or a president of a Land Central Bank.

Voting procedure

For the purposes of monetary policy decisions, the Governing Council makes its decisions by simple majority, with the president having the casting vote in the event of a tie.

Central Bank Council decisions are made by simple majority, with the president having the casting vote in the event of a tie.

Figure 10.4   Comparing the ECB and the Bundesbank

All quotations are taken from the relevant sections of the Maastricht Treaty and the Bundesbank Act

other central banks could probably be relied upon – Austria and, to a lesser extent, the Netherlands and Luxembourg.

There are two potential problems with this analysis. The most obvious is that the ability of a 'hard-core' of conservative central bankers to determine ECB policy decisions would clearly be at risk in an even wider monetary union. However, this should not be a major concern as the behaviour and reputation of the ECB are likely to be established in the very early years of its existence, when membership should be limited to the initial eleven countries.

The assumption that all Executive Board members will be 'hawks' might also be questionable. Admittedly, incoming EMI president Wim Duisenberg is a professional central banker, and he is currently in pole position to become the first president of the ECB. So too is Michel Camdessus, France's preferred candidate for the role. Nonetheless, it is disturbing that some EU countries seem to see advantages in securing an ECB president of their choosing.

The real threats to independence

Even allowing for some of the points raised in the last section, the Maastricht Treaty lays out a blue-print for a central bank which is at least the equal of the Bundesbank. Mr Issing, the Bundesbank's chief economist, is in little doubt of this – 'in terms of providing institutional protection to a monetary policy geared towards price stability, as much as can realistically be expected has been achieved'. However, Mr Issing goes on to say that 'the possibility of a dispute over the monetary policy stance of the European Central Bank remains'.

There are three areas in which a dispute between European governments and the ECB could emerge – exchange rate policy, employment policy and fiscal policy.

The exchange rate

'Among the criticisms frequently raised over the statute of the European Central Bank, the exchange rate problem vis-à-vis non-EU currencies has no doubt to be taken most seriously.'

Otmar Issing

The most likely area of dispute between the ECB and governments is over the appropriate level of the exchange rate. The Maastricht Treaty allows the European Council to enter exchange rate systems and agreements and,

Keeping the NCBs Independent

Institutional independence

The rights of third parties to:

- give instructions to NCBs or their decision-making bodies;

- approve, suspend, annul or defer decisions of NCBs;

- participate in the decision-making bodies of an NCB with a right to vote; or

- be consulted (ex-ante) on an NCB's decisions

...are incompatible with the Maastricht Treaty.

Personal independence

The statutes of the NCBs should ensure that:

- governors of NCBs have a minimum term of five years;

- a governor of an NCB may not be dismissed for reasons other than that he/she no longer fulfils the conditions required for the performance of his/her duties or if he/she is guilty of gross misconduct;

- other members of the decision-making process of NCBs have the same security of tenure as governors;

Functional independence

Requires the statutory objectives of NCBs to be in line with the ESCB's objective (i.e. price stability).

Figure 10.5   Ensuring the independence of national central banks
Source: Progress Towards Convergence 1996, European Monetary Institute.

most importantly, to 'formulate general orientations for exchange-rate policy' (article 109.2).

This represents a departure from the situation in Germany. Although the federal government reserves the right to choose the appropriate exchange rate regime for the Deutschemark (i.e. Bretton Woods, the ERM), the Bundesbank is in active control of exchange rate policy. This is one of the strengths of the Bundesbank Act, which charges the German central bank with 'safeguarding the currency'. If this is interpreted as applying to

Governing councils: ECB cf. Bundesbank

ECB Governing Council	Bundesbank Central Bank Council
Executive Board:	**Directorate:**
President, vice-president, between 2 and 4 other members	President, vice president, up to 6 other members
Normal representation: 6	Normal representation: 8
National central bank governors:	**Land central bank presidents**
Representation: 11 members[1]	Representation: 9
Total members: 17	**Total members: 17**

Figure 10.6   Comparing the ECB and Bundesbank Governing Councils
[1]*This depends upon the membership of the single currency. At present, there are 15 National Central Banks within the EU. The 11 members shown above reflects UBS's view that EMU will take place in 1999 and on a broad basis (i.e. including all EU countries except for Greece and the political 'opt-outs' – the UK, Denmark and Sweden.).*

the external (as well as the internal) value of the currency, the Bundesbank has a direct responsibility for exchange rate policy.

The ECB has no such responsibility or powers, and is involved in exchange rate policy purely on a consultative basis. Nonetheless, the Maastricht Treaty does state that any exchange rate decisions or orientations of the European Council must be 'without prejudice to the primary objective of the ESCB to maintain price stability'.

The key question is who decides whether or not a given orientation for exchange rate policy is consistent with price stability. In practice, the ECB is likely to decide for itself, but this could lead to a direct and damaging conflict with the European Council. Moreover, it is not clear that the ECB would win such a stand-off, particularly if concessions granted to France at the Amsterdam summit allow for an interpretation of 109.2 which favours the European Council.

Employment policy

The Maastricht Treaty calls upon the ECB to 'support the general economic policies of the Community with a view to contributing to the achievement of the objectives of the Community'. Among other things, the latter include

Independence & inflation:
the EU league table

	Independence rating[1]	Inflation rating[2]	Total rating[3]
Germany	4	4	8
Austria	4	4	8
Netherlands	3	3	6
Luxembourg	2	4	6
Belgium	2	3	5
Denmark	3	2	5
Ireland	3	1	4
France	2	2	4
Finland	2	2	4
Sweden	2	2	4
Greece	3	1	4
UK	2	1	3
Italy	2	1	3
Spain	1	1	2
Portugal	n/a	1	n/a

Figure 10.7   Central bank independence & inflation ratings of EU central banks
[1]*The independence rating is based on the findings of several studies, over varying time-spans pre-dating the Maastricht Treaty. A score of 4 represents the most independent type of central bank.*
[2]*The inflation rating is based on annual average inflation between 1960 and 1990. A score of 4 represents the most inflation-averse country.*
[3]*The total rating is the sum of the first two columns.*

a 'high level of employment and social protection'. Again, the Treaty makes it clear that this should be secondary to the primary goal of price stability and, it should be noted, there is a very similar clause in the Bundesbank Act. However, as with exchange rate management, there is a potential conflict of interests here, particularly if France is successful in its attempts to gain greater recognition for the social aspects of the Maastricht Treaty.

Fiscal policy

'If, even with the threat of non-participation, a member state is neither willing nor able to observe the limits for budget deficits and indebtedness, it is hardly likely that it will make increased efforts when such a strict sanction is no longer available.'

Otmar Issing

The Maastricht Treaty expressly forbids central bank financing of government deficits. In addition, the Stability and Growth Pact signed at the Amsterdam summit aims to place severe constraints upon the ability of governments to run 'excessive' budget deficits. However, liberal interpretation of the EMU entry criteria and continued watering-down of the stability pact raise serious question marks over just how binding these constraints are likely to be.

Should European governments run excessive budget deficits within EMU, and allow debt ratios to rise, then the independence of the central bank could be impaired. There are number of mechanisms through which this could work. First, in highly-indebted countries, political pressure for lower interest rates is immense and there is also a greater tolerance for high inflation. Second, it is difficult for a central bank in such countries to completely ignore the impact on government solvency of unrestrained interest rate hikes.

However, let us assume that the ECB refuses to finance an excessive deficit—as the Maastricht Treaty requires. The result would be higher interest rates and the crowding-out of domestic spending. This would be compounded if the resultant policy-mix led to an appreciating currency. The ECB would then be 'responsible' for weak growth (perhaps a recession) and a dramatic rise in unemployment, which would lead to enormous tensions. In these circumstances, the temptation to resort to indirect financing of deficits by intervention on the domestic money market (to prevent interest rates from rising) or the foreign exchange market (to prevent the currency from rising) is easy to see. Hence, Mr Issing's statement that 'regardless of the degree of independence, monetary policy will remain an integral part of the economic process'.

Conclusions

We have established that, on paper, the European Central Bank ought to be a fitting replacement for the Bundesbank. On most counts it scores as well, if not better than, the German central bank. In addition, it has the advantage of having its statutes enshrined in an international treaty which would require the unanimous agreement of all EU member states to change.

However, it is equally clear that the Bundesbank's position as the world's most credible central bank is not due simply to the Bundesbank Act. Rather, it reflects a domestic consensus in favour of low inflation which might not yet be shared by Europe as a whole. If not, then the ECB's ability to resist political pressures could be much reduced. As demonstrated by the recent gold revaluation debacle in Germany, that is the real strength of the Bundesbank.

Moreover, there are worrying signs. Having seen the consequences of a rigid commitment to fiscal rules and Bundesbank-style interest and exchange rate policies, the French government is beginning to shy away from the blue-print for monetary union signed at Maastricht. The Jospin government's insistence on a clarification of article 109.2 governing exchange rate policy, on an upgrading of the commitment to growth and employment, and on a downgrading of the commitment to fiscal discipline all represent potential threats to the independence of the central bank.

With the Amsterdam summit allowing for further discussion and negotiation of these points, it is impossible to give a conclusive view on the likely inflation credentials of the ECB. As the legislation stands, it is probably fair to say that the ECB will be a fitting substitute for the Bundesbank. However, if France succeeds in weakening the stability pact yet further, and in establishing an economic pillar to govern European exchange rate policy and act as a political counter-weight to the ECB, then there might come a day when many lament the passing of the Bundesbank.

Chapter
10

Appendix

The Maastricht Treaty and ECB independence

General objectives of the European Union

Article 2[1]

The Community shall have its tasks, by establishing a common market and an economic and monetary union and by implementing the common policies or activities referred to in Articles 3 and 3a, to promote throughout the Community a harmonious and balanced development of economic activities, sustainable and non-inflationary growth respecting the environment, a high degree of convergence of economic performance, a high level of employment and social protection, the raising of the standard living and quality of life, and economic and social cohesion amp solidarity among member states.

Objectives and tasks of the European System of Central Banks

Article 105

1.   The primary objective of the ESCB shall be to maintain price stability. Without prejudice to the objective of price stability, the ESCB shall support the general economic policies of the Community with a view

---

[1] *Note that, to maintain consistency throughout this book, certain typographical changes have been made to the extracts from original Community texts. These changes have no material affect on either the meaning or sense of the texts.*

to contributing to the achievement of the objectives of the Community as laid down in Article 2. The ESCB shall act in accordance with the principle of an open market economy with free competition, favouring an efficient allocation of resources, and in compliance with the principles set out in Article 3a.

2.   The basic tasks to be carried out through the ESCB shall be:

– to define the monetary policy of the Community;

– to conduct foreign exchange operations consistent with the provisions of Article 109;

– to hold and manage the official reserves of the member states;

– to promote the smooth operations of payment systems.

Independence of the European System of Central Banks

Article 107

When exercising the powers and carrying out the tasks and duties conferred upon them by this Treaty and the Statute of the ESCB, neither the ECB, nor a national central bank, nor any members of their decision-making bodies shall seek or take instructions from Community institutions or bodies, from any government of a member state or from any other body. The Community institutions and bodies and the governments of the member states undertake to respect this principle and not to seek to influence the members of the decision-making bodies of the ECB or of the national central banks in the performance of their tasks

Financing of government deficits

Article 104

2.   Overdraft facilities of any other type of credit facility with the ECB or with the central banks of the member states in favour of Community institutions or bodies, central governments, regional, local or other public authorities, other bodies governed by public law, or public undertakings of member states shall be prohibited, as shall the purchase directly from them by the ECB or national central banks of debt instruments.

Exchange rate policy

Article 109

1. By way of derogation from Article 228, the Council may, acting unanimously on a recommendation from the ECB or from the Commission, and after consulting the ECB in an endeavour to reach a consensus consistent with the objective of price stability, after consulting the European Parliament, in accordance with the procedure in paragraph 3 for determining the arrangements, conclude formal agreements on an exchange rate system for the Ecu in relation to non-Community currencies. The Council may acting by a qualified majority on a recommendation from the ECB or from the Commission, and after consulting the ECB in an endeavour to reach a consensus consistent with the objective of price stability, adopt, adjust or abandon the central rates of the Ecu within the exchange rate system. The President of the Council shall inform the European Parliament of the adoption, adjustment or abandonment of the Ecu central rates.

2. In the absence of an exchange rate system in relation to one or more non-Community currencies as referred to in paragraph 1, the Council, acting by a qualified majority either on a recommendation from the Commission and after consulting the ECB or on a recommendation from the ECB, may formulate general orientations for exchange-rate policy in relation to these currencies. These general orientations shall be without prejudice to the primary objective of the ECB to maintain price stability.

3. By way of derogation from Article 228, where agreements concerning monetary or foreign exchange regime matters need to be negotiated by the Community with one or more States or international organisations, the Council, acting by a qualified majority on a recommendation from the Commission and after consulting the ECB, shall decide the arrangements for the negotiation and the conclusion of such agreements. These arrangements shall ensure that the Community expresses a single position. The Commission shall be fully associated with the negotiations. Agreements concluded in accordance with this paragraph shall be binding on the institutions of the Community, on the ECB and on member states.

Structure of the European System of Central Banks

Article 106

1. The ESCB shall be composed of the ECB and of the national central banks.

3. The ESCB shall be governed by the decision-making bodies of the ECB which shall be the Governing Council and the Executive Board.

Article 109a

1. The Governing Council of the ECB shall comprise the members of the Executive Board of the ECB and the Governors of the national central banks.

2. The Executive Board shall comprise the President, the Vice-President and four other members. The President, the Vice-President and the other members of the Executive Board shall be appointed from among the persons of recognized standing and professional experience in monetary and banking matters by common accord of the Governments of the member states at the level of Heads of State or of Government, on a recommendation from the Council, after it has consulted the European Parliament and the Governing Council of the ECB. Their term of office shall be eight years and shall not be renewable. Only nationals of member states may be members of the Executive Board.

Article 109b

1. The President of the Council and a member of the Commission may participate, without having the right to vote, in meetings of the Governing Council of the ECB. The President of the Council may submit a motion for deliberation to the Governing Council of the ECB.

Protocol on the Statute of the European System of Central Banks

Article 10

2. Subject to Articles 10.3 and 11.3 each member of the Governing Council shall have one vote. Save as otherwise provided for in this

Statute, the Governing Council shall act by a simple majority. In the event of a tie the President shall have the casting vote.

4. The proceedings of the meetings shall be confidential. The Governing Council may decide to make the outcome of its deliberations public.

5. The Governing Council shall meet at least ten times a year.

Article 12

1. The Governing Council shall adopt the guidelines and take the decisions necessary to ensure the performance of the tasks entrusted to the ESCB under this Treaty and this Statute. The Governing Council shall formulate the monetary policy of the Community, including, as appropriate, decisions relating to the intermediate monetary objectives, key interest rates and the supply of reserves in the ESCB and shall establish the necessary guidelines for their implementation.

    The Executive Board shall implement monetary policy in accordance with the guidelines and decisions laid down by the Governing Council. In doing so the Executive Board shall give the necessary instructions to national central banks. In addition the Executive Board may have certain powers delegated to it where the Governing Council so decides.

    To the extent deemed possible and appropriate and without prejudice to the provisions of this Article, the ECB shall have recourse to the national central banks to carry out operations which form part of the tasks of the ESCB.

Article 14

2. The statutes of the national central banks shall, in particular, provide that the term of office of a Governor of a national central bank is no less than 5 years. A Governor may only be relieved from his office only if he no longer fulfils the conditions required for the performance of his duties or if he has been guilty of serious misconduct.

Clifford R. Dammers
Secretary General, International Primary Market Association

Chapter
11

The euro:
eliminating legal uncertainty

The voluntary adoption by a significant number of sovereign states of a single, new currency is unprecedented and has caused bankers, businessmen and lawyers to ask whether this momentous step poses legal problems. Few, if any, initiatives in European history have attracted so much interest in the legal aspects of a change in financial relationships.

The short answer is that for the vast majority of financial contracts and obligations — mortgages, bills of exchange, loan agreements, cheques — the substitution of a single currency for the national currencies of the EU member states which participate in the monetary union will not raise any legal problems. An obligation to pay in a national currency will be converted into euros calculated in accordance with the official conversion rates which are expected to be set some time in 1998. For example, a corporation which borrowed 10 million French francs from a bank on 5 January 1998 and promised to repay it on 5 January 2002 together with interest at 6 per cent p.a. will be required to repay the bank a sum in euros calculated at the official conversion rate. The term of the loan and the rate of interest — and all other terms and conditions — will remain unchanged.

The legislative solution

This result follows from the general principle of law that every country has the power to change its currency and all other countries must recognize and give effect to any such change. After unification the Ostmark was replaced by the Deutschemark and the change was recognized all over the world. Similarly, when France changed from the *ancien* franc to the *nouveau* franc, all other countries recognized the change. This legal principle is referred to in legal shorthand as *lex monetae*.

EMU is slightly different in at least two regards. First, the euro will be a new currency to be adopted by a group of sovereign states on a voluntary basis. It is not the imposition of an existing currency on to a country which was absorbed by another. For example, Nazi Germany absorbed Luxembourg into the Third Reich and replaced the pre-1939 Luxembourg currency with the Reichsmark. Second, the euro will substitute on a one for one basis for the Ecu, which is not strictly a currency but a currency basket.

The basic principle of *lex monetae*, however, does apply to financial obligations and the single European currency.

Early in the preparation for EMU legal experts became concerned that these two problems might lead to disputes and possible litigation; possibly in the case of run of the mill financial obligations but more realistically in more complicated contracts where it could be argued that the purpose of the contract had ceased to exist or that it was no longer possible to perform the contract in a meaningful way because one of the essential terms had disappeared, such as a pricing source. Those concerns were heightened by the confusion in the law of frustration of contract and impossibility.

These concerns led the European Commission to prepare European legislation which would provide the legal framework for the euro. The legislation takes the form of two European Regulation which were approved by the Dublin and Amsterdam summits respectively,

The Article 235 Regulation

The first, which was adopted on 17 June 1997 pursuant to Article 235 of the Treaty creating the European Community, resolves most of the legal uncertainty referred to above. It was adopted as early as possible so that the treatment of Ecu obligations and the issue of continuity of contract would be dealt with long before 1999 (see Appendix 1).

Article 2 of the Regulation provides for the conversion of the Ecu into the euro. The Ecu is to be converted into the euro, on a one for one basis, on 1 January 1999. By Ecu is meant the Official Ecu (as defined in Council Regulation 3320/94) and used by the European Union as its unit of account and the private Ecu if it is defined to be equal to or the same as the Official Ecu (as is the case in most Ecu-denominated bond issues and loan agreements). If a contract provides for payment in the private Ecu and does not contain such a definition, the Regulation provides a presumption that the Ecu was meant to be the same as the Official Ecu but this presumption ' is rebuttable taking into account the intention of the parties'. There do not seem to be very many, if any, contracts involving the private Ecu where the parties intended not to follow the Official Ecu.

Article 3 of the Regulation preserves the continuity of contracts. It is intended to ensure that neither party to a financial contract, such as a loan agreement or a derivative contract, has the right to terminate or amend the contact just because the national currency in which the payment obligations are denominated is converted into the euro or because of the introduction of the euro more generally. It reads as follows: 'The introduction of the euro shall not have the effect of altering any term of a legal instrument, nor give a party the right unilaterally to alter or terminate a legal instrument'. 'Legal Instrument' is given the broadest possible definition and includes all contracts and agreements, whether in writing or oral, unilateral legal acts and payment instructions.

The Article goes on to provide that if both parties to a legal instrument—a contract—agree otherwise, either at the time the contract was entered into or subsequently, they are free to amend or terminate the contract.

In addition to resolving any doubts about the status of the Ecu and continuity of contract, the Regulation sets the framework for the introduction of the euro in those areas where advance notice, with legal certainty, is necessary so work on changes which require a long lead time can be started.

Article 4 provides that the conversion rates (as one euro expressed in terms of each of the national currencies) shall be adopted on 1st January 1999 with six significant figures counting from the left.

The regulation also establishes rounding rules for conversions and cash payments and accounting.

The Article 109l (4) Regulation

The second regulation, the text of which has been approved by the Council of Ministers but which will not be enacted until 1998 when the member states which will participate in the first wave are known, will be adopted pursuant to Article 109l(4) of the Maastricht Treaty (see Appendix 2).

It will provide the monetary law for the euro. The Regulation will make the euro the currency for the participating member states.

Legal certainty beyond Europe

The Article 235 Regulation applies in all member states, whether or not they participate in monetary union. Many international financial contracts are governed by English law, even when the currency in question is not sterling.

Article 2 and 3 of the Regulation will resolve most questions involving the conversion of Ecu into the euro and continuity of contract for such contracts.

The question is less clear-cut if the parties have chosen the law of a non-EU member to govern their contract. For example, many master swap agreements are government by New York law and private placements and lease financings in Japan are frequently governed by Japanese law.

Lex monetae will provide for continuity of the vast majority of such contracts even though the Article 235 Regulation does not apply outside the European Union directly. However, under the principle of *lex monetae* the courts of New York and Japan will recognize the effect of the two Regulations. In fact, the Regulations will be helpful because they clarify the legal framework and make it easier for a foreign court to know exactly what the monetary law of the European Union is.

However, the more difficult cases, such as disappearing price sources and basis swaps, may prove to be more problematic where the contracts are governed by the law of a non-EU jurisdiction . The problem is probably most acute in the case of the law of the State of New York because many financial contracts are governed by New York law, the courts appear never to have referred expressly to *lex monetae* in their reported decisions and the judicial decisions applying the doctrines of frustration of contract and impossibility are relatively numerous and sometimes difficult to reconcile.

In order to resolve the potential legal uncertainty in New York and other jurisdictions, the interested international and national trade associations and legal working groups have drafted and introduced bills in the New York and Illinois State legislatures which provide for continuity of contract and the recognition of the conversion of the Ecu into the euro on terms very similar to the language of the Article 235 Regulation. At the time of writing, the legislation has been passed by the New York Senate and by both Houses of the Illinois Legislature (see Appendix 3).

Legal working groups are reviewing the law in California, Japan, Switzerland and other countries to determine if similar legislation is desirable or necessary in those jurisdictions.

Successor price sources

One of the remaining areas of legal (and economic) risk is successor price sources. When the euro is substituted for national currencies interest rates for the national currencies will disappear. If the Deutschemark disappears, the Frankfurt interbank offered rate for deposits in Deutschemarks will no longer exist. Long term contracts, such as revolving bank credits, floating rate notes and fixed/floating swaps, which provide for payments to be determined by reference to such price sources may be called into question.

Most such contracts have fallback provisions which tell the parties how to calculate the reference rate if the originally intended reference rate disappears. However, such provisions were drafted before or without reference to EMU.

Article 3 of the Article 235 Regulation sets forth the policy that such contracts are to continue but the Regulation does not and could not direct the parties as to how to calculate payments when the original price source disappears.

The international and national trade associations are working with the sponsors of the price sources and the data vendors such as Reuters and Telerate, who publish the reference rates, to provide for successor price sources. It is essential that these successor price sources are clearly identified as such and that the market accepts them without dispute as the proper successor to the original price sources.

This will happen if the new price sources make economic sense and the legal niceties are observed. For example, it is essential that the Reuters and Telerate pages be clearly labelled as 'successor pages'.

Most important there must be co-operation and good will from market participants.

Rider B

Continuity clauses

Transition periods can be especially difficult for legal relationships which span the transition period. The period leading up to 1 January, 1999 is no exception.

In addition to legislation, what can be done to ensure that contracts which are entered into before the introduction of the euro and require performance after 1 January 1999 are not subject to legal doubt? One solution is to include in new contracts provisions setting forth the parties' considered agreement as to what they want to happen after 1 January 1999. If the parties want the contract to continue unchanged in every respect except for the currency of payment, they can provide for that result. Alternatively, they can decide that the contract should terminate once the euro is substituted for the national currency or they can decide that some of the terms of the contract should be modified.

Most banks have decided that it is not necessary to insert continuity of contract clauses in their contracts. The approval of the Euro Regulations at the Dublin Summit encouraged those banks which had adopted this course of action.

A few banks and securities firms in New York, London and Frankfurt have decided to include continuity of contract clauses in certain types of contracts — e.g., derivative contracts and bond issues. In some cases the banks only do so if their customer is from outside the European Union, reasoning that such customers are less likely to be bound by the Euro Regulations or to be aware of the imminence of EMU.

Such clauses are usually disclosure clauses rather than operative clauses. In other words, they inform the investors or the bank's customer/counterparty that EMU may happen and that it could result in the conversion of the currency of payment.

The International Swaps and Derivatives Association published on 8 July, 1997 an EMU Continuity Provision for use in existing and future ISDA Master Agreements where the parties wish to document their intention that EMU should not affect the continuity of their contract (see Appendix 4).

The International Primary Market Association Working Group on Currency Continuity concluded that continuity of contract clauses are not necessary or desirable for bond issues or medium term notes, at least where they are governed by the laws of one of the 15 member states of the European Union — as is the case for almost all bond issues and medium term notes which are denominated in European Union national currencies.

Conclusion

The legal framework for the introduction of the euro is in good shape. The most important areas of legal uncertainty have been resolved and the remaining problems are much less difficult and more manageable. The work of the European Commission and the European Council is to be commended.

Section

IV

The *euro*

The foreign
exchange market

Pat McArdle
Ulster Bank Markets[1]

Chapter

12

Fixing euro exchange rates

Introduction and overview

The third stage of EMU will begin on 1 January 1999 and will extend to 30 June 2002, at the latest. From the beginning of this stage, the euro will become a currency in its own right and the conversion rates of the national currencies of those member states adopting the euro will be fixed irrevocably. National currencies will initially remain in circulation as sub-units of the euro. By 30 June 2002, at the latest, the euro will have fully replaced the national currency units of the participating member states.

The two basic texts governing the introduction of the euro are the Maastricht Treaty and the Madrid European Council conclusions. The Maastricht Treaty, a lengthy and complex document signed on 7 February 1992, deals with the institutional structures and start-up provisions for the single currency. The European Council, meeting in Madrid on 15 and 16 December 1995, reaffirmed the treaty provision that Stage Three of EMU will start on 1 January 1999 at the latest but went on to overlay this with an elaborate transitional arrangement whereby the new currency will be introduced in phases which will end no later than 30 June 2002. The Madrid Council also provided for the establishment of a legal framework for the euro by means of Council Regulation.

There is, therefore, no shortage of legal provisions regarding the introduction of the single currency. The existing corpus of legislation contains significant detail regarding the timing and method of introduction of the euro but is, however, largely silent on the key question of the setting of the irrevocably-fixed euro conversion rates. This silence is all the more

[1]
*The views expressed are personal and do not necessarily reflect those of Ulster Bank Markets.
The author is indebted to a number of people, in particular, John Corrigan, Elena Flores, Brendan
Halligan and André Louw, who kindly commented on earlier drafts.*

The Maastricht Treaty and the Madrid Summit on euro exchange rates[1]

'At the starting date of the third stage, the Council shall, acting with the unanimity of the member states without a derogation, on a proposal from the Commission and after consulting the ECB, adopt the conversion rates at which their currencies shall be irrevocably fixed and at which irrevocably fixed rate the Ecu shall be substituted for these currencies, and the Ecu will become a currency in its own right. This measure shall by itself not modify the external value of the Ecu. The Council shall, acting according to the same procedure, also take the other measures necessary for the rapid introduction of the Ecu as the single currency of those Member States.'

Article 109l(4) of the Maastricht Treaty

'The European Council therefore decides that, as of the start of Stage 3, the name given to the European currency shall be euro. . . . The specific name euro will be used instead of the generic term "Ecu" used by the Treaty to refer to the European currency unit'

Madrid Summit December 1995

'A Council regulation entering into force on 1 January 1999 will provide the legal framework for the use of the euro. From that date, the euro will be 'a currency in its own right' and the official Ecu basket will cease to exist. This Regulation will have the effect that the national currencies and euro will become different expressions of what is economically the same currency. As long as different national monetary units still exist, the Council Regulation will establish a legally enforceable equivalence between the euro and the national currency units ("legally enforceable equivalence" means that each monetary amount is assigned, in a legally enforceable way, an unchangeable counter value in terms of the euro unit at the official conversion rate and vice versa)'.

Madrid Summit December 1995

Figure 12.1

[1]*Note that, to maintain consistency throughout this book, certain typographical changes have been made to the extracts from original Community texts. These changes have no material affect on either the meaning or sense of the texts.*

surprising given that the setting of the rates is at the heart of and is, indeed, the very essence of the single currency project. From the beginning of 1999, until the middle of 2002 at the latest, the single currency will exist in the form of a set of fixed conversion rates. The success or failure of the project will, to a large extent, depend on how this critical phase evolves. One will, however, search the texts in vain for an indication of how these rates will be set or, more importantly, the precise levels at which they will be fixed. All we are told in the treaty is that the conversion rates will be set, on the basis of unanimity, by the Council at the starting date of the third stage and that this measure shall, by itself, not modify the external value of the Ecu (see Figure 12.1).

It is hardly surprising that this omission has led to a major debate regarding the fixing of the rates. The uncertainty and speculation which the current situation may engender has, in turn, led to various suggestions regarding the methodology which should be used to fix the rates and to calls for the preannouncement of this methodology, if not the actual rates. The objective would be to give greater certainty and avoid market turbulence in the run up to the start of Stage Three in 1999. The setting of the irrevocably-fixed conversion rates is one of the major outstanding issues in the context of the whole single currency project.

We will proceed to review the various suggestions that have been made but note at this stage that, whichever method is adopted, the rates chosen must conform to the economic reality that they allow for a sustainable locking of the currencies and economies of the participating member states and, ideally, they should also be close to existing market rates. The EU is in the happy position that these conditions appear to be satisfied by the bulk of the likely participant members, which are all trading close together and close to their existing EMS central rates. In many cases, these central rates have been in existence for up to a decade which, in turn, implies that they are sustainable economically. For such member states, the need is to avoid a possible build-up of speculation and a departure, by one or more of them, from the present equilibrium situation.

The Irish pound, however, is an exception in that it is currently trading well above its existing EMS central rates against the other member states. Whatever solution is adopted will, thus, present particular problems and challenges for the Irish authorities and these are also examined.

An alternative and earlier suggestion regarding the fixing of the euro rates was Lamfalussy's proposal that the rates be set at their three-year average. We note that there has been a tendency for the Lamfalussy Rule to be discarded in favour of the central rates proposal because the latter is more certain and transparent. We believe, however, that it is precisely these features which are the weakest points of the central rates proposal. This is because it gives the markets a windmill to tilt at and we conclude that central rates should only be used if they are accompanied by a public commitment on the part of the central banks to unlimited intervention to support them in the period between the announcement and the start of the third stage. We are sceptical that such a commitment can be secured, and, therefore, recommend that a modified form of the Lamfalussy Rule be adopted. The suggested modification would involve a commitment by the national authorities not to devalue or to seek to gain a competitive advantage by interfering with the otherwise orderly market evolution of the average. The Lamfalussy Rule is also preferable in the case of the Irish pound.

The uncertainty over euro rate fixing stems from the EMS

The legal framework for the introduction of the euro is contained in two Council regulations which have been promulgated as required by the Madrid Summit requirement.

One of them, Council Regulation (EC) No. 1103/97 on 'certain provisions relating to the introduction of the euro', was adopted in June 1997 and has entered into force. It contains provisions on matters which the financial markets felt were most in need of legal certainty, such as the 1:1 relationship between the Ecu and the euro, continuity of contract and rounding details. The second, 'on the introduction of the euro', will be formally adopted by the participating member states after they are chosen in May 1998. It provides for, *inter alia*, the name of the new currency and its substitution for the national currencies at the conversion rates. The legal provisions contained in the two regulations are reviewed in Appendix A at the end of this chapter. For our purposes, the essential point is that the key questions of how the conversion rates will be chosen and, in particular, how the treaty provision that the external value of the Ecu shall be maintained, are not addressed. The issue of the timing of any announcement regarding the setting of the rates is not specifically addressed either, though the presumption would appear to be that this will be done at the start of the third stage and the second Regulation includes a preamble which repeats the treaty reference to this effect. It follows that the question of an early announcement of the conversion rates and/or a preannouncement of either the rates, or the methodology to be used for setting them, remains open.

This is not entirely surprising given the historical experience. The Maastricht Treaty was negotiated at a time when the EMS was in its 'golden' period, currencies were close together and stable and the need for elaborate end-game methodologies was not obvious. Subsequently, exchange rate turbulence in 1992/93 caused the EMS narrow band to be effectively terminated and the legacy which this provides will have made the member states hesitant about giving hostages to fortune. The exchange rate provisions in the treaty are, moreover, grounded in the EMS ideology. In essence, this centered on taking the market by surprise when the matter of setting specific exchange rates arose.

This was most obvious at realignment time. Realignments were, for the most part, hastily convened affairs which took place over a weekend when the markets were closed with the new central rates being announced at the start of business on the following Monday. The legacy of the EMS is particularly obvious in some of the Maastricht Treaty provisions and we proceed now to consider one of them.

What is the 'external value' of the Ecu?

'This measure (the adoption of the fixed conversion rates) shall by itself not modify the external value of the Ecu'.

Article 109l(4) of the Maastricht Treaty

This provision is a critical one, which has neither been focused upon nor adequately considered in the debate so far. As we shall see, it will determine both when and how the conversion rates shall be fixed.

The connection with the EMS is striking. The provision is virtually identical to that in the Brussels Council Resolution of 5 December 1978 on the European Monetary System.

'The weights of the currencies in the Ecu will be reexamined and if necessary revised . . . . Revisions have to be mutually accepted; they will, by themselves, not modify the external value of the Ecu.'

Paragraph 2.3 of the Brussels Resolution

Council Regulation No. 1103 of June 1997 (Preamble 6) reiterates the treaty provision regarding the maintenance of the external value of the Ecu, but goes on to define this in the following terms:

'Whereas this means that one Ecu in its composition as a basket of component currencies will become one euro'.

This interpretation is not particularly helpful as it seeks to explain one requirement (unchanged external value) in terms of another (1 Ecu = 1 euro).

In so doing, it leaves open the question of how precisely the external value of the Ecu is to be maintained.

The weights of the currencies in the Ecu were revised twice, in 1984 and again in 1989, to bring them into line with developments in their economies and financial markets in the meantime. On both occasions, the date of the decision was known in advance to the markets and the parallels with the current situation are complete. There are, therefore, two precedents for the interpretation of the treaty provision regarding the maintenance of the external value of the Ecu. In both instances, the revised composition of the Ecu, i.e. the new amounts of the national currencies contained in the basket, were chosen in a way which ensured that at the closing rate on the eve of the recomposition[1], both the 'old' and the 'new' Ecu displayed identical values by reference to all other currencies. Put in other words, the value of the Ecu in its 'old' composition (as measured by the sum of the products of currencies' existing amounts times the market exchange rates on the last day before revision) was equal to the value of the 'new' basket (as measured by reference to the new currency amounts and the same market exchange rates of the day before the revision). Discrete movements in the value of the Ecu were thus avoided and the early Ecu rates on the day of the revision were practically identical to those of the day before, any minor differences simply reflecting exchange market developments in the meantime.

In this manner, the external value of the Ecu was completely and fully maintained in terms of its exchange rate *vis-à-vis* all currencies, i.e. both component and non-component currencies.

In the context of the fixing of the conversion rates, a similar approach would mean that the Ecu market rates of the participating currencies on the eve of the third stage should become the irrevocably-fixed conversion rates for the euro. In this way, and in this way only, can the external value of the Ecu in terms of all currencies be maintained. The statement in the treaty that the conversion rates shall be fixed on the starting date of the third stage of EMU, is reinforced by the practical consideration that the additional requirement regarding the maintenance of the external value of the Ecu can only be fully respected if the market rates on the eve of the third stage are used.

Ignoring precedent, and, presumably, based on the fact that, in practice, daily Ecu rates are calculated via representative market exchange rates for its component currencies against the United States dollar, some

---

[1] *In practice, the rates of the 2.15 pm concertation between the central banks were used.*

commentators have proposed that the treaty requirement regarding 'external value' can be interpreted as meaning that the dollar rate only of the euro must be identical to the Ecu's dollar rate at close of business on 31 December 1998. This, less restrictive, interpretation throws open the possibility that the chosen conversion rates between the Ecu and the participating component currencies could differ from the prevailing market exchange rates, as long as the weighted sum of the revaluations and devaluations offset each other exactly. Alternatively, a non-participant in EMU might allow the dollar rate of its component currency to be adjusted to the extent necessary to maintain the dollar value of the basket Ecu unchanged, thereby offsetting any net appreciation/depreciation of the participating component currencies. Such a scenario would, of course, necessitate last-minute adjustments to the exchange rates of EMS currencies prior to the introduction of the euro and would give rise to uncertainty as regards the setting of the euro conversion rates and, possibly, open up the prospect of competitive devaluations by some. It is, therefore, not to be recommended.

The only sure way to maintain the external value of the Ecu unchanged against all currencies is to follow precedent and adopt the market rates at the close of business on 31 December 1998 as the irrevocably-fixed conversion rates. Anything else, moreover, could well be open to legal challenge.

We have now dealt with the questions of when and how the conversion rates between the euro and the participating currencies should be fixed. The matters of the desirability and practicability of some form of preannouncement and the related questions of how any such announcement might influence the market rates on the last day remain open and will be examined in the next section.

The need for preannouncement of conversion rates

The Maastricht Treaty was drafted in a period of exchange rate stability prior to the turbulence of 1992/93. It can be inferred from the references to the membership criterion regarding exchange rates that the authors of the treaty envisaged a progressive narrowing of the then 2.25 per cent EMS bands as they approached the final stage of EMU[1]. Instead, the bands had

---

1
The word 'normal' instead of the then prevalent expression 'narrow' to refer to the EMS fluctuation band was used against a background where countries such as Belgium and the Netherlands were actively considering 1 per cent bands instead of the 2.25 per cent margins.

to be widened to 15 per cent in the face of market turbulence in August 1993. Phase A, i.e. the period between the decision in May 1998 on which member states qualify to participate and the fixing of the conversion rates on 1 January 1999, was designed to allow time for the practical actions necessary in order to make the new European Central Bank (ECB) operational. The time gap does, however, open up the possibility of destabilizing exchange rate speculation on the part of the markets and/or jockeying for competitive advantage by the national governments in the aftermath of the decision on which member states qualify for EMU.

The treaty's convergence requirement regarding exchange rate stability[1] applies to the period prior to the decision on membership being taken. It is silent on the period thereafter. While Article 109l(4) requires unanimity of participating member states as regards the fixing of the conversion rates, this does not rule out devaluations/deprecations prior to the setting of the rates which, as we have just seen, must, in all likelihood, be based on market rates on the last day of 1998.

Governments could seek to take advantage of this lacuna either by using the flexibility provided by the very wide bands to allow their currencies depreciate or, indeed, by outright formal devaluation. Prominent politicians in at least one country have already urged an effective devaluation. While this would, of course, be totally contrary to the spirit of the treaty, as things stand it cannot technically be ruled out[2].

Up to now, the fear of market speculation has received greater attention than the possibility of last-minute devaluations by participating member states. In the absence of countervailing action, the potential for speculation is, indeed, considerable. Borrowing and selling a weak currency, thereby driving down its rate against the Ecu, in the knowledge that this lower rate would shortly become the fixed euro conversion rate, could well become prevalent, giving rise to both speculative profits and to the possibility that some countries would be forced to enter EMU at market rates that would be inappropriate and/or unsustainable economically.

1
Article 3 of the Protocol on the convergence criteria specifies that a member state must have respected 'the normal fluctuation margins . . . of the EMS without severe tensions for at least the last two years before 'the examination' without devaluing 'its currency's bilateral central rate against any other member state's currency on its own initiative for the same period'.
2
Last minute devaluations may appear attractive to policy-makers in a situation where they might yield competitiveness gains without the usual inflation consequences if workers believed that the new ECB would not facilitate consequential wage rises. In this, fairly unique, set of circumstances, the trade-off between output and inflation is altered and the gains from devaluation are no longer transitory (Begg et al).

Were nothing to be done, the potential for uncertainty, speculation and tension amongst participating currencies could be quite high. There is, in consequence, widespread agreement that the current gap needs to be plugged by some form of preannouncement of the conversion rates. The objective would be to provide greater certainty regarding the conversion rates, and also to rule out both speculation by the markets and devaluation temptations on the part of the authorities.

Obviously, a simple public confirmation that the Ecu's market rates on the last day will be chosen as the euro conversion rates would not be adequate as it would not rule out the dangers identified above and, indeed, might well encourage them. Two possible solutions have been advanced.

Preannouncement—the Lamfalussy Rule

The Lamfalussy
market rates over a period prior to the end of December 1998 as the final conversion rates of the national currencies to the euro. Lamfalussy, in fact, proposed an average of the rates during the three-year period 1996-1998. The period could, however, be varied and, if necessary, weighted. The purpose of the weighting would be to increase the influence of the elapsed portion of the time period thereby increasing the predictive and stabilizing influence of the rule.

The advantage of the Lamfalussy Rule is that it would turn orthodox determination of exchange rates on its head — whereas normally buy and sell decisions are based on expectations of future exchange rates, under Lamfalussy's Rule, future exchange rates would be based on present and past buy and sell decisions.

In other words, the average and the eventual fixed conversion rate becomes increasingly dependent on its own history. Provided the rule was credible to the markets, exchange rates would become increasingly stable as they converged towards their own average, thereby reducing or eliminating volatility in the critical end period.

In recent debate, the Lamfalussy Rule has been overshadowed by a preference for ERM central rates. It has been argued that the rule can have counter-intuitive effects around the time of its announcement. Depending

---

1
Alexandre Lamfalussy, the first president of the European Monetary Institute (EMI).

on the prior evolution of the average, and the interest rate differentials which exist, it could lead to jumps in exchange rates at the time of announcement.

More importantly, the Lamfalussy Rule does not necessarily exclude a politically-inspired devaluation/depreciation, which could happen at any time and interfere with the otherwise smooth evolution of the rate towards its pre-depreciation average. On its own, therefore, the Rule fails to deliver the exchange rate certainty that is desirable. Any solution which allows the national authorities a greater degree of flexibility in the period after May 1998 than that provided by the Maastricht criteria in the run up to May 1998 is unsatisfactory. For the Lamfalussy Rule to work, it would need to be accompanied by an irrevocable commitment not to devalue in the run-up period.

Preannouncement—current ERM central rates

The defects noted above have caused the focus to shift away from the Lamfalussy Rule in favour of what is, in essence, the early announcement of the fixed conversion rates. This approach, it is argued, has the advantages of greater clarity, transparency and certainty. Successfully implemented, it would enable spot rates to converge smoothly, and, critically, it would rule out any prospect of last minute devaluations or depreciations by wayward governments.

Prior announcement of the fixed Ecu/euro conversion rates is, however, not possible. Since the Ecu is a basket, its rates are calculated rates which are derived from the market rate of each of its components. It is already clear that some of the component currencies will not participate in EMU. Their exchange rate behaviour cannot be predicted or limited and since their evolution affects the value of the Ecu, it follows that the end-1998 exchange rates of the Ecu against those components which become participating currencies are neither predictable nor determinable in advance.

1
See DeGrauwe, P paper. An example of such a jump in the case of the Irish pound is given later in this chapter.
2
Denmark has opted-out, Sweden has announced that it will not participate, Greece does not qualify and the UK is likely to opt out as well. We assume, for the purposes of this chapter, that the remaining 11 member states will participate. The fact that some non-component Ecu currencies, e.g. the Austrian schilling, are likely to participate in EMU is not relevant.

By a process of elimination, we are forced to fall back to the use of the fixed bilateral central rates in the EMS Exchange Rate Mechanism (ERM) as the means whereby the prior announcement of the conversion rates would be facilitated.[1] Following the announcement, market rates of the participant currencies would be expected to converge towards their central rates as interest rate differentials disappeared.

By 31 December 1998, at the latest, market rates would be identical to the central rates, as a transaction at any other rate would generate certain losses for one side and no rational operator would be party to it.

At the last moment, the focus would switch back to the market Ecu rates which would then be formally adopted as the irrevocable fixed rates.[2]

The wheel has now turned full circle and we are, in effect, back where we were in 1992, when the policy-makers seem to have envisaged that ever decreasing narrow bands would form the basis for the smooth glide into the single currency. It is worth recalling that the EMS bands are centered around the fixed bilateral rates and not, of course, the Ecu rates. The proposal to use the bilateral central rates as the basis for the conversion rates to the euro represents the extreme case in which the EMS fluctuation bands are reduced to zero. This, in turn, however, prompts the question — if the narrow bands could not be maintained in 1993, what certainty is there that the even more demanding spot central rates objective can be maintained throughout the period between the preannouncement and the actual fixing of the conversion rates on 1 January 1999? We will return to this topic later but, first, we will compare the two principal end-game solutions that have been proposed in terms of the fixed conversion rates that might result from their adoption.

End-game solutions compared

Given that most currencies are currently trading close to their bilateral central rates, (see Figure 12.2) use of either the Lamfalussy Rule or the bilateral central rates approach would, from a practical perspective and

[1]
We assume, for exposition purposes, that the bilateral rates would be expressed in terms of the Deutschemark.

[2]
Though the bilateral rates of the participating currencies would have been constant at their central rates, their Ecu rates would, of course, have continued to fluctuate under the influence of movements of the non-participating Ecu component currencies. Crossing the new fixed Ecu rates would, however, give bilateral rates which would be identical to the central rates save for minor rounding differences.

Most currencies are close to Deutschemark parities

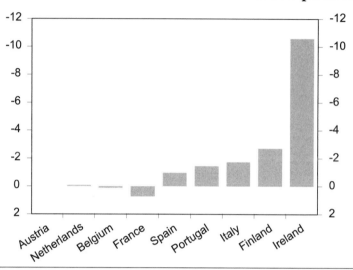

Figure 12.2   Divergence form DM central rates*
*Rates used are those of 17 July 1997

assuming that things went smoothly, make little difference to the eventual conversion rates chosen. This is particularly true of the six core EMS currencies, viz. Deutschemark, Austrian schilling, Belgian franc, Luxembourg franc, Dutch guilder and French franc, which in July 1997 were all trading within half a per cent of their central parities. Three other currencies, the Spanish peseta, the Portuguese escudo and the Italian lira, were less than two per cent away from their central rates and the Finnish markka not much further away. The currency movement required to achieve their central Deutschemark rates would, thus, in all cases be relatively modest.

The classic example is provided by the Dutch guilder (see Figure 12.3), the exchange rate of which against the Deutschemark was virtually invariant at 0.89 for the 18 months to mid-1997. Short-term interest rates in the Netherlands had, moreover, converged on German levels, with the result that the interest-rate differential was zero. In these circumstances, the announcement of a Lamfalussy-type three-year average as the basis for the choice of fixed conversion rates would have absolutely no impact on the existing spot rate of the currency. The guilder would stay at its then current level of DM0.89 for the remaining 18 months giving a three-year average also of 0.89.

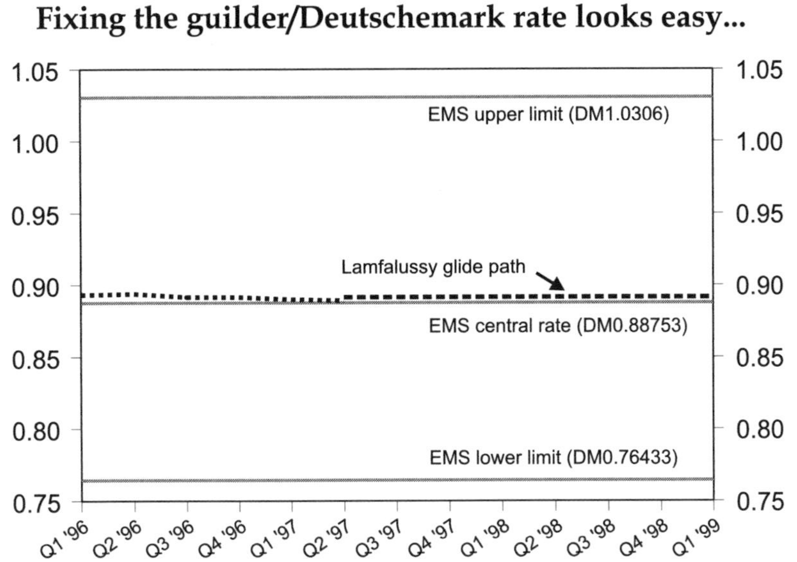

Fixing the guilder/Deutschemark rate looks easy...

Figure 12.3   Deutschemark/Dutch guilder end-game exchange rates

As the Deutschemark/Dutch guilder bilateral central rate is 0.89 too, the use of central rates as the mechanism to set the conversion rates would similarly have no impact on the spot rate.

The Irish pound, on the other hand, provides the most complex end-game exchange rate scenario. In mid-1997, there was a three percentage point gap between short-term Irish and German interest rates. As long as there is a differential between the respective interest rates, it will pay investors to hold the Irish pound and the IR£/DM exchange rate will glide towards its ultimate destination, arriving there when the interest rate differential is zero.

We, first of all, look at the impact which the announcement of a Lamfalussy three-year average might have on the Irish pound's exchange rate. Various possibilities,[1] are set out in Figure 12.4. It can be seen that the outcome will vary depending on the interest rate differential. If the interest rate differential were zero, the exchange rate would go to DM2.48, its average against the Deutschemark in the 18 months to mid-1997, and

[1]
Based on the methodology adopted by Honohan.

...but Ireland...

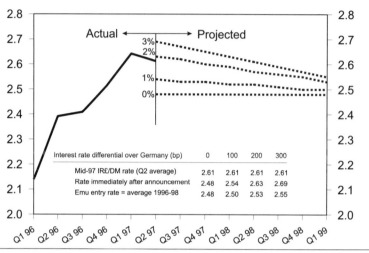

Figure 12.4   Lamfalussy exchange rate glide paths under various interest rate scenarios (IR£/DM)

...is at the other extreme

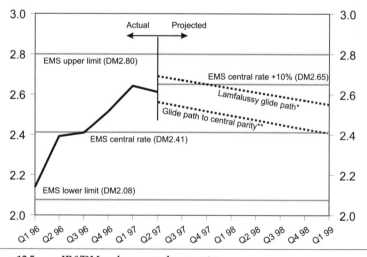

Figure 12.5   IR£/DM end-game exchange rates

*Assumes that current 3.0 percentage points short-term differential between Irish and German interest rates continues until end-1998 giving an average of DM2.55 over the 3-year period 1996-1998.

**Also assumes that current 3.0 percentage points differential remains.

would remain there until EMU entry. In the other extreme, a continuation of the three per cent interest rate differential until end 1998 would imply that the spot rate would jump from its mid-97 reading of 2.61 to a starting point of 2.69 and would then decline gradually to an entry level of 2.55. Smaller interest rate differentials would give intermediate outcomes. It is noteworthy, however, that the gap between the likely final entry rates is quite small — the range is from DM2.48 to DM2.55 — if Lamfalussy averages are used.

The evolution depicted in Figure 12.4 assumes that the respective interest-rate differentials remain constant for the remainder of the period. Irish interest rates could be expected to remain above German levels if, for example, the Central Bank of Ireland felt that higher Irish short-term interest rates were appropriate given the economic circumstances. In practice, however, they would be likely to have difficulty in maintaining such a stance and it may well be that differentials would decline over time while still remaining positive. This would imply that the eventual outcome would be some combination of the first three lines in the graph and that the final IR£/DM rate would be close to but slightly below DM2.55. For ease of exposition, however, we will adopt the hypothesis that the existing 3 per cent differential remains constant right until the end of 1998, when it collapses to zero. As already indicated, this would yield a three-year average and an entry rate of DM2.55.

A comparison of the glide path implied by the Lamfalussy Rule, assuming that the current three percentage point interest rate differential is maintained, with that which would obtain if bilateral central rates were chosen as the fixed rates, is shown in Figure 12.5. Just as the Lamfalussy Rule implied an upward jump in the spot rate at the time of announcement, the adoption of the central parity proposal would imply a downward shift. This reflects the fact that the forward market was discounting a rate higher than DM2.41 and it is assumed that the credibility which would accompany the announcement would cause this to be corrected.

For the Irish pound, therefore, there is potentially a significant difference in the conversion rate depending on which methodology is chosen. The Lamfalussy Rule, combined with our interest rate assumption, would imply a Deutschemark conversion rate of 2.55 which is significantly above the existing central rate of DM2.41. For reasons which will become clear later, the situation assuming a 10 per cent revaluation of the Irish pound's ERM central rate to DM2.65 is also shown in Figure 12.5.

We conclude that, for currencies which are currently trading close to their ERM central rates, there is little to choose from as between the two methodologies. The use of preannounced ERM bilateral central rates has, however, the advantages of greater clarity and certainty. The Irish pound is a special case—irrespective of which methodology is chosen. For this currency, the Lamfalussy Rule would be preferable in that it would give rise to less exchange rate movement and would result in a fixed rate which, while it would be lower than the rates prevailing in mid-1997, would be significantly above the existing ERM central rate and, would, as we shall see later, be more in keeping with the needs of the economy.

The deficiencies of the central rates proposal

Two problems with the preannouncement that existing ERM central rates will be used to set the conversion rates can be identified—one specific and one general.

The specific problem relates to the Irish pound and is examined in detail in Appendix B. While most of the likely participant currencies are trading close to their central rates, the Irish pound is a clear outlier and a substantial fall in its spot rate would be necessary to reach the central rate. The percentage move from the mid-1997 rate is so big as potentially both to be disruptive and to have undesirable economic consequences in the form of a temporary boost to inflation.[1]

This difficulty could be overcome by raising the pound's central rate within the ERM, but we see this as a solution which is inferior to the Lamfalussy Rule which, as we have seen earlier, would result in a conversion rate close to DM2.55 for the Irish pound.

The second and overriding problem with the preannouncement that existing ERM central rates will be the conversion rates relates to the difficulty of enforcing them should the market seek to test the authorities' commitment in the knowledge, gained in 1993, that their war chest is not unlimited. This is even less tractable than the Irish pound problem and can, in fact, only be fully remedied by a change in the game plan which is more far-reaching than anything that has been considered so far.

If the market rate of any one of the EMU candidate currencies were to be bid well away from its central rate, the rule would no longer be compatible with the adoption of unchanged Ecu market rates on the last day. This, in turn, has led to the suggestion that governments of the prospective EMU member states should strengthen the credibility of the

---

[1] *The movement required could be greater or lower depending on the situation at the time of the announcement. On 17 July 1997, for example, the DM rate was 2.70 and the required fall would have been almost 11 per cent.*

announcement by committing their central banks to intervene in the markets, if necessary, in order to force the market rates to equal their central rates on the last day. The parallels with the EMS situation are, again, striking.

A *de facto* advancement of EMU?

The effective breakdown of the EMS in 1992/93 reflected the refusal of the central banks, in particular the Bundesbank, to intervene in a genuinely unlimited manner. This will change dramatically in the single currency environment and it is precisely this potential for unlimited intervention that will be the key to the sustainability of the fixed conversion rates during the transitional phase between 1 January 1999 when they are set, and late 2001 when euro notes and coin replace national currencies.

Suppose, for example, that, after the start of EMU, market operators decide to sell the Belgian franc in favour of the Deutschemark, both of which currencies will continue to exist (in the guise of non-decimal expressions of the euro) until the end of the transition period. In reality, they would merely be selling one part of the euro in favour of another part of that same euro and the central banks, as reconstituted in the form of the ECB, would be happy to supply them with Deutschemarks indefinitely. There would, of course, be no net impact on liquidity within the euro area.

To be fully credible, any preannouncement of the conversion rates would need to be backed up by similar institutional safeguards. The national authorities and the European Commission will, no doubt, be comforted by the impressive economic convergence in recent years and the current exchange rate tranquility. We believe that any such complacency is misplaced, and that a re-run of the 1993 crisis could well occur in the absence of watertight safeguards. The announcement of the conversion rates would have to be accompanied by the bringing forward of the guarantee that such rates will be maintained by means of unlimited intervention, should this prove necessary.

In short, this boils down to the suggestion that the new ECB, which will be formally created at the time of the decision on membership in May 1998, should also be accorded *de facto* operational responsibility from that date. Though the ECB is due to be established in May 1998, it will not become operational until January 1999, and any central bank co-operation in advance of that would have to be informal. In essence, what would be needed would be an effective early start to EMU, in so far as intervention and currency support is concerned. Anything less would risk further destabilizing speculation on the lines of that which occurred in 1992/93.

Such a radical proposal is, of course, highly controversial. The ECB and the national central banks have to be made fully independent by the time of the May 1998 decision on the establishment of the ECB. They are unlikely to want to contemplate an unlimited intervention role in the absence of a very specific mandate from a supreme authority. Even then, some might well feel that this would be incompatible with their statutes. The Bundesbank, which would have to be a key player in any such scheme, has the statutory obligation of safeguarding the Deutschemark and is, moreover, not noted for its pro-EMU sentiment. It might take the view that an excessive supply of Deutschemark liquidity in the period prior to the commencement of EMU would conflict with its statutory objectives.

On the other hand, many commentators hold that any boost to the money supply in the run-up to EMU would not be inflationary because there would not be time for the effects to percolate and the liquidity released by the intervention would, in any event, most likely be neutralized once EMU commenced. In extreme circumstances, all the intervention required could take place on the last day before EMU, because it is only on this day that the market rates must be identical to the central rates for the preannouncement to work.

While recognizing the difficulties, we conclude that anything other than a *de facto* advancement of EMU is excessively risky in that it opens up the potential for speculation and a repeat of the 1993 EMS crisis. If the preannouncement of the irrevocable central rates as conversion rates cannot be accompanied by a commitment to unlimited intervention, it should be discarded in favour of the Lamfalussy Rule, supplemented by a binding commitment from the member states to rule out competitive devaluations/depreciations.

The timing of the announcement

The desire for certainty has prompted some commentators to urge an early preannouncement. The most notable of these was the call by the Bundesbank president for a resolution of the issue at the September Ecofin meeting in Luxembourg. Prior to that, the Luxembourg prime minister, Jean-Claude Juncker, also called for the fixing of the bilateral central rates during his presidency. The unusual thing about these calls is that they have come so early. They are, also unusual in that in many other areas, e.g. the fixing of the date for the introduction of euro notes and coins, the member states have pointedly deferred making a decision until May, when the participating member states will be known.

We see three main objections to the idea of an early announcement, in particular to a preannouncement of central rates. First, Article 109l(4) makes it clear that the decision on rates must be unanimous and this would, presumably, also apply to any preannouncement. The Irish, at least, have a strong incentive not to agree to any early preannouncement of central rates, as they seek to avoid giving hostages to fortune in the context of further sterling fluctuations (see Appendix B).

Secondly, it seems unlikely that the opt-out countries, or for that matter, doubtful candidates, would wish to tie their hands in advance by acquiescing in an announcement that the central rates would be used in advance of the decision on membership. Non-qualifiers might, for example, see their currencies initially depreciate sharply relative to the euro, leaving them with a difficult task to regain the announced conversion rate.

Thirdly, and most importantly, there is the need, adverted to earlier, for the preannouncement to be accompanied by a commitment to unlimited intervention. This will be difficult to achieve at any stage and, it would seem, practically impossible in advance of the decision on participating member states. Central bank reservations regarding such intervention would, however, be likely to be considerably reduced in the aftermath of the decision on the participants.

These arguments are primarily directed at the central rates option. They are less compelling if the Lamfalussy Rule (reinforced by a non-devaluation commitment) is to be adopted though, in this case, too, we believe that it is preferable that the announcement be made in May 1998. The announcement of the qualifying member states will be a watershed. It provides the most logical and realistic time for the preannouncement of the conversion rates assuming that such a preannouncement is to be made.

Conclusion

The existing provisions for the introduction of the euro are lacking in that they do not provide adequately for the methodology to be used in the fixing of the euro irrevocable conversion rates. Precedent and the Maastricht Treaty, however, indicates that there is little option other than to use the Ecu market rates on the eve of Stage Three. The risk of destabilizing speculation points to a need for some form of official guidance in the interim. For technical reasons, this can only come in the form of rules regarding the bilateral rates of the participating currencies. The Lamfalussy suggestion — that an average of market rates over a number of years be used — has been discarded in favour of the transparency and certainty that use of the existing bilateral ERM central rates would bring. This route is seen to have the added advantage that all of the likely participants, with the exception of the Irish pound, are currently trading close to their bilateral central rates. The specific problem of the Irish pound could be overcome by revaluing its central rate in order to give a more realistic starting point.

There is, however, a more general problem associated with the central rates proposal in that there is no obvious mechanism to enforce it should the market, for whatever reason, decide to challenge one or more of the bilateral rates. A commitment on the part of the authorities to unlimited intervention to support a currency under attack in the run-up to Stage Three of EMU is the only sure way to deal with this problem. Such a commitment will be an integral part of the institutional framework once the single currency has started. This mechanism, however, is not available in advance of January 1999 and the institutional set-up which confers independence on the central banks, renders such a commitment difficult to envisage in practice. The authorities should agree on the methodology to be adopted, but should only announce it if they are confident they can combat any speculation which might seek to drive the market rates away from the chosen parities.

General assurances are unlikely to be sufficient and we are sceptical that more watertight arrangements can be put in place. We conclude, therefore, that it would be impracticable to use the EMS central rates as the basis to fix the conversion rates.

The Lamfalussy Rule is, in fact, preferable from the point of view of avoiding destabilizing speculation. As we have seen, there is little difference in practical terms between it and the alternative, in so far as the vast bulk of the likely participants is concerned. In the case of the Irish pound, it would avoid the need for a revaluation and would give an intermediate outcome with a Deutschemark rate close to 2.55, i.e. below the DM2.65 rate which can be justified, but well above the 2.41 existing central rate which would be tantamount to a competitive devaluation.

Apart from the somewhat lesser degree of clarity which the Lamfalussy Rule entails, its main drawback is the fact that it does not rule out devaluation by a member state. This could be overcome by the simultaneous announcement of a commitment by participants that they would not devalue. We, therefore, recommend the use of the Lamfalussy Rule in this modified form. This could be announced at any time, but for maximum impact and, in particular, in order to gain maximum credibility, it would be best done in May 1998, when the participating member states are being announced.

Chapter
12

Appendix A

Interpreting the Regulations

Regulation No. 1103 of June 1997 'on certain provisions relating to the introduction of the euro' confirms the 1:1 conversion rate between the official Ecu and the euro. It, thus, clarifies that the official basket Ecu is to be converted at par into the euro regardless of the number of member states participating in EMU and of the combined weight of their currencies in the Ecu. In so doing, it rules out suggestions that the euro might merely replace the combined weight of the 'ins' in the Ecu. This is in keeping with the spirit of the provision in the treaty that the Ecu shall become the common currency.[1]

The 1:1 conversion applies in the first place to the 'official Ecu' as referred to in Article 109g of the Maastricht Treaty and other Community legislation. But it also applies to all contracts under private law (the 'private Ecu') that make explicit reference to the Ecu as defined in the treaty and other Community legislation. The draft Regulation, moreover, establishes a presumption that all references to the Ecu are to be read as references to the Ecu as defined in Community legislation. This presumption is based on the premise that practically all parties intended to make reference to the official Ecu, even if this intention was not always properly reflected in the wording of their contracts. The presumption, however, is rebuttable with the agreement of both parties to the contract, respecting the principle of freedom of contract.

This Regulation also sets out some aspects of how the conversion rates will be fixed. It stipulates that only the conversion rate of 1 euro in terms of each of the participating currencies shall be fixed. These rates will, moreover, be adopted by the Council with six significant figures, e.g. 1 euro

---

[1] *Albeit as amended by the Madrid Summit which ruled that Ecu was a generic term and that the Ecu, when shedding its basket definition to become a currency, shall be called the euro.*

equals BFr40.1234, or 1 euro equals DM2.12345, which must not be rounded or truncated when making conversions. This follows from the practice of the definition of central rates in the Exchange Rate Mechanism (ERM) of the EMS, which are also expressed to six significant figures.

Furthermore, the rates adopted by the Council must be used for conversions between the euro and the national currency unit and vice versa. The Regulation sets out how to convert from one national currency unit to another. The first step is to convert from the national currency unit into the euro unit and, the second step is to convert that euro amount into the other national currency unit. The alternative of defining bilateral rates would have opened up the possibility of profit-making through conversion operations from one national currency unit to another and has, accordingly, been ruled out. The use of inverse rates is similarly banned because of the rounding inaccuracies and potential profit-making opportunities it would give rise to and any reversion to the original currency must also be done via the euro. This clearly implies that bilateral rates between the national currency units will not be defined by the Council.

The draft Regulation 'on the introduction of the euro' which is to be adopted in May 1998 provides, *inter alia*, that 'from 1 January 1999 the currency of the participating member states shall be the euro. The currency unit shall be one euro' and 'the euro shall be substituted for the currency of each participating member state at the conversion rate'. The conversion rate, in turn, is defined as the 'irrevocably-fixed conversion rate adopted for the currency of each participating member state'.

The provisions referred to above represent a development of Article 109l(4) of the Maastricht Treaty which reads as follows:

'At the starting date of the third stage, the Council shall, acting with the unanimity of the member states without a derogation, on a proposal from the Commission and after consulting the ECB, adopt the conversion rates at which their currencies shall be irrevocably fixed and at which irrevocably-fixed rate the Ecu shall be substituted for these currencies, and the Ecu will become a currency in its own right. This measure shall by itself not modify the external value of the Ecu. The Council shall, acting according to the same procedure, also take the other measures necessary for the rapid introduction of the Ecu as the single currency of those member states.'

The treaty text quoted above, however, appears to refer to two types of fixed rates, viz. the fixing of the bilateral conversion rates between the participating currencies and the fixing of conversion rates between each participating currency and the euro. We have seen above that the idea of formally fixing bilateral conversion rates was dropped because of the rounding and profiteering difficulties it would give rise to.[1]

It is clear from Article 109l(4) that the irrevocable conversion rates are to be fixed on the starting date of EMU, viz. 1 January 1999.[2] This provision is repeated in the third preamble of Regulation No. 1103 of June 1997, but is not specifically provided for in the body of the Regulation. This may be because the authors felt there was no need to repeat what is already in the treaty. On the other hand, and as we have seen above, many of the provisions in the Regulations are merely repetitions of treaty provisions and the failure to nail down the question of when the conversion rates will be set was a surprising omission against the background of the active debate in financial markets on when this will occur.

---

[1] *The notion of having two types of fixed rate – fixed bilateral rates between participating currencies and fixed Ecu rates between each participant and the Ecu - may now appear strange. It must be remembered, however, that in 1992, when the treaty was drafted, there was still some uncertainty as to how quickly the new currency would come into being. Hence the provision, also in Article 109l(4), that 'the Council shall .. .also take the other measures necessary for the rapid introduction of the Ecu as the single currency of those member states'. Any delay in the acceptance of the Ecu as the single currency would, as seen earlier in the main portion of the text, rule out the adoption of fixed Ecu rates because the Ecu would continue to fluctuate under the influence of movements in component currencies that did not participate in EMU. Now that the Ecu or, more precisely, the euro, is, de facto, to immediately become the single currency of the participants, it is neither necessary nor appropriate to have two sets of fixed rates. More importantly, perhaps, the reference point in 1992 would have been the EMS which, in essence, consisted of fluctuation margins around fixed bilateral central rates, supplemented by fixed Ecu central rates. Against this background, the juxtaposition of the two is not so surprising.*

[2] *As 1 January 1999 is a Friday and a holiday, the fixed conversion rates will, in practice, come into effect on the following Monday, i.e. 4 January 1999.*

Chapter
12

Appendix B

The case of the Irish pound

As we have seen, the adoption of the central rates as conversion rates would, given the current constellation of the Irish pound's exchange rates, be tantamount to calling for a competitive devaluation of the pound. The simplest solution to this problem would be to revalue the pound's rate within the ERM, thereby limiting the fall in the spot rate that would be required in order to reach the central rate. It is assumed that this would be done in the context of a preannouncement of the conversion rates though action might be necessary if the pound was to reach an upper EMS limit prior to a preannouncement. The economic case for a revaluation of the Irish pound is examined below, where it is concluded that a revaluation of up to 10 per cent, which is what would be required to prevent it falling significantly from mid-1997 levels, is justified.

Some may question the feasibility of a revaluation in the context of the treaty provisions. As noted earlier, the convergence criteria rule out devaluation against any other currency but are silent on the question of revaluation which is, therefore, permitted. There is, however, a further requirement regarding the respect of the fluctuation margins 'without severe tensions'. This, too, is not defined in the treaty, but the indications from official sources are that a revaluation designed to prevent a substantial fall in the real exchange rate would be acceptable.

Recent movements in Irish pound exchange rates are depicted in Figure 12.6. This shows that, while movements in the key bilateral rates of sterling and the Deutschemark have been considerable, they have tended to offset each other, with the result that the pound's trade-weighted index (TWI) has been relatively stable. Irish exchange rate policy has, however, clearly been bedeviled by sterling volatility and it is this which complicates enormously the task of fixing an appropriate conversion rate.

The starting point of the graph is 1987, i.e. the beginning of the 'new EMS' period of tranquillity. Virtually all of the currency volatility in the interim has been due to sterling movements which had to be offset by counterbalancing movements against the Deutschemark. It is noteworthy that the IR£/DM rate is, in broad terms, now back where it was originally.[1]

Similarly, the IR£/sterling rate is once again close to where it was in the late 1980s. It is not surprising, therefore, that the TWI, too, is little changed.[2] Nominal exchange rates, as measured by the TWI, thus indicate that the pound was fairly valued at mid-1997 levels. The purpose of a revaluation would be to avoid a precipitate fall from those levels.

Variant B of the trade-weighted index in Figure 12.6 depicts the outcome if the IR£/DM rate were to fall to the central rate of DM2.41 in the context of an early preannouncement that existing central rates would be used as conversion rates, i.e. a depreciation of 11 per cent. The associated TWI value would be well below anything encountered in recent years. Variant C shows the projected outcome in 1997 if the central rate were revalued by 10 per cent to DM2.65 and if this were to be used to fix the conversion rate. The implied fall in the spot rate would be correspondingly less and the additional fall in the TWI would also be modest. The TWI would, however, still show a 3 per cent fall in 1997 as compared with 1996.

In Figure 12.7, the nominal movements in the pound's trade-weighted exchange rate are supplemented with cost data in order to obtain an index of competitiveness.[3]

It can be seen that the fall in the trade-weighted index in the period to July 1997 has already brought the index to its lowest level in a decade. The further improvement in competitiveness which a depreciation to DM2.41 − Variant B − would imply is quite dramatic. It would give rise to a real exchange rate which would be more that 10 per cent below anything experienced over the past decade.

Even with the more limited depreciation to DM2.65 which would be necessitated in the context of a 10 per cent revaluation of the ERM central rate, Variant C, the real exchange rate index would still be 4 per cent below the 1996 level and well below the average of the past decade.

1
   The IR£/DM rate averaged 2.67 between 1987 and 1991 as compared with DM2.70 on 17 July 1997 − the devaluation of 1992 had, thus, been completely unwound.
2
   The 1997 values for sterling and variant A of the trade-weighted index in Figure 12.6 are also the 17 July rates, viz. GBP0.90, DM2.70 and TWI 66.85.
3
   The data are based on relative hourly earnings in a common currency instead of the more usual relative unit wage costs in manufacturing. Had the latter been used, the improvement in competitiveness would have been much more dramatic as the index has fallen by more than 30 per cent since 1987. These data are eschewed in favour of hourly earnings because they may be distorted by supernormal productivity gains in those sectors of manufacturing where multinational companies predominate.

Ireland would be very competitive...

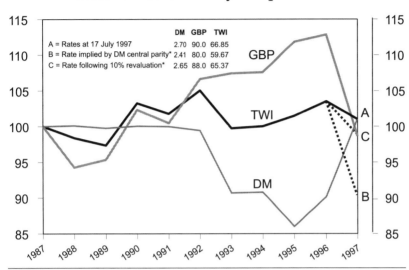

Figure 12.6   Nominal IR£ exchange rates. (Base 1987=100)
Other things being equal, i.e. assuming that sterling remains at its 17 July rate of DM3.0.

...if the Irish pound fell to its Deutschemark central rate

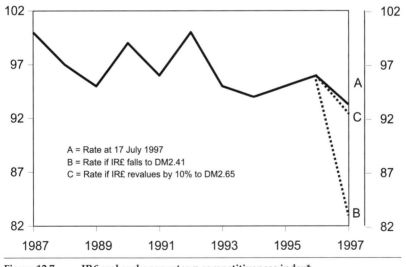

Figure 12.7   IR£ real exchange rates = competitiveness index*
Relative hourly earnings in a common currency; Central Bank of Ireland (Base 1987 = 100)
N.B. Fall in real exchange rate = improvement in competitiveness

Competitiveness considerations, albeit a relatively imprecise guide, strongly indicate that, other things being equal, the setting of the conversion rate at DM2.41 would give an enormous further boost to the Irish economy. A revaluation of the central rate prior to EMU entry would be necessary if a very substantial fall in nominal exchange rates and an unwarranted gain in competitiveness were to be avoided.

The case for revaluation is bolstered by real economy considerations. GNP growth in recent years has averaged over 7 per cent per annum, exports have risen at over 14 per cent per annum, inflation has remained low and the balance of payments surplus is of the order of 4 per cent of GNP. The fundamental situation in the Irish economy would, thus, support the case for revaluation or, more precisely, the avoidance of any precipitate fall in the trade-weighted index from current levels.

Any such fall would be likely to have a temporary impact which would last, perhaps, two years during which time output would rise further and, critically, price inflation would accelerate. The small open nature of the Irish economy means that falls in the trade-weighted exchange rate are rapidly reflected in prices and the consumer price index would likely rise to 4 per cent or more for a time as compared with the 1997 level of about 1.5 per cent.[1]

Put simply, a sharp decline in the TWI from current levels is the last thing that is required against a background of a booming economy, rapid asset price inflation, the prospect that short-term market rates will fall by up to three percentage points in the run up to EMU (the precise extent of the fall will depend on how much German rates rise in the meantime) and a fiscal policy that is mildly expansionary.

The analysis thus far has been conducted in a static type of situation — we have assumed, for example, that sterling would remain unchanged at its mid-1997 level against the Deutschemark. In fact, sterling at this level was generally regarded as substantially over-valued and could be expected to weaken. In normal circumstances, and assuming they were not constrained by preannounced EMU conversion rates, the Irish authorities could maintain effective exchange rate stability should sterling weaken by allowing recent Irish pound movements against both sterling and Deutschemark to unwind, thereby keeping the TWI unchanged and effectively reverting to the situation which obtained in 1996.

---

[1] *The inflationary impact might be attenuated or avoided entirely if the depreciation were to be delayed until shortly before the start of EMU — see earlier reference to study by Begg et al.*

The dilemma for the Irish authorities is that the preannouncement of a particular rate against the Deutschemark would remove this flexibility and give rise to a situation where the pound's trade-weighted index, under the influence of a subsequent fall in sterling, could rise significantly. Even when it comes to the fixing of the irrevocable exchange rates, sterling is a factor of such importance to the Irish economy that it cannot be ignored.

The impact on Irish competitiveness of a number of alternative sterling scenarios is illustrated in Figure 12.8. In this graph, the central scenario is depicted by the heavy black line which is based on Variant C of Figure 12.4, viz. a situation which the Irish pound is revalued by 10 per cent to DM2.65 which becomes the effective conversion rate in an EMU context while sterling remains at its 17 July 1997 level of DM3.00. In choosing a conversion rate, the Irish authorities have to reckon with the possibility that sterling might rise further before falling back. Variant C(i), thus, looks at the impact on competitiveness of a sterling/DM3.30 rate. The real exchange rate of the Irish pound would fall by a further 2.5 per cent and competitiveness would improve accordingly.

It is not possible, and would be wholly inappropriate, for the Irish authorities to try to devise an exchange rate policy based on extreme sterling movements. The problem is that there is no knowing if and when sterling will fall. It is appropriate, therefore, to consider the long-term equilibrium sterling exchange rate. We start by noting that forward exchange rates are implicitly discounting a depreciation of sterling *vis-à-vis* the Deutschemark of about 6 per cent over the final 18 months to EMU. This seems relatively modest, a view which is supported by the fact that sterling is well above the levels indicated by Fundamental Equilibrium Exchange Rates (FEERs). For 1998, these are calculated by Goldman Sachs, for example, at around DM2.50.

sterling will fall by nearly 17 per cent. Other things being equal once again, a fall in sterling to DM2.50 would imply a rise in the Irish pound TWI of the order of 4 per cent and an equivalent loss in competitiveness.

---

[1]
The weights and composition of the Irish trade-weighted index are secret. For the purposes of this chapter, we have assumed a weight of 25 per cent. This corresponds with the 1996 share of exports to the UK. Private sector simulations point to the actual weight being less than the bilateral trade share. In the early eighties, the use of double export weights became common but it is not known whether or not they are used to calculate the Irish TWI. Such weights take account of competition in third markets and are generally regarded as superior. The most recent EC calculation gives a double export weight for Ireland in relation to 23 industrial countries of 23.1 per cent in 1995.
[2]
Other estimates range from DM2.40 to DM2.60. The figure used is, thus, around the centre of the range.

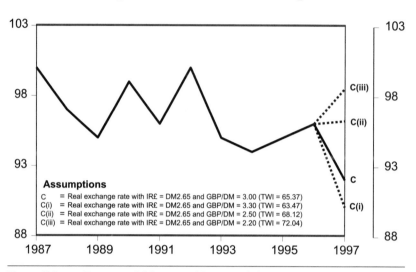

Figure 12.8   **Impact on Irish competitiveness of alternative sterling scenarios**
N.B. Fall in real exchange rate = improvement in competitiveness and vice versa

This, central, outcome is depicted by Variant C(ii) in Figure 12.5. Competitiveness in 1997 would be little changed by comparison with 1996 and would be close to the average of the last decade, a situation that looks like it would be both sustainable and acceptable to the Irish authorities.[1]

For completeness, the impact of an overshoot in the sterling/DM rate to its recent low of approximately 2.20, is modeled in Variant C(iii). In this scenario, the real IR£ exchange rate would rise strongly and competitiveness would be significantly eroded. This outcome might, however, be tolerable against the background where a fall in sterling to such low levels would be unlikely to last for long.

1
If the Irish authorities wish to give themselves greater room for manoeuvre, they could limit any revaluation of the Irish pound to a figure somewhat less than the 10 per cent that we have assumed. Crossing the respective DM rates gives an implied equilibrium IR£/sterling rate of 1.06, slightly higher than the previous high of 1.04 in August 96. Though probably justified in fundamental economic terms, the prospect of breaking new ground against sterling might, however, prompt the authorities to opt for a slightly lower Deutschemark conversion rate.

The difficulties outlined above, together with the natural desire to hedge their bets, have led some (Honohan) to suggest the introduction of a safety valve into any preannouncement formula for Ireland. The objective would be to avoid any further steep falls against sterling, while at the same time also protecting against a sharp rise in that currency. This would take the form of announcing that Ireland would join at the Deutschemark parity of 2.41, or as close to that rate as would place its sterling value above a certain level, say, 87p. Crossing those two rates gives a GBP/DM threshold of 2.77. If sterling were still above DM2.77 at end 1998, say DM3.00, the Irish pound would be revalued to DM2.61 which would maintain the Ir£/GBP 87p rate. Conversely, if sterling had fallen to DM2.50 the IR£/DM rate would be set at 2.41 which would give a cross rate of GBP 96p.

The associated falls in the real exchange rate would be considerable, of the order of 5 per cent and 9 per cent, respectively, as compared with 1996 but this is deliberate on the part of the author who sees advantages in joining EMU at an enhanced level of competitiveness. This type of safety valve arrangement would be ideal if it could be negotiated but must be considered doubtful against a background where the purpose of the preannouncement of the conversion rates is to give certainty and transparency. It is likely also that such a stratagem would be seen as tantamount to setting the rate by reference to sterling, something which might not be acceptable to all the other member states in a context where exchange rate decisions have to be unanimous.

Against this difficult background, the policy stance of the Irish authorities is likely to be to put off the evil day for as long as possible thereby retaining maximum flexibility. If they are forced to make an early preannouncement of a fixed conversion rate against the Deutschemark, it is likely that this would be accompanied by a significant revaluation of the existing Deutschemark central rate. To do otherwise would in all probability imply an unacceptably large fall in the real exchange rate. The size of the revaluation required could, moreover, be up to 10 per cent, considerably greater than anything mooted so far.

From the perspective of the Irish pound, the use of the Lamfalussy Rule instead of the bilateral central rates as a preannouncement mechanism to determine the euro conversion rates would clearly be preferable, in that it would give rise to a market led outcome and avoid the need to confront the issue of revaluation.

Bibliography

- Begg, D., F. Giavazzi, J. von Hagen and C. Wyplosz (1997) *EMU - Getting the End-game Right*, CEPR.
- Louw, A. (1997) *The Irrevocable Fixing of the Conversion Rates*, Editions Ecu Activities No. 39.
- Honohan, P. (1997) *The Tortuous Path to EMU Entry*, IEA.
- De Grauwe, P. (1996) *How to fix conversion rates at the start of EMU*, CEPR.
- Arrowsmith, J. (1996), *Pitfalls on the Path to a Single Currency*, EUI Working Paper RSC No. 96/21.
- Arrowsmith, J. and C. Taylor (1996), *Unresolved Issues on the Way to a Single Currency*, Occasional Papers 49, NIESR.

Paul Temperton

The Independent Economic Research Company (TIER)

Chapter

13

The euro, the yen and the dollar

Will the euro be a strong currency?

Perhaps the most frequently asked question about the euro is whether it will be a 'strong' or a 'weak' currency. But when phrased in such a general sense the question is so vague as to be almost unanswerable. At one level, the question is about whether the euro will be a suitable replacement for the Deutschemark and particularly whether inflation in the euro area countries will be as low as in Germany. The answer to that question relates to the nature of the European central bank and the countries that are included in the euro area, issues which are addressed elsewhere in this book.

The question we seek to answer in this chapter is whether the euro will be a strong or a weak currency in relation to the two other main world currencies — the yen and the dollar. In order to answer the question we look at key factors that will affect the demand for the euro when it is launched: changes in the demand for the US dollar and the euro within foreign exchange reserves; changes in institutional demand for the US$ and the euro; the use of the euro as a currency for denominating international trade; and the issue of whether the euro will be launched at an appropriate equilibrium exchange rate.

The euro as a reserve currency

EU central banks may want fewer dollars...

There has been much comment about whether, following the euro's introduction, Europe's foreign exchange reserves will, in some sense, be 'excessive'. A simple calculation shows why this might be the case. At the moment the fifteen EU countries have combined foreign exchange reserves in excess of $360bn. The statutes of the ECB provide for up to Ecu50bn

(US$62.5bn) to be transferred to it from the national central banks following EMU. National central banks can keep any of their reserves not transferred but they will have to be held in non-EU currencies and, in practice there will be little need for them to hold reserves as intervention will be carried out by the ECB. Thus there could be excess holdings of as much as $300bn and, it is argued, attempts to reduce these reserve holdings will put severe downward pressure on the dollar, leading to a stronger value of the euro against the US$.

Such calculations are too simplistic and overstate the savings in reserves that can be made.

- First, reserve holdings of the most likely initial group of countries adopting the euro (i.e. Germany, Austria, France, Belgium, the Netherlands, Luxembourg, Ireland, Finland and Spain) are only around $200bn.
- Second, foreign exchange reserves are often built up by foreign exchange borrowing. If both sides of the national central banks' balance sheets are run down, this will have no net effect on the demand for dollars.
- Third, even after 2002 when national currencies have disappeared, there is no reason to think that there will be a big drop in the level of reserves. There is no 'correct' level for reserves. For example, combined foreign exchange reserves for the eight euro area countries would be around 4 per cent of GDP compared with 1 per cent of GDP in the USA; but Japanese reserves amount to 4.6 per cent of GDP. Furthermore, given that the first few years (at least) of the European Central Bank's existence will see the ECB striving to establish its credibility, it would be imprudent to run reserves down too quickly.

Thus although there may be some excess of dollars as a result of pooling of foreign exchange reserves, it is easy to overestimate the size of that excess and in any case it is likely to be run down only gradually. This possibility of a reduced demand for US dollars should be seen in a longer-term context. A process of diversification of official foreign exchange reserves away from the dollar has been taking place over a long period of time: between 1973 to 1994, the yen's share of official reserves grew from 0.1 per cent to 8.5 per cent and that of the Deutschemark from 7 per cent to 15.5 per cent, while the dollar's share fell from 76 per cent to 63 per cent.

...and other central banks may want to hold euros...

At the same time as there may be reduced demand by euro area central banks to hold dollars, other central banks may seek to increase holdings of the euro. EU countries which do not join the first wave of countries moving to EMU may well want to hold a larger proportion of their foreign exchange reserves in euro. 'EMS II' which will be established when the euro area is formed will set fluctuation bands against the euro for those European currencies not using the euro. Although these will be 15 per cent bands, as with the current ERM, some countries—especially those who are close to joining the euro area—may want to keep their currencies in narrower bands and in those circumstances it would be appropriate to hold a large proportion of foreign exchange reserves in euro.

Central and eastern European countries may also come to frame their foreign exchange management policy in terms of fluctuations against the euro and they may also have a strong demand to hold the euro as a reserve currency (see Chapter 14).

...so central banks' reserve holdings will exert some upward pressure on the euro

On balance, therefore, changes in the demand for foreign exchange reserves are likely to exert some upward pressure on the euro against other currencies although this is likely to be a force that is of a longer-term structural nature.

How will institutional holdings be affected?

Institutional investors already have very diversified portfolios. As is shown in Figure 13.1, at the end of 1995, foreign investors held over $1 trillion of bond and equity investments in countries that are likely to join the euro area. Changes in the preferences of those investors could clearly have a very significant effect on the value of the euro, much larger than any potential change in foreign exchange reserves. How might foreign preferences for European assets be affected?

From the standpoint of a foreign investor, one advantage of investing in a range of European financial assets at the moment is that a certain degree of diversification is achieved. As the euro supercedes these national currencies, that benefit will be lost. However, even before the euro is launched there is a strong correlation between the currencies and asset markets of those countries. likely to be included in EMU so this potential 'loss' should not be overstated. Furthermore, many global fund managers are restricted in the extent to which their portfolios can deviate from a 'benchmark', usually defined in terms of market capitalization. Financial assets will not be created or destroyed by the move to EMU, so a 'euro' benchmark will be equivalent to the sum of the previous national

International portfolio diversification

	Total outstanding	...of which held by foreigners
	(US$ billion)	(%)
Australia	386	16
Belgium[1]	392	17
Canada	781	33
Denmark	346	16
France	1559	20
Germany	2855	20
Italy	1160	20
Japan	7501	8
Netherlands	642	21
Spain	373	28
UK[2]	1901	22
USA	15,517	9
Total	*33,413*	*12*

Figure 13.1   Total outstanding bonds and equities
[1]*data for end-December 1994*
[2]*data for end-June 1995*

Source: JP Morgan

benchmarks which have been subsumed into the euro. In this sense, one would not expect benchmark portfolio preferences to change.

It is also often argued that after EMU European market will come to resemble US asset markets more closely, with more active corporate bond markets, for example, If this were to be the case, foreign investor interest in the euro may well be stimulated.

Ultimately, however, portfolio preferences will depend on how investors see prospects for growth, inflation, interest rates and so on. Such factors are essentially cyclical and it is very difficult to ascertain in advance how these might be affected by the creation of the euro.

How actively will the euro be traded?

Every three years, a survey is conducted[1] on the size and structure of the foreign exchange market. The last one, conducted in 1995, showed that the currencies of the countries likely to be included in the euro area accounted for around 30 per cent of global foreign exchange market turnover. That market share was well ahead of turnover in the yen (12 per cent) but still significantly behind the dollar bloc (44 per cent) (see Figure 13.2)

Of course, many of the transactions between European currencies (selling French francs and buying Deutschemarks, for example) will disappear once the euro is introduced, and it is therefore not particularly sensible to aggregate turnover data in national currencies to obtain an estimate of turnover in the euro. Bank of England data show that around 10 per cent of foreign exchange turnover in London is between likely euro

The dollar's huge share of forex turnover...

	US$ billion	%
US$	656.7	41.8
Likely euro area currencies[1]	469.4	29.9
Sterling	80.0	5.1
Yen	185.7	11.8
Other	180.0	11.4
Total	1571.8	100.0

Figure 13.2   **Foreign exchange turnover (daily averages of spot, forward and swap transactions)**
[1]*Not all of the smaller currencies were identified in the study. The total is for Deutschemark, French franc, Italian lira and Dutch guilder*
Source: BIS (1996) Central Bank Survey of Foreign Exchange

---

[1] *By the world's leading central banks. The study is co-ordinated and published by the Bank for International settlements.*

area currencies. If this disappears completely then the euro would be involved in around 20 per cent of foreign exchange turnover. This would make the euro twice as important as the Yen; around half as important as the dollar. In terms of turnover, therefore, the euro looks set to be the second most important world currency.

...is not due to the US economy's importance

| Country | Share (%) of: | |
	Actual world exports	World exports denominated in the currency of that country[1]
US	13	48
Five European countries	31	31
of which, Germany	*11*	*16*
Japan	8	5

Figure 13.3   Shares of world exports by country and currency
[1]*That is, 48% of world exports are denominated in US dollars, etc.*
Note: the five European countries are Germany, France, Italy, the UK and the Netherlands
Source: OECD Economic Outlook, June 1997

Will the euro be used as a 'vehicle' currency?

The euro may, however, come to be far more important in the world currency market than the above calculations suggest. At the moment around 48 per cent of world exports are *denominated* in US dollars even though the US accounts for only 13 per cent of actual exports. For five European countries — Germany, France, Italy, the UK and the Netherlands — their proportion of world exports (31 per cent) is in line with exports denominated in their currencies (see Figure 13.3). Clearly, there is scope for more world trade to be denominated in euro, at the expense of the US dollar. This would almost certainly increase the demand for euro. As roughly, imports hold cash balances in the invoicing currency of around 10 per cent of the value of imports.

As with the considerations regarding foreign exchange reserves, such changes in the demand for euro are longer-term and structural in nature.

Will the euro trade at the 'right' level against the yen and the dollar?

Of more immediate concern is whether the euro will trade at a level against the other main world currencies which is appropriate, given economic fundamentals. The question can be answered in two parts: whether the three main world currencies (yen, Deutschemark and dollar) are currently trading at an appropriate rates against each other; and second, whether the likely euro area currencies are trading at an appropriate level against the DM.

There are various gauges as to the appropriate values for exchange rates between the major currencies. Perhaps the most popular guide is to look at purchasing power parity (PPP) between the countries. Perhaps the most popular variant of this approach is the 'Big Mac' method popularized by The Economist [1] This assesses the exchange rates between countries which would be needed for the Big Mac to cost the same everywhere. Such Big Mac exchange rates show that the Deutschemark should currently be trading at DM2.02/US$ and the yen at ¥121/$. Exchange rates on 1 September 1997 showed the yen very close to that level; the Deutschemark still slightly undervalued (i.e. the Deutschemark should have been stronger against the dollar than its actual exchange rate at that time). The

G3 currencies

	DM/US$	Yen/US$	Yen/DM
Big Mac PPP	2.02	121	60
OECD PPP	2.04	169	83
'Fair value'	1.72	90	52
Actual rate, 1 September 1997	1.80	120	67

Figure 13.4   PPP and 'fair value' estimates

[1] See The Economist, April 12-18 1997, page 107.

The DM is fairly valued vs. the US dollar...

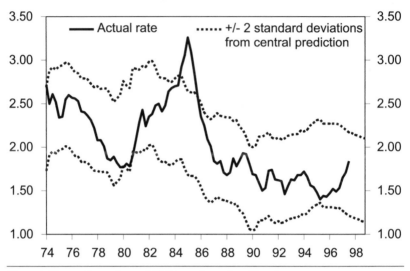

Figure 13.5   Deutschemark/dollar and predicted bands

...but the yen is too weak

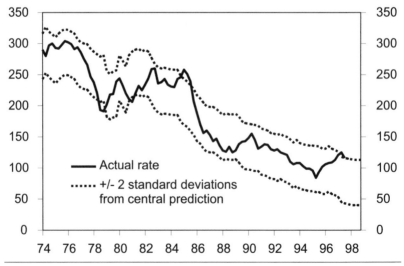

Figure 13.6   Yen/dollar and predicted bands

Most of the likely euro area currencies are fairly valued

PPP level versus the DM

	Big Mac[1]	TIER estimate[2]	Actual rate 01 Sep 97	% over (+) or under (-) valuation vs. DM[3]
Portuguese escudo	n/a	134	101	24.0
Danish krone	5.26	3.87	3.81	16.6
British pound	2.71	2.49	2.92	12.4
Swedish krona	5.31	4.58	4.36	11.8
Irish pound	n/a	0.39	0.37	5.3
Belgian franc	22.2	20.8	20.6	3.9
French franc	3.57	3.23	3.37	0.9
Finnish markka	n/a	3.00	3.01	-0.5
Austrian schilling	6.94	n/a	7.04	-1.4
Dutch guilder	111	106	113	-3.9
Spanish peseta	76.5	85	84	-4.4
Italian lira	939	912	978	-5.7

Figure 13.7   **Purchasing power parity and actual exchange rates of European currencies**
[1] Source: The Economist, 12 April 1997
[2] As estimates by TIER (The Independent Economic Research Company), using 1987 as a base period and relative prices since then.
[3] + indicates the currency is stronger than its purchasing power parity rate versus the DM (taking the average of the two measures of PPP).

OECD's estimate of the PPP rate for the DM/US$ is actually very similar to the Big Mac rate. Other approaches to exchange rate determination take into account the trend in the current account balance and differences in real interest rates between countries to come up with measures of 'fair value' for currencies. One such approach (see Figure 13.4) suggests an exchange rate of DM1.72/$. Moreover, on the basis of this approach the dollar has moved from a very weak rate against the DM (at the start of 1995) to a level which is more appropriate. (see Figure 13.5). On similar considerations, however, the yen seems too weak against both the dollar and the DM (see Figure 13.6).

What about other European currencies' values against the DM?. Once again the PPP method can be used and Figure 13.7 sets out two estimates: the Big Mac and those estimated by TIER. For a large group of countries actual exchange rates were close to PPP levels on 1 September 1997. Nine countries (Ireland, Belgium, France, Finland, Austria, the Netherlands, Spain, Italy and Luxembourg) had exchange rates within 6 per cent of the estimated PPP level versus the DM.

Conclusions

When the euro is created there are two important longer-term factors which may lead to an increase demand for euro at the expense of the US dollar: a change in foreign exchange reserves and in international trade invoicing patterns. Changes in international portfolio preferences could, however, be much larger than these effects but it is difficult to ascertain how these might be affected. If current exchange rates are broadly maintained, however, the euro looks likely to be launched at broadly appropriate exchange rates. The Deutschemark is currently fairly valued against the US$; and the countries likely to be in the first wave of EMU are also fairly valued against the DM. In this sense, there is no fundamental reason to expect the euro to strengthen or weaken after it is launched.

Chapter
14

David Abramson
Bank Credit Analyst Forexcast[1]

The euro and central European currencies

In sharp contrast with the obsession in several European Union (EU) countries, there is no government in emerging central Europe whose main focus is on European monetary union. Investors and analysts alike reacted with surprise and amusement in early 1997 when the Polish Finance minister remarked out of the blue that the country would be ready for EMU in the year 2006.

Central European countries such as Poland, Hungary and the Czech Republic (CE3) attach much higher priorities to joining Nato and the EU for obvious military, historical and agricultural reasons. However, the importance of monetary union can only grow as the longstanding twin goals of Nato and EU membership are achieved by the early part of the next decade. Nato membership has already been promised for the CE3 countries by April 1999. Negotiations for EU membership will begin in early 1998.

In addition, most central European countries are acting as if they want to satisfy the Maastricht criteria – albeit without the formal commitment made by western European policymakers. The economic orthodoxy and convergence-orientated logic of the Maastricht criteria are less controversial than they were when the western European periphery tried to stabilize their currencies and reduce inflation and budget deficits in the late 1980s. The Czech currency turmoil in May 1997 has further concentrated the minds of central European policymakers on the role of their exchange rate in relation to the Deutschemark and, soon, the euro.

1
Max Tessier, Tom Fahey and Stine Madsen made significant editorial and technical contributions. Special thanks to Mehran Nakhjavani of the BCA Emerging Markets Strategist for comments.

Public attitudes also play a role. It is telling that *Eurobarometer,* the publication that surveys European attitudes, does not even bother to question the public behind the former Iron Curtain about EMU. Nevertheless, the central European public has a positive view towards both the European Union and market reforms in general although support has eroded in the past few years (see Figure 14.1 a,b,c). One would expect the pattern to extend to the popularity of the single European currency, as is already evident in the peripheral countries being considered for the first round of EMU, such as Italy, Spain and Portugal.

These trends imply that the central European currencies will eventually be ready to adopt the euro. However, they also imply that exchange rate stability will increasingly be viewed as a policy target — rather than simply a policy tool in the CE3 countries. That leaves room for trouble, and even a 1992-style currency crisis on the path to convergence. The key questions for investors are: When will the CE3 be ready for EMU? What are the preconditions? Will there be bumps along the way and are there reliable early-warning signs of trouble?

This chapter sets out to answer these questions in seven sections. The **first section** maps out the current attitude of central European central bankers to European monetary integration. The **second section** provides a thumbnail sketch of the transition that the CE3 have already made and compares their situation with the western European peripheral countries that are likely to be in the first round of EMU. The conclusion is that the economic transition in central Europe has been impressive and rapid but still has a long way to go; the **third section** underscores this point with comparisons to Finland. The **fourth section** provides a paradigm for anticipating the currency bumps along the way as central Europe tries to converge with western Europe. The **fifth section** provides practical early-warning indicators in line with this paradigm and uses them to compare the 1995 Mexican peso turmoil and the 1997 Czech koruna devaluation. The **sixth section** compares the present central European currency environment with that preceding the 1992 ERM crisis for the western European periphery. The **seventh section** lists the conclusions.

Central Europe's view of the euro

A desire to join the euro club...

A starting point for understanding how the central European currencies will interact with the euro is to examine the attitude of CE central banks towards EMU. The overall impression is of an outsider wanting to 'join the club'. The conclusion is that CE central banks will increasingly view currency stability *vis-à-vis* Europe's core as an end in itself, rather just an instrument of policy.

Czech National Bank governor Josef Tosovsky gave an address in early 1997 at the London School of Economics, entitled 'European Monetary Integration from the Perspective of Central European Countries'. His discussion makes clear that, while CE is not thinking much about EMU, these countries are on a Maastricht-orientated inflation and fiscal convergence path. It also suggests that, while CE central bankers realize the benefits of a floating exchange rate in theory, in practice they usually prefer a stable or strong exchange rate.

Tosovsky emphasizes three points. First, he recognizes the notion of a dynamic optimal currency area as an argument for fixing an exchange rate to a hard money anchor 'early'. An optimal currency area is usually a static concept in which a fixed exchange rate zone makes sense for countries that tend to be affected in the same way by most economic shocks and have a high degree of factor mobility between the member countries. The dynamic version notes that a country can achieve macroeconomic convergence, and trade integration more rapidly, if the exchange rate is used to tie the hands of policymakers. As an example of a dynamic optimal currency area, Tosovsky refers to the Austrian experience which benefited from linking to the Deutschemark before they were strictly ready.

The second point is that the CE has already made a major transition from looking east for its trade in the Communist era, to trading with the European Union. The bulk of this shift was achieved in the late 1980s. This development increases the odds that CE policymakers will believe that a currency link to the euro, possibly an irreversible one, makes sense.

...but much work remains to be done

The final point is that central bankers realize that a lot of work remains to be done on the central European economies before they can consider monetary integration with the euro. In particular, there is a lot of ground to cover in the area of labour market reform and banking system/capital market liberalization.

Institutional exchange rate arrangements are consistent with CE central bankers attempting to reduce currency volatility and link to a European currency anchor wherever possible. Czech authorities have stated that the koruna will shadow the Deutschemark following the 1997 depreciation. Hungary reduced the depreciation rate of their currency basket from 1.1 per cent to 1 per cent per month in early 1997. Estonia and, more recently, Bulgaria have adopted currency boards that tie the hands of their central banks with rigid exchange rate links to the Deutschemark.

Western Europe's attitude to EMU*

	1990	1991	1992	1993	1994	1995	1996
Italy	61	57	65.5	68	61	62.5	n/a
Spain	n/a	n/a	n/a	n/a	n/a	40	47
Portugal	n/a	n/a	n/a	n/a	n/a	25	30

Figure 14.1a
* Percentage of respondents who are 'positive' minus percentage who are 'negative'
Source: Eurobarometer

Central Europe's attitude to the EU*

	1990	1991	1992	1993	1994	1995
Czech Republic	47	43	42	27	28	19
Poland	43	46	43	28	35	39
Hungary	49	38	28	28	24	21

Figure 14.1b
* Percentage of respondents who are 'positive' minus percentage who are 'negative'
Source: Eurobarometer

Central Europe's attitude to market reform*

	1990	1991	1992	1993	1994	1995
Czech Republic	54	39	24	15	11	6
Poland	47	28	33	29	26	46
Hungary	47	52	39	21	20	5

Figure 14.1c
* Percentage of respondents who are 'positive' minus percentage who are 'negative'
Source: Eurobarometer

Central Europe's economies: a snapshot

CE has made an impressive, rapid transition...

Economic indicators for the three large CE countries confirms that they are on a path that would eventually lead to sustainable EMU membership. Figures 14.2 and 14.3 demonstrate that these countries have come a long way in a relatively short period of time.

Figure 14.2 looks at the CE3 from the narrow Maastricht point of view. The Czech Republic has held inflation down to single digits for four years and more than satisfies the fiscal criteria, in part because the split with lower-income Slovakia made the adjustment easier. Hungarian inflation is barely in double digits and the fiscal criteria are not much different than some of the western European countries that are candidates for the first round of monetary union. Poland has the highest inflation rate of the CE3 — but even that is below 20 per cent. The Polish budget deficit is less than 4 per cent of GDP and the public debt is only 54 per cent of GDP.

This Maastricht scorecard is even more impressive when judged against the transition that these countries had to endure after the Iron Curtain was lifted. Figure 14.3 shows that these countries underwent their most intense reforms in either 1990 or 1991, depending upon the country. The World Bank calculates a summary measure of liberalization for developing countries based on internal, external and private sector criteria. The measure ranges between 0 (minimal liberalization) and 1 (strong liberalization). In each of the CE3 countries, this liberalization measure rose from extremely low levels (between 0.16 and 0.34) in 1990, to quite high levels (between 0.86 and 0.9) only four years later. The private sector in each of the CE3 has mushroomed to account for more than one-half of total production.

Figure 14.3 also illustrates the noticeable payoff in standard economic aggregates as the shock phase of the transition vanishes in the rear-view mirror. Foreign exchange reserves have risen, external debt burdens have shrunk, economic growth has strengthened, inflation has declined and capital spending is booming. The main cost has been higher unemployment, but this comparison may have been distorted by a different definition of an unemployed person under the Communist regime.

...but still has a long way to go

The difficult path already travelled by the CE3 and the ability to endure shock treatment (the exception to shock treatment was the Czech Republic — but they had easier starting conditions), suggest that central

Catching up: on Maastricht criteria

CE not so far behind Western periphery on narrow Maastricht view

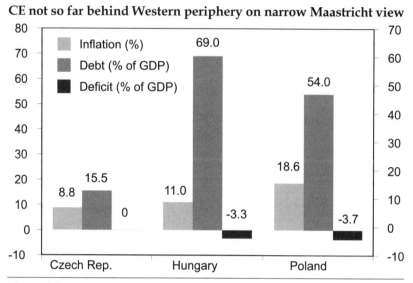

Figure 14.2

European policymakers will set their sights on EU macroeconomic norms in the long term. In fact, such economic goals may occur sooner rather than later once the political goals of Nato and EU membership seem assured. Part of the success of the transition has related to foreign direct investment (FDI) inflows that can only increase as the CE3 become more integrated with western Europe. FDI can help attract portfolio capital inflows, accelerate economic convergence, and stimulate the tradable goods sector of the economy.

Such a strategy should eventually work, but that leaves room for bumps – or even crises – along the way. There are plenty of differences between the CE3 and those peripheral countries of western Europe that are set to participate in EMU. Jeffrey Sachs and Andrew Warner have noted that, even though the CE3 have come a long way, these countries are still far behind in terms of per-capita income levels. Figure 14.4, reproduced from the Sachs/Warner study, shows that CE3 income levels range from one-third to one-half of the EU average. In contrast, 'poor' potential first round EMU participants like Ireland, Portugal and Spain still have income levels ranging from 72 to 84 per cent of the EU average.

From an economic perspective, large income differences make it difficult for a single currency area to function, at least without some

Catching up: on economic criteria

	Czech Rep.	Hungary	Poland
S&P debt rating	A	BB+	BBB-
Net external debt/exports (%)			
1987-1996	5	161	235
1996	-14	88	55
Reserves/imports (months)			
1987-1996	4.1	4.3	3.5
1996	6.5	6.0	6.8
Real GDP (% change)			
1987-1996	-2.7	-0.8	-0.9
1996	5.5	3.0	5.5
CPI Index (% change)			
1987-1996	13.3	23.8	85.2
1996	8.5	25.0	19.5
Unemployment (% of workforce)			
1987-1996	2.0	6.7	9.3
1996	3.0	10.0	14.0
Real investment (% change)			
1987-1996	0.8	-0.5	3.7
1996	15.0	8.0	14.9
Private sector output/GDP (%)			
1987-1996	5.0	19.0	27.0
1996	69.0	60.0	58.0
% trade with EU			
1989	27.2	26.6	32.9
1996	65.2	62.8	83.5
Year of most intense reform[1]	1991	1990	1990
Prior level of liberalization[2]	0.16	0.34	0.24
Liberalization level in 1994[2]	0.9	0.86	0.86

Figure 14.3

[1] *Source: Åslund, Boone, Johnson, 'How to Stabilize: Lessons from Post-Communist Countries'; Brookings Papers on Economic Activity, no.1, 1996.*

[2] *The World Bank Index of liberalization is a weighted average of change from 0 to 1 along three dimensions: internal prices, external markets, and private sector entry. Prior level refers to the index reading in the year before the most intense reforms were implemented.*

mechanism for redistributing income from rich to poor. From a political perspective, the EU would be unwilling to boost structural aid to offset the huge income differential between the CE3 and the rest of the European Union.

It is therefore important to get an idea of at what pace the CE3 will rise towards EU income levels. Figure 14.4 shows some of the variables that determine the pace of development. The CE3 has low tariff levels, although they are still slightly higher than in the European Union. Government spending is also not much greater than for the EU periphery. Savings rates are quite high, but the inadequate pension system stifles the potential for an even greater pool of savings. However, the large tax wedge in central Europe represents a major disincentive to job creation.

All in all, this is not a bad picture. The difficulty is that the CE3 need to have even stronger fundamentals than the 'poor' western European countries in order to catch up. Figure 14.5 provides the Sachs/Warner calculations for when the CE3 would reach 70 per cent of the EU per-capita income (still slightly below Ireland, Portugal and Spain) under three different growth scenarios. Note that a natural tendency for poor countries to converge towards richer neighbours over time is embedded in all the scenarios.

The key factors in each of the scenarios are the degree of economic openness, the domestic savings rate (both public and private) and an Index of Economic Freedom.[1] Of course, these measures are by their nature rough, but they provide a good approximation of why growth rates in differing countries and regions differ over the long term.

The first scenario assumes that the CE3 pursue their current set of policies, the second scenario assumes that they follow policies similar to the EU average and the third scenario assumes that they follow policies similar to eight very fast growing developing economies (VFGE).

Under the optimistic 'harmonize with VFGE' scenario, it will still take between 10 and 21 years for central Europe to achieve the status of the poor western European countries expected to take part in EMU. Moreover, the CE3 are unlikely to imitate the extreme free market, savings-inducing

---

1

According to Sachs and Warner, 'the Index of Economic Freedom (IEF) aims to measure the extent of market distortions in 140 economies focusing on market distortions caused by government intervention and the absence of well-defined property rights ...(t)here are sub-indexes for trade policy, taxation, government consumption, monetary policy, capital flow and FDI restrictions, banking restrictions, wage and price controls, the absence of property rights, regulatory policy, and black market activity.' For details, see 1996 Index of Economic Freedom, The Heritage Foundation, Washington, D.C.

Catching up: on market reform

	Czech	Hungary	Poland
GDP per capita in PPP prices percent of EU average, 1994 (%)	53	48	36
Average tariff, 1994 (%)	5.0	13	14
Government spending, 1995 (% of GDP)	50.9	54.6	49.4
Tax wedge[1], 1994	128.5	223.8	128.5
Savings, 1995 (% of GDP)	21.2	17.1	18.8
Investment, 1995 (% of GDP)	30.4	21.3	16.9
Index of economic freedom[2]	2.1	2.8	2.9

	Ireland	Portugal	Spain
GDP per capita in PPP prices percent of EU average, 1994 (%)	84	72	81
Average tariff, 1994 (%)	3.6	3.6	3.6
Government spending, 1995 (% of GDP)	45.1	47.3	46.0
Tax wedge[1], 1994	101.6	96.2	114.6
Savings, 1995 (% of GDP)	20.7	20.4	21.0
Investment, 1995 (% of GDP)	17.6	28.5	23.3
Index of economic freedom[2]	2.3	2.3	2.3

Figure 14.4
[1] *Cost of labour to the firm as a percentage of real take-home pay of the average worker*
[2] *EU average*

Source: 'Achieving Rapid Growth in the Transition Economies of Central Europe';
Unpublished paper by Jeffrey Sachs and Andrew M. Warner, July 1996, Harvard Institute
for International Development

Catching up: by when?

	1993 GDP as a % of EU average	'Policy' action	Growth prospects	Years to raise GDP to 70 per cent of EU average
Czech Rep.	53	Keep current policies	3.6	23
		Harmonize with EU	3.5	36
		Harmonize with VFGE	6.6	10
Hungary	48	Keep current policies	1.9	n/a for current prices
		Harmonize with EU	2.8	45
		Harmonize with VFGE	4.6	13
Poland	38	Keep current policies	3.8	104
		Harmonize with EU	4.3	66
		Harmonize with VFGE	6.1	21

Note: VFGE = very fast growing economies: Chile, Hong Kong, South Korea, Malaysia, Mauritius, Singapore, Taiwan and Thailand

Figure 14.5

VFGE policies. The central European public already had its share of shock treatment in the early 1990s and the support for market reforms peaked a few years ago, as shown in the polling data in Figure 14.1.

Adopting the norms of EU structural policies is a more realistic scenario given the political, economic and historical tendency of the CE3 to take their cues from Europe's core. It would take the CE3 somewhere between 36 and 65 years to be on a par with Ireland, Spain and Portugal by following the EU model. Carrying on with the status quo, perhaps if the public becomes even more apprehensive of the structural change caused by earlier market reforms, would be a disaster for Poland and Hungary in terms of trying to catch up to 70% of the EU average income. The Czech Republic would require 23 years to reach the 70% barrier.

These estimates confirm that CE3 convergence will be a multi-year process, although they overstate the amount of time that it will take. The earlier examples of Ireland and Portugal demonstrate that EU membership jump-starts FDI inflows and productivity in countries with low labour costs and skilled labour forces. This is also true for the CE3 countries, since they boast relatively literate, well-educated workers and good infrastructure. Of course, EU transfers also helped Ireland and Portugal to get a leg up and this will also be the case for the CE3 once they join the EU.

What does this mean for exchange rate policy? The most likely outcome is that CE policymakers will strive for currency stability relative to the euro in the early part of the next decade. Such a stance would allow for bouts of currency turmoil. The CE3 would be under pressure to achieve a higher growth path than western Europe, but hesitant to let their currencies bear the burden of adjustment as their business cycles overshoot and undershoot Europe's core.

Starting with the Finnish

The Finnish experience supports the notion that central Europe has made an impressive transition, but still has a long way to go. Finland and the CE3 (Poland, Hungary and the Czech Republic) share striking similarities:

Both underwent gut-wrenching monetary and fiscal adjustments as their largest trading partner, the Soviet Union, collapsed in the early 1990s. From 1989 to 1993, real GDP contracted by 11.5 per cent in Finland and by 16.1 per cent in the CE3.

Public sector adjustment in both regions was different, but equally difficult. The priority in Finland was to cut back the welfare state and introduce reforms that would bring public finances into balance and increase market flexibility. In the CE3, there was more emphasis on privatization and deregulation, as well as bringing social transfers in line with the new market reality. However, many of the effects of this adjustment were similar in both regions: rising structural unemployment and declining public sector spending.

Both Finland and the CE3 successfully altered their trade patterns towards western Europe (see Figure 14. 6) rather than 'turning inward'. The EFTA was absorbed into the EU and the trading bloc under Soviet influence (COMECON) fell apart, forcing a realignment of trade toward the EU. Figure 14. 6 reveals that the CE3 trade shift started two or three years after Finland. The chart also suggests that CE3 trade with the EU may keep rising; it has already reached two-thirds of total trade for Hungary and Poland, and will increase upon accession to the EU.

Despite these similarities, Finland is virtually guaranteed a berth among the first round of EMU participants yet the CE3 will not even be in the running until the latter part of the next decade. Problems of a structural

Lessons from Finland's transition:
Increased trade with the EU...

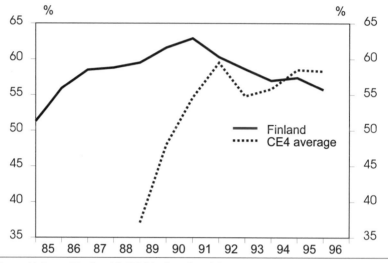

Figure 14.6a   Trade with EU (% of total trade)

...can quickly replace lost trade with eastern Europe

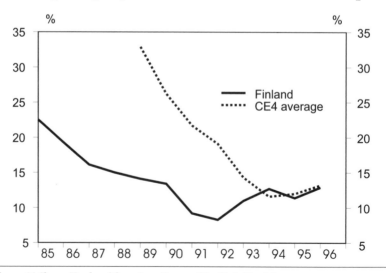

Figure 14.6b   Trade with eastern Europe (% of total trade)

nature that Finland did not have to deal with in the late 1980s are likely to surface if central European integration is too rapid. Integration hurdles to monitor can be grouped in four categories:

Economic structure:	The CE3 economies have not completed the shift away from the industrial sector into services. In Finland, services account for 65% of employment, whereas that number averages less than 50% in the CE3 and is dominated by the public sector.
Investment needs:	The ongoing transition requires additional investment for the CE3 economies; fixed capital formation is about 24% of GDP for the region versus 15% in Finland, with the difference explaining much of the current account shortfalls and interest rate differentials.
Wealth difference:	Finnish GDP per capita is about 5 times the CE3 average.
Free market institutions:	Liberalization and stabilization have done much to put the CE3 on the road to transition. Strong market-orientated institutions and a comprehensive legal framework must be in place before full integration can take place.

Ultimately, the reduction of these four barriers will result in interest rate convergence and greater exchange rate stability for the CE3 *vis-à-vis* the EMU bloc. The CE3 has a much larger labour cost advantage than Finland and relatively-skilled labour supply; both factors have attracted, and will continue to attract, large quantities of FDI to central Europe. Nevertheless, the Finnish markka meltdown of 1992 warns that the integration process will be difficult to manage and that the currency anchor may need to be periodically adjusted.

Currency turmoil: how to anticipate it

Thus far in this chapter, we have argued that CE economic convergence towards the European norm is at least a decade-long process, but that central European policymakers may try to 'put the cart before the horse' and stabilize their currencies vis-à-vis the euro. The combination of these two factors is a recipe for occasional bouts of currency turmoil. We now provide some indicators to predict when such turmoil is imminent.

To determine when an emerging currency is heading for trouble, it is important to recognize that successful emerging countries often run large current account deficits. That is because investment opportunities are so prevalent, and the rate of return on capital so high, that foreign capital floods in. The counterpart of massive capital inflows is a current account deficit.

Instead, the emphasis should be on whether a current account deficit is sustainable. The emerging currency paradigm developed by Mehran Nakhjavani of the BCA Emerging Markets Strategist lists five criteria to monitor for signs of trouble. The factors shown in Figure 14. 6, four domestic and one external, all can be applied to the Polish zloty, Hungarian forint and Czech koruna.

- What is the nature of the **foreign capital** flowing into the country? Is the inflow accelerating at a sustainable rate? Are domestic interest rates competitive in relation to foreign benchmarks, both before and after 'adjusting' for the capital gain/loss of recent exchange rate movements?

- How big is the country's stockpile of **forex reserves** that will help to fend off speculators in case of temporary 'bad news' or a chronic exchange rate misalignment?

- How **competitive** is the currency? Are export profit margins high or low? Is the exchange rate expensive or cheap in real, trade-weighted terms relative to its history? Is productivity in the traded goods sector rising rapidly enough to allow the real exchange rate to appreciate? Has the country been subject to a terms-of-trade shock?

- How rapidly is the **current account deficit** increasing in relation to the growth in income? How big is the current account deficit after adjusting for the fact that foreign direct investment often involves an initial surge in capital goods imports before the export-related benefit shows through?

- Finally, on the **external front**, what is the state of monetary and business cycle conditions in the major developed countries? In the case of the eastern European currencies, the actions of the Bundesbank and Federal Reserve are particularly important because of the importance of the Deutschemark and dollar.

Based on this paradigm, a typical deteriorating picture for an emerging currency would consist of shrinking interest rate spreads, a slowdown in

Emerging markets currency paradigm

The 'emerging market' paradigm implies: a rapid increase in inward investment, accelerating GDP growth and globalization and tariff deregulation

Therefore, Current Account Deficits (CADs) are the norm, not the exception

For industrialized countries, this would imply steadily depreciating nominal exchange rates, but in the emerging markets paradigm, CADs can (and indeed *must*) persist for a long time

For the investor in emerging markets, the issue is whether a country's CAD is sustainable. CAD sustainability needs to be monitored from different perspectives

Capital flow	**Reserve management**	**Competitiveness**	**Debt management**
• A proxy indicator of overall capital flow measures the aggregate change in the capital and the service accounts • The spread between domestic and foreign interest rates, expressed in nominal terms, in inflation-adjusted terms and in FX-adjusted terms	• The rate of change in official FX reserves • The size of official FX reserves relative to the volume of imports • Efficiency of sterilization, as measured by the size of official FX reserves relative to M1	• The rate and scale of recent changes in the real effective exchange rate • The rate of productivity growth, factor substitution, labour training issues • Micro-reforms affecting labour and other operating costs	• Composition of CAD: FDI vs. portfolio flows, export sector vs. consumption • CAD vs. GDP growth (i.e. rate of growth of foreign debt) • Relative size and servicing requirement of foreign debt

```
The POLICY FILTER
How do domestic politics respond to the need for policy change?
What is the predictability of the policy environment?
How vulnerable is the system to political shocks?
```

External shocks
e.g. shrinking Japanese current account surplus
FOMC policy, German re-unification

Figure 14.7

the pace of currency appreciation and foreign exchange reserve accumulation, an overvalued exchange rate, a dramatic deterioration in the current account deficit and a decline in net foreign direct investment inflows. Tightening global monetary conditions would also darken the outlook for an emerging currency already showing signs of wear and tear.

Is the emerging currency paradigm practical for spotting warning signs of trouble in the real world? We have selected two well-known episodes of exchange rate turbulence and compared them to central European currency examples. We examine the warning signs that preceded the 1995 Mexican peso crisis and compare them with the 1997 Czech koruna devaluation. The analysis then proceeds to the 'quest for European convergence' that took place among the western European peripheral countries of Sweden, Italy and Spain that ended in the ERM blow-up of 1992. The comparison here is with the CE3 currencies.

We conclude in both episodes that, while the timing is never perfect, a simple checklist of indicators can alert the investor to when a major depreciation is imminent. This is even the case if the depreciation represents a transitory event on the path to convergence, as is our long-term view for the CE currencies. Note that both the peso and the western European peripheral currencies (WEP) ultimately stabilized after a year or so and no longer exhibit any obvious signs of sustained wear and tear.

Currency turmoil: early warning indicators

The Mexican peso lost 52 per cent of its value against the dollar in only three months after three years of generally stable trading. Likewise, the koruna fell by 8 per cent against its targeted Deutschemark and dollar currency basket in less than a month after four years of virtual stability.

Figure 14.8 depicts summary variables for the four domestic criteria in the EM currency paradigm. In the 1994/95, these variables predicted the Mexican devaluation:

- **Capital flows:** The best symptom of a deteriorating capital flow backdrop was the return to dollar-based investors in Mexican short-term assets (Figure 14.8a). This measure peaked in early 1994, nearly a year before the peso meltdown. The reason for this early-warning signal was that Mexican authorities manipulated the peso to stay stable even as the bloom slowly came off the rose for foreign investors in Mexico.

- **Reserve management:** An excellent indicator of the clash between an overvalued currency and a stubborn central bank is the import coverage of forex reserves. Mexican reserves peaked above four months' worth of imports. Mexican authorities then had to eat into their stockpile of dollars, beginning in early 1994, to pay for a rising demand for 'cheap imports' without depreciating the peso. In fact, reserves are such a good indicator that the Mexican authorities hid the deterioration initially by not publishing timely reserve data (this is no longer the case).

- **Competitiveness:** The peso was grossly overvalued more than a year before the turmoil, both on a purchasing power parity basis and judging from four consecutive years of real effective exchange rate appreciation. It does not help that Mexico has a relatively low share of fixed investment versus GDP. Investment can be a proxy for future productivity if used efficiently.

- **Debt management:** Developing countries frequently run current account deficits owing to prevalent investment opportunities but few countries can run external deficits in excess of 6 per cent of GDP for very long. By mid-1994, it was clear that Mexico's current account deficit-to-GDP ratio was heading for a record 8 per cent. Moreover, the dependence on short-term capital increased steadily, judging from the decline in the stock of long-term financial liabilities in the early 1990s. On the surface, the jump in foreign direct investment during 1994 flies in the face of an expensive currency. But this reflects the 'Walmart phenomenon', where foreign firms entered Mexico to sell to the domestic markets and buy real estate, rather than produce for export.

This analysis also predicted the rising strains on the Czech koruna in 1997, but there were several signs that a Mexican-style smash-up was not in the cards:

- The returns to dollar-based investors from Czech short-term assets peaked in the middle of 1995, along with investor euphoria over the 'central Europe turnaround story'. These returns tumbled to new lows only a few months before the devaluation.

- Forex reserve import cover peaked about one year before the koruna devaluation. However, the level of import coverage was still high when contrasted with the Mexican example.

- Competitiveness had deteriorated to an extreme — whether calculated on the basis of PPP or real, trade-weighted index (TWI) measures. A one-time real exchange rate appreciation was inevitable

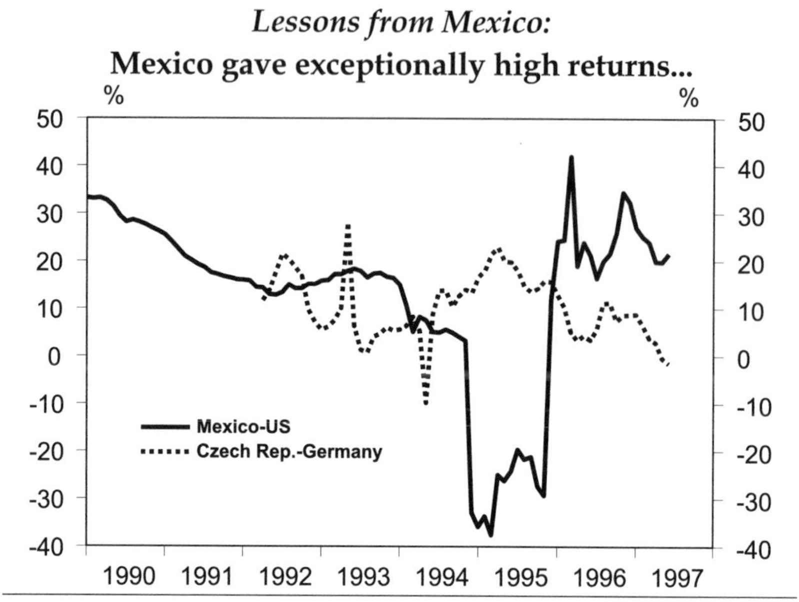

Lessons from Mexico:
Mexico gave exceptionally high returns...

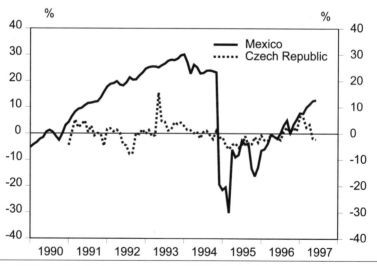

Figure 14.8a   Short-term returns converted to dollars

...until a clearly overvalued currency...

Figure 14.8b   Purchasing power parity (PPP) valuation*
*koruna versus D-mark and peso versus US$.

...could no longer be defended

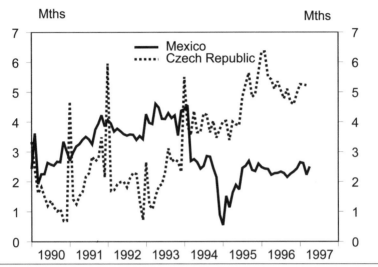

Figure 14.8c   Import cover of forex reserves

The current account recovered quickly...

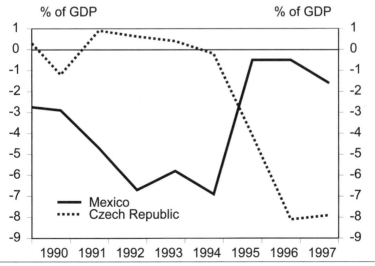

Figure 14.8d   Current account balance

...as competitiveness improved...

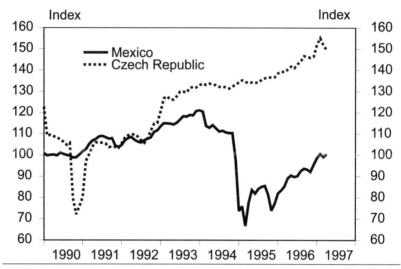

Figure 14.8e   Real effective exchange rate

...and foreign debt declined

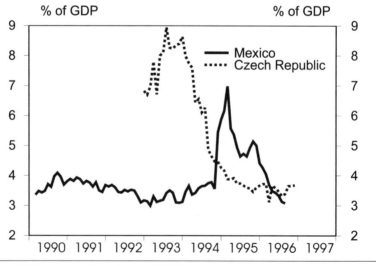

Figure 14.8f   Long-term foreign liabilities

Fixed investment has recovered...

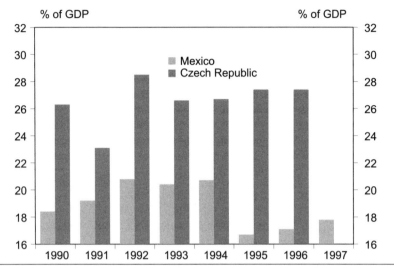

Figure 14.8g   Fixed investment share of GDP

...aided by healthy FDI inflows

Figure 14.8h   Foreign direct investment

after the Iron Curtain fell, owing to the low level of labour costs and productivity 'catch up'. But the real TWI had been rising for six consecutive years! Nevertheless, the much higher investment-to-GDP ratio than in Mexico also warned against expecting a meltdown.

–   Neither the size nor the rate of deterioration of the Czech current account deficit was sustainable. Moreover, the rundown of both long-term financial liabilities and FDI pointed to a rising dependence on short-term capital flows.

The external environment in 1997 is more hospitable to overvalued currencies than it was in 1995. Interest rates in western Europe and Japan are much lower this year than two years ago, at both ends of the yield curve. In addition, the U.S. Federal Reserve is much less intent on tightening liquidity conditions because it perceives inflation to be less of a threat than at the time of the Mexican turmoil.

Lessons from 1992 for the big three CE currencies

We know in retrospect that Italy, Spain and Sweden converged with the DM-bloc of countries, but there was a confidence-shattering explosion along the way in 1992. The lira, peseta and krona declined by 39 per cent, 32 per cent and 33 per cent, respectively against the Deutschemark from their 1992 peaks, before bottoming in 1995. The current environment for the 'eastern periphery' shares enough similarities with the 'western periphery' in the fall of 1992 to suggest that the convergence path in central Europe will not be smooth even if we are correct that CE policymakers will stay on a convergence path.

Figure 14.9 compares the criteria that got the western European peripheral (WEP) currencies into trouble with the current reading for the zloty, forint and koruna. Figure 14.9 (a-d) depicts an accident waiting to happen among the WEP currencies in 1992: overvalued exchange rates,[1] large current account deficits by developed country standards, industrial

---

[1] *the PPP level is measured by using 1987, first quarter, as the base period and then using the average of four cost and price indices (consumer prices, wage costs, export prices and producer prices) from that date to track the PPP path versus the DM*

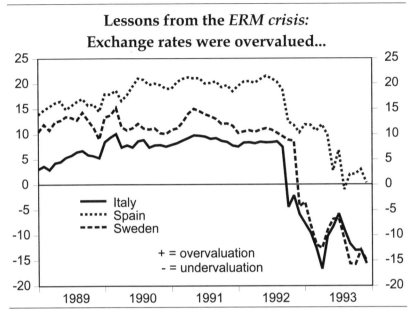

Lessons from the *ERM crisis*:
Exchange rates were overvalued...

Figure 14.9a   Deviation from PPP values

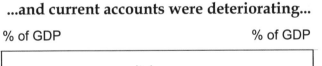

...and current accounts were deteriorating...

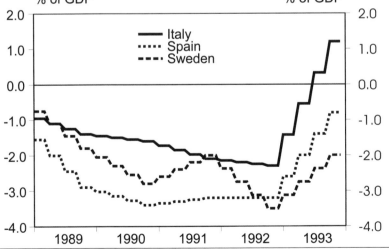

Figure 14.9b   Current account balance

...but activity recovered soon afterwards

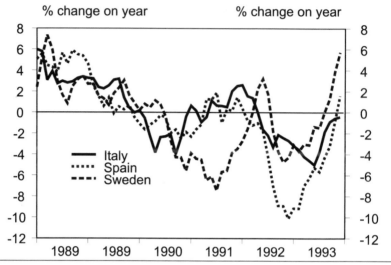

Figure 14.9c   **Industrial production**

Central banks were unable to defend their currencies

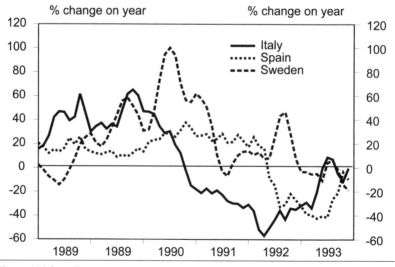

Figure 14.9d   **Forex reserves**

The CE country with the 'strongest' exchange rate...

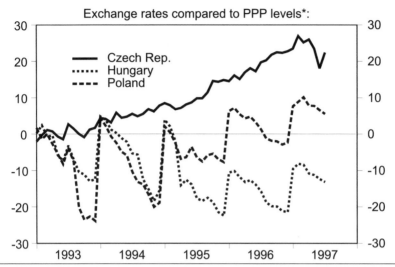

Figure 14.9e   Deviation from PPP values
* over (+) or minus (-) valuation compared to TIER estimate of the PPP

...had by far the biggest current account deficit

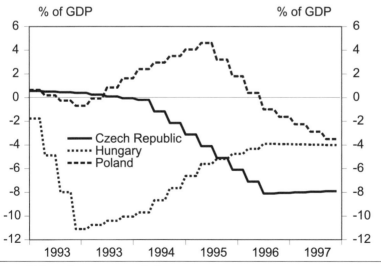

Figure 14.9f   Current account balance

The koruna undermined Czech economic health...

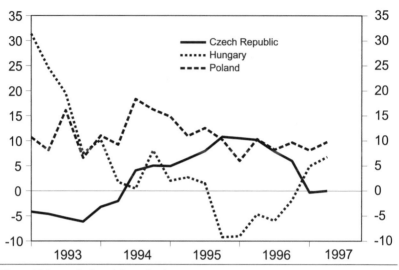

Figure 14.9g   Industrial production

...and drained forex reserves

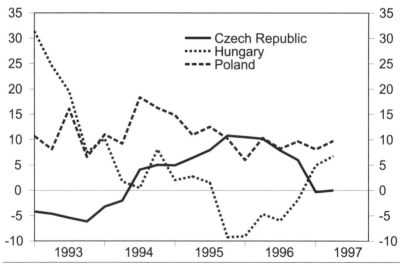

Figure 14.9h   Forex reserves

production stagnant—or worse—as these countries sacrificed their economies to stick with the Deutschemark anchor, and slowdowns or outright contractions in central bank foreign exchange reserve positions.

Similar indicators are shown for the CE3 in Figure 14.9 (e-h). As with the Mexican comparison earlier, the Czech koruna stuck out like a sore thumb: currency overvaluation, an unsustainable current account deficit—even by developing country standards, falling industrial production, and contracting forex reserves.

The Polish zloty and Hungarian forint give more of a mixed picture based on the comparison with the ERM crisis. Imbalances are slowly building. There would need to be more warning signs before expecting these currencies to deviate from their targeted rates of devaluation. In Poland, the zloty is getting pricey, but the current account deficit is not yet at danger levels, while production is expanding at a healthy rate and forex reserves are rising. Correspondingly, Hungary has a cheaper currency than Poland or the Czech Republic but that advantage is eroding rapidly.

An erosion in Hungarian or Polish production or worsening current account positions would be necessary before their authorities would even consider devaluing. In fact, Hungary and Poland are more likely to reduce the prescribed rate of devaluation in the coming years if their economies stay buoyant and the 'Czech fuss' dies down. That would increase the long-term commitment to an eventual link with the euro, but also boost the chances of periodic episodes of currency turmoil.

Conclusions and extensions

Being part of EMU is an inevitable goal of the CE3, now that Nato and EU membership are in their sights. These countries are sufficiently far along in their economic transition to eventually be part of the euro zone, but far enough behind western Europe that it will take at least a decade. There will be plenty of bumps along the way as the uneven convergence path for both macroeconomic criteria and per capita incomes causes the eastern European currencies to ebb and flow relative to the euro.

Simple economic and financial variables can be used to predict when CE currencies are approaching a period of maximum danger. This is the case even though it is likely that the Polish zloty, Hungarian forint and Czech koruna are on a gradual convergence path towards western European norms for per capita income levels, inflation and fiscal accounts.

To evaluate investment risks fully, it is necessary to go beyond the warning signs developed in this chapter. The next step is to gauge how policymakers will react when faced with an unsustainable exchange rate level. Taking the example of the koruna devaluation of 1997, the Czech authorities waited until the forex reserves were plunging and the current account deficit had gone to unreasonable extremes before acting. However, it still seems clear from the koruna devaluation that the Czech National Bank will be more flexible about the exchange rate anchor than Spain, Italy and Sweden were before the 1992 ERM crisis forced their hand.

One can speculate on the implications for the broader range of eastern and central European currencies described in the Appendix at the end of this chapter.[1] There will continue to be a wide variety of arrangements, ranging from a currency board to a 'dirty float'. The tightest arrangements, and therefore the easiest to make the transition to the euro, are the iron-clad Estonian and Bulgarian currency board links to the Deutschemark. However, all of these countries will increasingly view currency stability versus the euro as a goal of policy, as well as an instrument.

---

[1] *The Appendix gives details of various eastern and central European currency arrangements which are beyond the scope of this chapter.*

Chapter
14

Appendix

Institutional exchange rate arrangements

ESTONIA

Estonian kroon

Estonia was the first of the 15 ex-Soviet Republics to leave the rouble zone and circulate its own currency. The Estonian kroon was first circulated on 12 June 1992. The kroon is pegged to the D-mark in the framework of a currency board system. The kroon is fully convertible at the fixed rate of EEK 8.00 = DEM 1. There are no major foreign exchange restrictions. The government and the central bank remain committed to the currency board and no major policy changes are expected in this area of policy for the time being.

Estonia: selected indicators for 1996:

Growth of real GDP (ann. % chg.):	4
Consumer prices (ann. % chg.):	15
Unemployment (%):	6
Fiscal balance (% of GDP):	-2
Current account (% of GDP):	-10.2
Forex reserve import cover (months):	2.5
External debt (% of exports):	16.8
External debt service (% of exports):	1.2
Total public debt (% of GDP):	6.2

LATVIA

Latvian lats

The exchange rate of the lats, introduced on 5 March 1993, is a managed floating currency. Occasionally, the central bank intervenes so that the lats generally moves with the SDR rate. The Latvijas Banka sells foreign currency unconditionally to any commercial bank in Latvia to ensure full convertibility. No major changes in Latvia's foreign exchange policy are expected for the time being.

Latvia: selected indicators for 1996:

Growth of real GDP (ann. % chg.):	3
Consumer prices (ann. % chg.):	13
Unemployment (%):	7
Fiscal balance (% of GDP):	-2
Current account (% of GDP):	-9
Forex reserve import cover (months):	3.8
External debt (% of exports):	32.4
External debt service (% of exports):	4.5
Total public debt (% of GDP):	13.4

LITHUANIA

Lithuanian litas

The litas was first introduced on 25 June 1993. As of 1 April 1994, the litas has been pegged to the US dollar at the rate of LVL 4 = US$1 in a currency board arrangement. Plans are on the table to remove the currency board by the fall of 1997. The litas is fully convertible.

Lithuania: selected indicators for 1996:

Growth of real GDP (ann. % chg.):	4
Consumer prices (ann. % chg.):	13
Unemployment (%):	6
Fiscal balance (% of GDP):	-1
Current account (% of GDP):	-8.2
Forex reserve import cover (months):	2.1
External debt (% of exports):	34.1
External debt service (% of exports):	4.3
Total public debt (% of GDP):	17.1

BULGARIA

Bulgarian lev

The lev was a free-floating currency, but the conventional monetary policy was pre-empted by a currency board mechanism in July, 1997. The currency board is being introduced as a cornerstone of the new governments stabilization program The lev is pegged to the Deutschemark at a rate of BGL 1000 = DM1. The lev has certain current and capital account payments restrictions.

Bulgaria: selected indicators for 1996:

Growth of real GDP (ann. % chg.):	-10.9
Consumer prices (ann. % chg.):	311
Unemployment (%):	12.5
Fiscal balance (% of GDP):	-11
Current account (% of GDP):	-2
Forex reserve import cover (months):	1
External debt (% of exports):	159
External debt service (% of exports):	17.9
Total public debt (% of GDP):	175

SLOVENIA

Slovenian tolar

The free-floating tolar was introduced on 8 October 1991. The central bank intervenes occasionally. The tolar is fully convertible for current account transactions, but payment restrictions exist on the capital account.

Slovenia: selected indicators for 1996:

Growth of real GDP (ann. % chg.):	3.5
Consumer prices (ann. % chg.):	8.8
Unemployment (%):	7.3
Fiscal balance (% of GDP):	0
Current account (% of GDP):	0
Forex reserve import cover (months):	3
External debt (% of exports):	38.3
External debt service (% of exports):	9.1
Total public debt (% of GDP):	28.5

ROMANIA

Romanian leu

The leu is a free-floating currency, but the central bank intervenes regularly. Current and capital account restrictions exist. The exchange of foreign currency was liberalized in February 1997, with the view of full currency convertibility. One option under consideration for the stabilization of the exchange rate is to switch to a crawling-peg.

Romania: selected indicators for 1996:

Growth of real GDP (ann. % chg.):	4.1
Consumer prices (ann. % chg.):	57
Unemployment (%):	8.5
Fiscal balance (% of GDP):	-6
Current account (% of GDP):	-6.6
Forex reserve import cover (months):	0.8
External debt (% of exports):	85
External debt service (% of exports):	14.5
Total public debt (% of GDP):	23.6

SLOVAKIA

Slovak koruna

The Slovak koruna was first issued on 8 February 1993, following the dissolution of the currency union with the Czech Republic. Since 14 July 1994, the koruna has been pegged to a trade-weighted basket of currencies consisting of the Deutschemark (60 per cent) and the US$ (40 per cent). The koruna is convertible for current account transactions, but restrictions remain on capital account transactions. The index against the DM/US$ basket is allowed to float +/- 7 per cent against the central parity.

Slovakia: selected indicators for 1996:

Growth of real GDP (ann. % chg.):	6.9
Consumer prices (ann. % chg.):	5.4
Unemployment (%):	12.5
Fiscal balance (% of GDP):	-1.3
Current account (% of GDP):	-10.2
Forex reserve import cover (months):	3.8
External debt (% of exports):	71.5
External debt service (% of exports):	10.2
Total public debt (% of GDP):	32.4

HUNGARY

Hungarian forint

The Hungarian forint is managed as a crawling-peg. The peg is to a basket of currencies that includes the Deutschemark (70 per cent) and the US dollar (30 per cent) and the monthly devaluation is 1 per cent. The high D-mark weighting is a reflection of the successful redirection of trade flows from the former CMEA members to the EU countries, which now represent almost two-thirds of Hungary's export market.

The exchange rate regime is determined by the central bank in agreement with the government. Exchange rate adjustments of up to 5 per cent can be made independently by the central bank. More dramatic changes require the government's consent.

Hungary has full convertibility of the current account, but capital account restrictions still apply.

Hungary: selected indicators for 1996:

Growth of real GDP (ann. % chg.):	1
Consumer prices (ann. % chg.):	20
Unemployment (%):	11
Fiscal balance (% of GDP):	-3.3
Current account (% of GDP):	-3.7
Forex reserve import cover (months):	7.1
External debt (% of exports):	144
External debt service (% of exports):	28.9
Total public debt (% of GDP):	69

CZECH REPUBLIC

Czech koruna

Following its devaluation in June 1997, the koruna now operates as a managed float. The new exchange rate policy under consideration is an ill-defined 'shadowing' of the Deutschemark. From 1993, the Czech koruna was pegged to a currency basket consisting of the Deutschemark and the dollar, which were weighted at 65 per cent and 35 per cent, respectively. The central bank used to allow the koruna to fluctuate within a +/- 7.5 per cent band. Current account transactions are fully convertible, but capital account restrictions still apply.

The move to the two currency basket, from a five currency basket, reflects the growing importance of the Czech Republic's trading partner's in the DM-bloc.

Czech Republic: selected indicators for 1996:

Growth of real GDP (ann. % chg.):	4.4
Consumer prices (ann. % chg.):	8.6
Unemployment (%):	3.5
Fiscal balance (% of GDP):	0
Current account (% of GDP):	-8.6
Forex reserve import cover (months):	4.1
External debt (% of exports):	68.7
External debt service (% of exports):	13.7
Total public debt (% of GDP):	15.5

POLAND

Polish zloty

The Polish zloty is managed as a crawling-peg, which targets a basket of currencies and devalues by 12.7 per cent per annum. The basket includes the dollar (45 per cent), the D-mark (35 per cent), pound sterling (10 per cent), French franc (5 per cent) and Swiss franc (5 per cent). The authorities are moving to liberalize foreign exchange transactions.

The zloty is a fully-convertible currency for all current account transactions, but some capital account restrictions remain.

Poland: selected indicators for 1996:

Growth of real GDP (ann. % chg.):	6
Consumer prices (ann. % chg.):	18.6
Unemployment (%):	13.5
Fiscal balance (% of GDP):	-3.7
Current account (% of GDP):	-1
Forex reserve import cover (months):	6
External debt (% of exports):	139
External debt service (% of exports):	8.1
Total public debt (% of GDP):	54

Sources

Euromoney, 'The 1996 Guide to Emerging Market Currencies', supplement to the June 1996 issue.

Union Bank of Switzerland, *Exchange Rate Arrangements and Regulations*, ed. H. Theiler, November 1994.

Section
V

The
euro

The euro and
financial markets

Chapter
15

Mary Pieterse-Bloem
Paribas[1]

The euro and government bond markets

Introduction

The euro will mark a significant change for European bond markets. Its introduction essentially implies the instant merger of a number of domestic markets creating one large 'home' European bond market which, in terms of size, will be one of the largest bond markets in the world, as we will see. However, the merger of these European bond markets which, over time, have developed their own characteristics in terms of instruments, issuing procedures, investor behaviour, regulatory environment etc. will create a market which, in aggregate, is as unique as its individual components.

In this chapter, we will take a detailed look at the implications of the euro on European government bond market. For ease of reference, the sections are numbered. In Section 1, we discuss the features of this new market in terms of both size and liquidity. Understanding the credit implications of the euro, as outlined in Section 2, is necessary for analysing the type of debt which will become the benchmark, which is covered in Section 3. The implications for investors and borrowers are reviewed in Sections 4 and 5, respectively, while Section 6 contains our concluding remarks.

[1]
Mary Pieterse-Bloem is the Ecu/EMU Bond Strategist in the International Research Department of Paribas and chairman of the Euro Committee, sub-committee of the EFFAS European Bond Commission. The chapter draws heavily from the research conducted by Paribas' research department on the implications of EMU on capital markets and published in their bi-monthly 'EMU Countdown' document.

1. Features of the new market

Currently, the US dollar market is the largest government bond market in the world, with a total amount of US$4.9 trillion outstanding in US public debt (marketable Federal debt and municipal securities) as at the end of March 1997. Disregarding eurobonds – but including corporate bonds and bonds issued by the financial sector – the size of this market is US$8.2 trillion. The Japanese market follows in second place. The public debt sector in this market accounted for ¥344 trillion (US$2.9 trillion) as at the end of June 1997 and, if one includes the domestic and corporate sectors, the size rises to ¥480 trillion (US$4 trillion).

Strictly speaking, the largest government bond market in Europe is that of Italy, with the total amount of government bonds outstanding being L1933 trillion (US$1 trillion). In Germany, however, where the size of the domestic sector (which incorporates all bank bonds) is larger than the total amount of outstanding German government bonds, the overall size of the market is larger than the lira market, at US$ 1.7 trillion. The French market is the third-largest in Europe, with an amount outstanding of FFr7338bn (US$ 1.2 trillion) in public debt instruments and domestic bonds. The other European markets are all relatively small, with none of them exceeding US$300bn.

The creation of the euro merges all the markets of the participating currencies into one large domestic 'euro' bond market. Judging from the current size of the prospective EMU-entrants, it can be seen that a small composition of the euro will create a euro market which will be the third largest market in the world. This can be seen in Figure 15.1, where the German, French, Benelux and Ecu markets comprise a market (Euro 1) with a size of US$3.3 trillion, and a sovereign sector of US$1.6 trillion. Including the relatively large markets of Italy and Spain (Euro 2) creates a market with a total size of US$ 4.8 trillion, and a sovereign sector of US$ 2.9 trillion. This market will be larger than that of Japan and will thus take the world's second place in terms of size.

The same picture is revealed by the swaps market. According to a survey conducted by the International Swaps and Derivatives Association (ISDA) for the end of 1995, the largest swap amounts outstanding in any currency were in US$ (in both interest rate swaps and currency swaps), accounting for nearly 35 per cent of the total outstanding (see Figures 15.2 and 15.3). The Japanese yen followed in second place, with nearly 23 per cent of interest rate swaps and 17 per cent currency swaps outstanding in this currency as at the end of 1995. However, a small composition of the euro, Euro 1 (including only the Deutschemark, French franc, Dutch guilder, Belgian franc and the Ecu), creates a swaps market which is already larger

The euro debt market: #3, or even #2, in the world

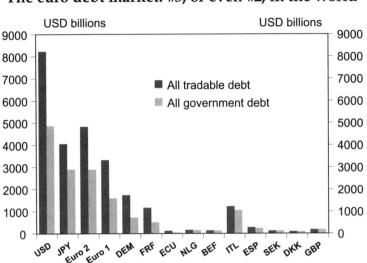

Figure 15.1   Amounts outstanding in the international bond markets
Notes:
i) All tradable debt excludes eurobonds
ii) All public debt includes government debt, debt of local authorities and, in some cases, government guaranteed bond
iii) Size of individual markets are converted to USD at exchange rates as of 1/8/1997
Source: Paribas

than the yen market. On the basis of a simple summation of the underlying markets, this euro swap market would account for some 24 per cent of interest rate swaps and some 19 per cent of all currency swaps. Including Italian lira and the Spanish peseta creates an even bigger market – increasing the market share for interest rate euro swaps to 28 per cent and, for euro currency swaps, to 23 per cent. That being said, although it is without doubt that the creation of the euro will create one of the largest swaps markets overnight, a simple summation of the amount outstanding in the underlying currencies may give the wrong impression. This is particularly true for currency swaps as these instruments are often being used for hedging exposure to moves of exchange rates between European currencies, such as Deutschemark/French franc, Deutschemark/Spanish peseta, Dutch guilder/Italian lira, etc. This activity may, or may not, be replaced by US dollar/euro and Japanese yen/euro currency swapping.

Interest rates swaps in euro: #2 in the world...

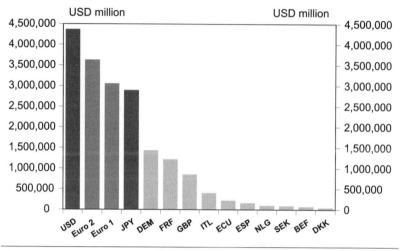

Figure 15.3   1995 year-end swap outstandings (interest rate swaps in US$m)
Note: Euro 1 = DEM, FRF, NLG, BEF, ECU; Euro 2 = Euro 1 plus ITL and ESP
Source: International Swaps and Derivatives Association

... currency swaps in euro also possibly #2

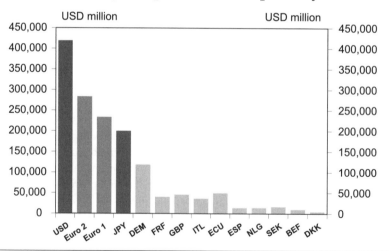

Figure 15.2   1995 year-end swap outstandings (currency swaps, in US$m)
Note: Euro 1 = DEM, FRF, NLG, BEF, ECU; Euro 2 = Euro 1 plus ITL and ESP
Totals are adjusted to account for both sides of a currency swap
Source: International Swaps and Derivatives Association

Despite the fact that the size of the euro bond market will be large, it will by no means be a homogenous market, since the domestic participants all inherit their own unique characteristics from the past. The composition of each market differs. For example, the domestic bond sector is larger than the government bond sector in Germany – but virtually non-existent in the Netherlands and Italy. There is a wide variety of instruments, with a number of countries being the proud owner of a form of debt which is unique to their own market – Pfandbriefe in Germany and CTEs in Italy being just two examples. With regard to government debt, issuing procedures differ, and while most governments operate some form of primary dealership system, Germany, the Netherlands and Denmark have a separate system. Maturity structures of the debt also vary considerably, from an average maturity of government securities of over nine years in the UK, and as low as three years in Spain. Similarly, the size of benchmark issues show a wide variation: from anything between US$1-2.5bn in countries like Portugal, Sweden and Austria, to almost US$20bn in France. Last, but not least, market conventions can differ not only from country to country, but also from instrument to instrument, with yield and accrued interest being calculated on different day-count rules (30/360, actual/360, actual/actual etc.), a coupon frequency of both annual and semi-annual depending on the type of instrument and some bonds being quoted in decimal prices (100.50), or in terms of yield (6.38%), with others shown in fraction prices (116 12/32).

As a result of these disparities, domestic investors – being most comfortable with their own market practices – have traditionally held a clear advantage over foreign investors and have thus tended to dominate their own market. However, with mounting pressure on fund managers to perform, and with governments becoming increasingly cost-conscious, the European capital markets have slowly implemented reforms. Among these are the abolition of withholding tax for residents in both Spain and Italy, the introduction of 6-month Bubills, 2-year Schatze and strips in Germany and the 1997-introduction of strips in both Spain and the UK. Of course, with the prospect of EMU serving to increase competition between financial centres, the introduction of these reforms has accelerated. Figure 15.4 summarizes some of the recent changes, innovations and trends in various European markets.

At the start of 1997, with less than two years to go before EMU, a discussion was initiated in the market-place on the harmonization and re-denomination of European national bond markets. Working parties and euro project groups realized that the introduction of the euro is a unique opportunity to create one large homogenous market. Although both harmonization and re-denomination are often mentioned in one breath – and may have the same goal of the creation of a large, liquid,

The prospect of EMU acclerates market reform

	Recent changes/innovations	Trends
Austria	Strip facility created in 1996. Creation of an option market in 1996.	3-day settlement for Vienna Stock Exchange transactions starting in 1997.
Belgium	OLOs first became strippable in 1992. Creation of controlling body under the supervision of the Banking and Financial Commission.	None.
Denmark	Reform of the stock exchange in 1996, allowing non-members to trade Danish securities. Also issuance of collateralized government bonds.	June 1997 agreement between Stockholm and Copenhagen Stock Exchanges on a common trading system and standards may suggest a future common Stock Exchange.
Finland	Bearer-form government bonds have been replaced by book-entry form only.	Main focus in the coming months is on the development of the repo market.
France	New auctions calendar from July 1997 including regular Ecu auctions on the same date as French franc issues.	Development of fungible auction programmes in January and July.
Germany	Creation of 6-month Bubills, 2-year Schatze, 30-year government bonds in 1996. Launch of strips market, repos transacted in Frankfurt no longer subject to minimum reserve.	Expected: combination of Federal government and special fund issues under the single denomination of 'Federal Republic of Germany'.
Ireland	At the start of 1997 the Treasury moved to a more regular funding calendar (monthly).	Main focus in the coming months is on the development of the repo market.

Cont.

	Recent changes/innovations	Trends

(cont.)

Italy	From 1997, Italian corporations and foreign residents in countries with a double taxation agreement are exempted from withholding tax.	Revision of auction frequency of bonds and bills. Introduction of strips is under discussion.
Netherlands	A version of tap issue called issue portfolio was introduced in 1997.	Cash management through Treasury certificates is taking over issuance in the bond market.
Portugal	Creation of a repo market in 1997 and a futures market in 1996.	Launching of regulations to develop the repo market. A reform of the primary auction system allowing for the participation of foreign players is foreseen for 1999.
Spain	From 1997, the Bank of Spain accepts private paper as repo collateral. Strippable issues are exempt from withholding tax for Spanish corporations.	Issuance of the first strippable bonds in July 1997 that can only be stripped once the size of the bond reaches 1 trillion.
Sweden	In 1996 a requirement for primary dealers to hold a minimum 2.5% market share in both primary and secondary market was introduced.	Development of the index-linked bond market is underway. A stripping facility under study was forecast for introduction in 1997 but did not come into effect because of an adverse tax regulation on strips.
UK	Creation of an open repo market in 1996. Also tax reforms in 1996 and abolition of the ex-dividend period.	Creation of a gilt strips market starting in Autumn 1997.

Figure 15.4

transparent and efficient market—they involve different processes. Harmonization seeks to standardize the market rules and conventions of the various bond markets which participate in the euro. Re-denomination, however, relies on the decision of an issuer to change the denomination of its existing debt from a participating national currency to the euro.

With regard to harmonization, the consensus was that such a step is 'not necessary but desirable'. The discussion culminated in a joint statement in July 1997 from market representative groups and market associations recommending a set of harmonized conventions for new euro-denominated instruments. For bond markets, the recommended conventions are actual/actual for the day-count basis, decimals for quotations, Target operating as the factor for setting the business days, no standardization of coupon frequency and a T+3 business days rule for settlement. In their conclusive report, published in July 1997, the consultative group on the impact of the introduction of the euro on capital markets for the European Commission, chaired by Mr A. Giovannini, recommended broadly the same standard conventions. Although these preferred conventions cannot be forced upon the market, the industry-wide support they enjoy, suggests that they will be adopted for newly issued euro-denominated debt.

As far as re-denomination is concerned, the discussion is still ongoing at the time of writing. Although the advantages of re-denomination seem clear at first sight, since the translation of securities from national currency denomination into euro at the six-decimal conversion rate is very unlikely to result in whole numbers of euro—or even whole numbers of euro-cent—the main technical difficulty involved with re-denomination lies in how this problem can be overcome.

As part of the changeover scenario to the single currency, which was adopted by the EU heads of state at the Madrid Summit meeting in December 1995, it was agreed that participating countries of EMU are obliged to issue new debt in euro. However, the re-denomination of tradable or existing debt would be subject to the principle of 'no compulsion, no restriction'. The French government was the first to announce (as early as November 1995) that it intended to re-denominate its debt into euro as soon as possible in 1999, thus signalling to the market-place its strong political commitment to Europe's single currency. Other governments have followed France's example—the most recent case being Germany whose Ministry of Finance announced in July 1997 that it had decided in favour of converting German government debt on 1 January 1999. Figure 15.5 summarizes both the official and unofficial commitments of the various EU member states to re-denomination of tradable debt. It can be seen that, whereas only four countries have made official

Re-denomination of debt will be widespread

Member state	Re-denomination		Bonds affected
	Y/N	*Date*	
Germany*	Yes	1 January 1999	All government debt (excluding *Schatze*)
France*	Yes	1 January 1999	All government debt
Belgium*	Yes	2 January 1999	Dematerialized debt (OLOs & T-certs.)
Netherlands	Yes	January 1999	All tradable debt
Ireland	Yes	1 January 1999	All government debt
Italy*	Yes	1 January 1999	All tradable debt
Spain	Yes	January 1999	All public debt held at central depository
Sweden	Yes	Joining date	n/a
Finland	Yes	2002	n/a

Figure 15.5 **Position of major EU member states on re-denomination of government debt**
States where official statements on re-denomination have been made

announcements to re-denominate, virtually all those member states that are widely expected to join EMU from the start have serious intentions to convert their debt from their national currency into euros.

On 8 July 1997, the French government became the first to reveal their method of re-denomination although, at the time of writing, the exact method of re-denomination is still under discussion with other governments. In an official statement issued by the French Treasury, it said that 'amounts of bonds held in French francs will be multiplied by the conversion rate to the euro and then rounded down to the nearest euro. To take the remainder into account, holders will receive a compensatory cash payment, valued at market price, of less than one euro per issue held by each account'.

For example, a line of 5,000 securities of FFr2000 each, i.e. total holding of FFr10m, converted at a (hypothetical) rate of 6.63552 translates into 1,507,040.89506 euros (10,000,000/6.63552). The holder will receive 1,507,040 securities with a par value of 1 euro each and a cash payment of 0.89506 euro (market price as at 31 December 1998 + accrued interest).

The re-denomination will occur on Friday, 1 January 1999 and, as of that date, debt previously denominated either in French francs or in Ecu and newly-issued debt will be fungible.

To summarize, the euro implies the creation of a domestic European bond market that will rival the US dollar and Japanese yen market in size. However, as the participating markets all bring their own unique characteristics to the party, the euro bond market will have a segmented character, particularly during the first few years of its existence. Harmonization of market conventions for all the newly-issued euro-denominated debt is clearly an important attempt to create one large liquid and homogenous market which can be accessed easily by international investors and borrowers. Over time, the trends that have been set in motion to reform and modernize European national capital markets will work towards a greater transparency and liquidity of the euro bond market too. The denomination of the debt in the transition phase (1999-2002) is not an issue, at least in theory, as legally the euro and participating currencies are denominations of one and the same money. In practice, however, investors may prefer euro-denominated debt if this is perceived to be more liquid, especially if the larger part of the tradable debt is in euro. The latter seems to be the most likely scenario as most governments have already announced, either officially or unofficially, their intention of re-denominating their existing debt, and are obliged to bring new debt in euro. Non-government debt which is not re-denominated to euros is therefore likely to constitute the 'odd' part of the euro bond market for which investors are likely to receive a liquidity premium.

2. Credit aspects

The elimination of currency risk within the EMU zone means that the valuation of securities in the euro bond market will largely be determined by credit considerations, liquidity, and a residual set of factors such as name recognition and investors' preferences. Presently, government bond yields in Europe are, in the main, determined by a country's exchange rate, short- and long-term interest rates, and the direction of German government bond yields, a fact which is borne out by various econometric studies. The remaining influence on government bond yields reflects the market's perception of a sovereign's creditworthiness.

Ratings assigned by rating agencies like Moody's and Standard & Poor's reflect the probability of default, i.e. failure of timely repayment of debt obligations.

To the credit rating agencies, EMU represents a unique case. The closest comparison of an EMU member state is perhaps a Canadian provincial government. However, the absence in Europe of a supranational power like the Canadian federal government clearly makes the two very different. There are at least two other distinguishing features of EMU. Firstly, the individual member states will continue to have extensive tax raising powers — within the boundaries of the recently-agreed stability pact. Secondly, the member states are subject to the 'no bail-out' clause of the Maastricht Treaty (article 104b) which stipulates that neither the Community, nor a member state, will be liable for the debts of either a member government or its public authorities. The approach of the major international credit rating agencies to sovereign risk analysis is changing in the light of EMU to incorporate a larger focus on the 'financial flexibility' of a member state as measured by, say, its tax competitiveness, indebtedness, unfunded pension liabilities, etc.

The two leading credit rating agencies, Moody's and Standard & Poor's, have both outlined their approach in analysing credit risk. Both rating agencies plan to establish a triple-A ceiling for the EMU zone. A critical assumption in this is that EMU is irreversible. A residual foreign currency risk brought about by the possibility of partial break-up of EMU would justify a lower overall rating for the EMU area.

As far as their approach to sovereign ratings are concerned, however, the two leading agencies do not have similar views. Standard & Poor's is of the opinion that the euro should be considered as a foreign currency debt obligation, since a participating member state gives up the right to monetize its debt. Moody's, on the other hand, would rate a country's euro-denominated debt at the same level as its local or domestic currency debt rating, on the basis that participating member states still have extensive national tax raising powers in the euro.

Figure 15.6, which lists the current ratings that both agencies have assigned to EU member states' foreign and domestic debt, allows us to analyse the implication of both approaches. It will be observed that both Moody's and Standard & Poor's have assigned a number of countries the same rating, triple-A, for their local and currency debt obligation and only in the unlikely event that any of these will be downgraded prior to the start of EMU will their different assessment have any implications. Where their opposing views clash on the basis of current ratings is, for example, in the case of Ireland and Finland. Their foreign and local currency debt rating could be equalized at triple-A by Moody's post-1999, whereas Standard & Poor's might re-rate these countries domestic debt to the lower level foreign debt rating, implying an effective downgrade. As markets will be left to

Credit ratings: not much agency agreement...

	Moody's		Standard & Poor's	
	Foreign	*Domestic*	*Foreign*	*Domestic*
Austria	Aaa		AAA	AAA
Belgium	Aa1	Aa1	AA+	AAA
Denmark	Aa1	Aaa	AA+	AAA
Finland	Aa1	Aaa	AA	AAA
France	Aaa	Aaa	AAA	AAA
Germany	Aaa	Aaa	AAA	AAA
Greece	Baa1	A2	BBB-	A-
Ireland	Aa1	Aaa	AA	AAA
Italy	Aa3	Aa3	AA	AAA
Luxembourg	Aaa		AAA	AAA
Netherlands	Aaa		AAA	AAA
Portugal	Aa3	Aa2	AA-	AAA
Spain	Aa2	Aa2	AA	AAA
Sweden	Aa3	Aa1	AA+	AAA

Figure 15.6　**EU member states' credit ratings**

chose who to believe, price anomalies may occur as a result of these significant rating discrepancies.

As a consequence of the triple-A ceiling for the EMU area, some companies, banks or local authorities could end up with higher credit ratings than their 'parent' government if the latter indeed has a lower credit rating. Both Moody's and Standard & Poor's have confirmed this possibility—however, if it happens at all, it is likely to be confined to regional, municipal or government controlled institutions rather than to private sector corporations.

If, in fact, the importance of credit in the assessment of relative bond yields will increase, then where will credit spreads of the EU sovereign states trade in the euro market? Unfortunately, there is no definitive way of determining a fair price for the difference in credit risk. A starting point

...and distorted spreads among the sovereigns

	3-yr	5-yr	7-yr	10-yr	30-yr
Austria	15bp	11bp	9bp	23bp	n/a
Belgium	19bp	20bp	n/a	25bp	n/a
Finland	n/a	n/a	23bp	24bp	n/a
Ireland	13bp	4bp	n/a	n/a	n/a
Denmark	n/a	7bp	n/a	n/a	n/a
Sweden	-12bp	8bp	15bp	n/a	n/a
Italy	5bp	11bp	n/a	n/a	15bp
Portugal	n/a	11bp	n/a	n/a	n/a

Figure 15.7   **EU sovereign spreads in the eurodollar sector**
Spreads as of 31 July 1997

may be to assess where eurobonds trade relative to the local currency benchmark curve. Taking the largest eurobond market, the eurodollar market as an example, one could argue that, in theory, the basis point yield spread of a eurodollar bond to the interpolated US Treasury curve reflects the perceived credit risk of the issuer to the 'risk-free' curve, both bonds already having identical currency risk. Figure 15.7 lists the spread as at 31 July 1997 for a number of EU member states and it can be seen, that apart from the US dollar Italy-Global 2023 which traded at 57 basis points over the US Treasury curve, the widest spread was for a Belgium 10-year bond at 25 basis points. However, this analysis is hampered by a number of factors. First, the two largest member states which are certain to join EMU when it starts, Germany and France, do not issue in a foreign currency (with the exception of the Ecu, in the case of France). Secondly, of those member states who do issue in US dollars, the issues outstanding are not numerous enough to enable a thorough comparison and thus an analysis on the basis of the available data cannot go beyond the level of broad statements. Thirdly, the price of an issue in eurobond markets is heavily influenced by the demand generated by the syndicate of banks at launch, familiarity of retail investors with an issuer's name, the size of the issue, etc., and it is therefore difficult to derive the pure credit element of the spread. That being said, given that the economies of the participating member states should have converged prior to entrance to the monetary union, credit spreads should not really be in excess of 50 basis points, unless there are special circumstances involved.

Another very important reason why the spread levels quoted in Figure 15.7 can give a distorted picture of the size of the credit spreads that may prevail in the future euro market, is that these spreads are a reflection of the current global bond market environment. They are very much a snapshot of the current situation. Figures 15.8 and 15.9, showing an Italian and Belgium 7-year eurodollar bond relative to the US Treasury curve, show that credit spreads have not always been so tight. The relative spread has been as high as 50bp in 1995 in the case of the Belgium bond, and 85bp in the case of the Italian bond.

With short-term interest rates at a low around the globe, resulting in relatively low long-term rates (with 10-year bonds at 2.3 per cent in Japan, 6.2 per cent in the US and 5.7 per cent in Germany), investors have been looking to put their money to work in higher-yielding assets. This has driven spreads down of traditionally higher-yielding eurobonds and domestic bonds within markets. With the next move in short-term interest rates more likely to be up than down, credit spreads would tend to widen. Furthermore, with a larger focus on credit in general in the euro bond market and the kind of credit rating discrepancies noted earlier, not only might credit spreads be higher than is currently anticipated, but they might also be more volatile.

In summary, one of the main implications of the advent of the euro will be the larger role that credit will play in the valuation of securities. With regard to sovereign ratings, EMU represents a unique situation for the credit rating agencies, since comparisons with other nations like Canada only work to a limited extend. It is unfortunate that the two major credit rating agencies do not seem to agree on their approach towards sovereign ratings, although both have confirmed a triple-A rating as a sovereign ceiling. Several studies on the size of sovereign credit spreads in a euro environment are underway. A possible starting point for such studies are the spreads levels which can be observed in the eurodollar market. As a final comment, it should be mentioned that, driven by the prospect of the euro, developments in the credit domain of the non-sovereign sector are also already under way. Amongst the most important of these is a deeper and more liquid corporate bond market, which will include the likely development of a high-yield market in Europe. In this more credit-dominated environment, the 'winners' will be those with a fundamental understanding of credit risk.

The Italy-US credit spread has not always been tight...

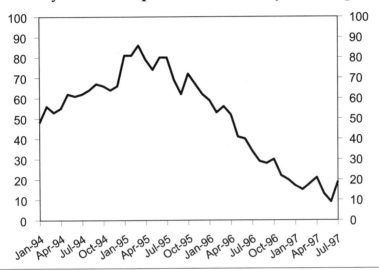

Figure 15.8   ITALY 2003 vs. interpolated US Treasury curve

...neither has the Belgium-US spread

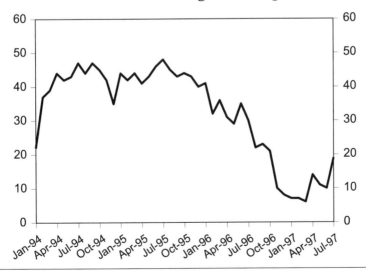

Figure 15.9   Belgium 2003 vs. interpolated US Treasury curve

3. Benchmark

The main conclusion that can be drawn from the analysis in the previous section on sovereign credit risk is that it would be conceptually wrong to think that there will be one euro yield curve, at least in the early days of the euro. The reason is that, even among member states with a similar credit rating, differences in credit risk will exist as there will be differences in the level of financial flexibility of each state. It may appear as if securities of the various participating governments in the euro all lie on the same curve — assuming that the states have very similar economic and fiscal profiles, and no serious political tensions are present. But, however small these differences may be, if the credit risk of a country suddenly deteriorates, a rapid rise in the yield of its debt relative to the others will be observable. Therefore, debt of different sovereign borrowers should still be thought of as making up individual yield curves. At the very short end of the curve, money market rates will be much more — if not entirely — similar for all, as a result of the fact that the ECB will set one level of short-term interest rates for the whole EMU zone.

With the various yield curves still (theoretically) in existence, but trading much closer to each other as a result of the elimination of currency risk, the question arises as to which of these yield curves will become the benchmark. Before we try and answer this, it should be noted that, by comparison to the current situation, there is a shift in the whole concept of benchmark status in the case of the euro. The reason is that a benchmark curve in a market is usually the government bond yield curve, since it comes closest to the risk-free rate of return — a concept born out of financial theory. However, under EMU, and as already identified by the credit rating agencies, governments lose their ability to monetize their debt and, as a result, government bond yield curves will contain default risk, albeit at small absolute levels. The effect is that government bond yield curves become poorer approximations for the risk-free rate of return. It is for this reason that some have suggested that the euro swap curve, of which there will presumably only be one, will become the benchmark in the euro market. However, we reject this idea, as swap rates represent counterparty risk — in that it contains default risk at the level of the counterparty in the swap.

Currently, the German government bond yield curve is the benchmark in Europe. The two principal factors behind this status are the size of the German economy (the largest in Europe in terms of GDP), and the proven ability of the Bundesbank in securing low inflation and a stable currency. However, with the creation of the euro, these factors will be shared with the rest of euroland: Germany's economy will be absorbed in the single market and monetary policy will be set by the ECB—of which the Bundesbank is only one constituent. In the euro environment, it will be factors like liquidity, depth, sophistication and transparency of a market and its procedures that will be key in determining the benchmark. Comparing France and Germany on these factors (see Figure 15.10), shows that France is ahead of Germany, although the gap is closing due to recent innovations which the Germans have introduced to their capital market.

France and Germany vie for the benchmark crown

	France	Germany
Size (public and domestic debt)	US$ 1.2 trillion	US$ 1.7 trillion
Typical size of benchmarks	BTANs: DM20bn Oats: DM30bn	OBLs: DM10-15bn Bunds: DM20bn
Benchmark effect	Limited	Severe
Instruments	BTFs, BTANs,OATs strips since 1991	Bubills, Schatze, OBLs, Bunds strips since 1997
Issuing procedures	Primary dealership	Federal bond consortium
% held by foreigners	7%	36%
Liquid futures contracts	3-month Pibor 10-yr MATIF Notional	3-month DEM Libor 10-yr LIFFE Bund contract
Repo market	Efficient	Not so efficient

Figure 15.10 **The structure of the French and German government bond markets**

The typical size of benchmarks is larger in France, while issuing procedures, both in terms of the issuing calendar and the issuing method, contribute more to the efficiency and liquidity of the market in France than in Germany. However, the most important differences between the French and German markets lie in the fact that the repo market has always been more efficient in the former and also that, in France, strips are actively traded. This would support the argument that France is better positioned to become the benchmark in the new market, with the only contra-indication being the fact that a much smaller proportion of their debt is held with non-domestic investors (7 per cent in France, against 36 per cent in Germany). However, with the abolition of minimum reserve requirements in Germany, and the introduction of a strips facility, the Deutschemark market is definitely making up ground on France.

To summarize, the benchmark status for the euro market is up for grabs — with both Germany and France playing hard to win the honours. The question as to which curve will become the benchmark lies with Germany's ability to catch-up with France in terms of modernizing its capital market in the time that is left before the euro is introduced. However, Germany does have the additional advantage of being currently seen as the benchmark in Europe. Also, international investors tend to have a larger holding in the German market than in the French market.

4. Implications for investors

For investors, who face a challenge in adapting to this new world, the most noticeable impact will be on the composition of their benchmark index. Most fund managers measure their performance against a benchmark index. They allocate a certain weight to each market, for example 38.1 per cent to the US$-bloc in the case of the Salomon Brother index. On a frequent basis, fund managers decide how much the exposure of their investments should deviate from that of their index (where exposure is a combination of total allocation to a market and the duration of the allocation). A relatively higher exposure in an upward-trending market generally results in a better return relative to the index, and vice versa.

As can be seen from Figure 15.11, the largest component in the most widely-used benchmark indices is currently the US$-bloc, with an allocation of between 38 per cent and 43 per cent, followed by Japan with an allocation of between 14 per cent and 19 per cent. The largest European market, Germany, has an allocation of only between 6 per cent and 9 per cent. Based on a simple summation of the percentage allocation to the individual EU markets, the arrival of the euro is expected to create one single component of between 23 per cent and 25 per cent, if participation in EMU is limited to the very core countries in Europe (Euro 1 in Figure 15.11). A wider participation in the monetary union results in a total percentage weight of between 31 per cent and 34 per cent of the indices (Euro 2).

The effect of this larger euro component on portfolio allocations is likely to differ with the domestic base of investors. No large portfolio shifts should be expected from European investors, since most of them naturally hold a diversified European portfolio already. That being said, though, their traditional liking for currency diversification may encourage some to start including more non-EMU countries in their index. The most likely

The euro: set to be the #2 benchmark index component

	Salomon Brothers	JP Morgan (traded)	EFFAS
US-bloc[1]	38.1	44.3	43
Japan	18.8	14.3	19
Germany	9.4	8.9	9
France	7.5	8.1	6
Netherlands	3.4	3.6	3
Austria	0.9	n/a	n/a
Belgium	2.6	2.9	3
Ireland	0.4	n/a	n/a
Finland	0.5	n/a	n/a
Italy	6.3	4.9	5
Spain	2.8	3.1	2
Denmark	1.6	1.8	1
United Kingdom	5.8	6.4	5
Sweden	1.6	1.7	2
Switzerland	0.4	n/a	n/a
Euro 1[2]	24.7	23.5	23[4]
Euro 2[3]	33.8	31.5	31[4]

Figure 15.11   Composition of benchmark indices
[1] *United States, Canada*
[2] *Euro 1 = Germany, France, Netherlands, Austria, Belgium, Ireland and Finland*
[3] *Euro 2 = Euro 1, plus Italy and Spain*
[4] *Includes 2% weight for the Ecu bond market*

candidates for inclusion are Norway, and countries like Poland and Czech Republic which have recently sought admission to the EU. Non-European investors, on the other hand, may have had a tendency to marginalize Europe in their benchmark, as a heavy involvement in European markets would require knowledge of the economic and political situation of each individual country. Also, a number of European markets have hitherto been too small to accommodate large-scale trading, with the result that they have usually been the first to be removed from the benchmark. The euro,

Currency decisions have greatly affected performance...

	1991	1992	1993	1994	1995	1996
Performance						
WM Composite	19.1	6.6	15.8	-2.5	19.1	8.7
Salomon Brothers Index	15.8	5.5	13.3	2.3	19.0	3.6
Outperformance	3.3	1.1	2.5	-4.8	0.1	5.1
Attribution						
Currency allocation	1.1	1.4	-0.8	-2.6	-0.8	2.7
Country allocation	0.3	-0.5	0.9	0.1	-0.1	1.6
Duration	1.4	0.2	2.1	2.20	1.1	0.5

Figure 15.12   **Attribution to relative performance of fund managers**

which will constitute a large part of their index, will thus provide these investors with one large domestic market, representing the same currency risk, and in which they can seek the instruments which represents the best risk/reward relationship. It is from these non-European investors that we can expect portfolio shifts into the euro, particularly if the euro establishes itself as a credible currency.

In general, in their quest to outperform their benchmark, fund managers will have to review what type of decision constitutes the largest contributor to their relative performance. Studying some data on the attribution to the relative performance of fund managers over the period 1991 to 1996 (see Figure 15.12) reveals some interesting points. First, the level of performance of all fund managers on average — as represented by the WM composite relative to the Salomon Brother's world government bond index — has been positive, with the exception of the bear market year of 1994. Secondly, breaking down the attribution of the currency move, country allocation and duration decision to this relative performance, it can be seen that currency decision is by far the largest contributor to performance, accounting on average for 46 per cent of relative performance between 1991 and 1996. Duration or stock selection is the second largest contributor, accounting on average for 38 per cent. Country selection only comes third place with an average contribution of 16 per cent.

..with yen/dollar moves of great importance

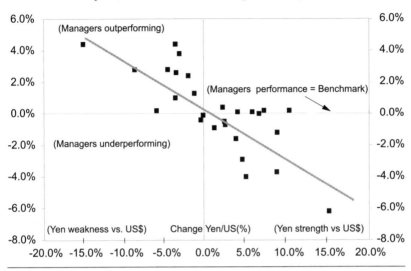

Figure 15.13   **Fund managers' performance versus USD/JPY**
Source: DICAM London

The greater the risk, the higher the reward

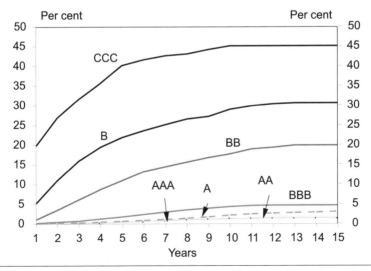

Figure 15.14   **Static cumulative default rates**
Source: Standard & Poor's

Thus, the value added and importance of country allocation is generally over-emphasized. This reflects the higher historic volatility of foreign exchange rates and bond yields (i.e. duration risk) compared to the variance yield differentials between government bond markets. In fact, there is further evidence that managers' relative performance is largely determined by the main currency moves, i.e. US dollar/Deutschemark and US dollar/Japanese yen (see Figure 15.13). Performing a linear regression of the WM composite relative performance to the dollar/yen shows that there is a negative relationship between yen strength versus the dollar and managers' performance: managers have only outperformed when the yen was weak.[1]

To summarize, in the brave new world, there will be a reduced capacity to perform from country allocation for fund managers. This implication will particularly be felt with European investors, who traditionally have had a liking for diversification. In this environment, the first concern of a fund manager should be to get the dollar/euro and dollar/yen moves right, and the second concern is with the optimal exposure or duration of the overall position in a market. Country allocation has the smallest share in total outperformance. The latter is where credit risk, once again, becomes an important factor since a thorough credit analysis will not only help fund managers in the selection of stocks, in particular non-government bonds, but will also allow them to enhance the performance of their portfolio. This is demonstrated in Figure 15.14, which shows the static cumulative default rate, per level of credit as the number of years on the debt increase.

As can be seen, this cumulative default rate anywhere between triple-A and triple-B rated debt does not differ a great deal, in particular where the maturity of the debt is kept below 10 years. However, yield levels can differ a great deal in this credit range, thus significantly rewarding an investor for the perceived extra risk that is taken.

5. Implications for borrowers

Without doubt, the euro also has important implications for issuers, not least the fact that they would be well advised to move in tandem with investors if they are to maintain competitive bids for funds. With the focus on credit increasing, in particular for European investors — which lag their

---

[1]   *The author is grateful to DICAM London Ltd. for pointing this line of analysis out to her.*

US counterparts in this respect—the key to a successful placement programme will be an issuer's perceived credit status.

Borrowers have already started to act in anticipation of the single currency. January 1997 marked the birth of a new 'euro-style' bond market. Since then, a growing number of borrowers have been issuing bonds designed for the euro, with some 62 issues (for a total of US$26.3bn) placed by end-July 1997. The spectacular growth of this new market segment is illustrated in Figure 15.15, which shows the cumulative issuance of euro-style bonds since the start of 1997.

Euro-style issuance takes off in 1997

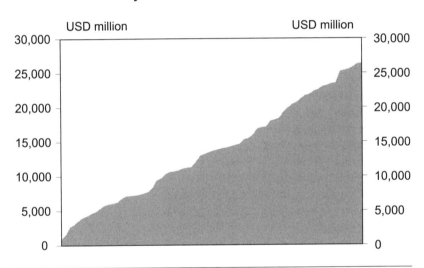

Figure 15.15   Cumulative issuance of euro-style debt (US$m, Jan-July 1997)

The rationale for tapping into the euro market, in one form or another, is obvious. With an overwhelming majority of investors convinced that EMU will be established in 1999,[1] euro-style issues have shown healthy demand.

There are, of course, other specific advantages for euro issuers:

---

[1] *The Paribas April 1997 EMU Investor Survey revealed that 97% of the respondents believe that EMU will start in 1999.*

- Through launching euro-style issues, a borrower can create large, liquid issues, particularly as the specific clauses included in the prospectuses of many of the bonds allow for a consolidation of a number of issues into one large size euro-denominated bond;
- A euro-style issue allows borrowers to position their credit ahead of EMU. In particular, issuers who have infrequently tapped the individual European markets can pre-market their credit strength and enable their name to become familiar amongst a diverse range of domestic EU investors;
- Issuers acting on behalf of those sovereigns which have a positive attitude towards participation in EMU have been able to send a strong signal to the market, underlining their commitment to the euro, through the issuance of euro-style bonds;
- A euro-style issue has proven an excellent vehicle to tap into a wide and growing investor base. Demand for these euro-style bonds has been good, and has emanated not only from across the whole of Europe, but also from the Middle East, Asia and the United States.

Euro-style issues have been launched in a variety of shapes and forms. Broadly speaking, three main structures can be distinguished: an exchangeable issue, a parallel bond and a euro issue. Below, we discuss each in turn:

Exchangeable bond

Through an exchangeable bond, a borrower issues a eurobond, denominated in one of the currencies which is expected to participate in EMU, carrying the same coupon and maturity as a specific domestic issue. After EMU has started, both bonds will be re-denominated in euro allowing for an exchangeability between the two. A schematic representation of an exchangeable issue is given in Figure 15.16.

In the launch of its very first euro-style bond, the Republic of Austria introduced the first exchangeable bond. In this particular case, the exchange is unilateral from the eurobond into the domestic issue and is at the bonds holder's discretion. The Kingdom of Spain went one step further in July 1997, by issuing a eurobond compulsorily exchangeable into a domestic issue.

Parallel bond

Through a parallel bond, a borrower launches two bonds with identical terms and conditions in two different currencies which are both expected to participate in EMU. After EMU has started, both bonds will re-denominate into euro, allowing for the consolidation of both issues into

The exchangeable bond

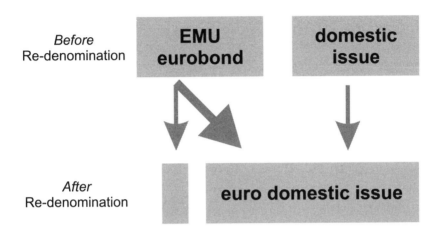

Figure 15.16

The parallel bond

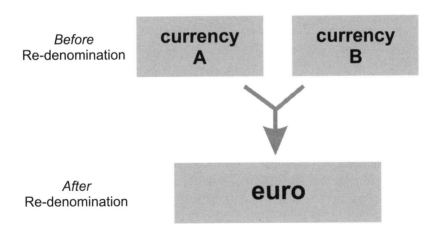

Figure 15.17

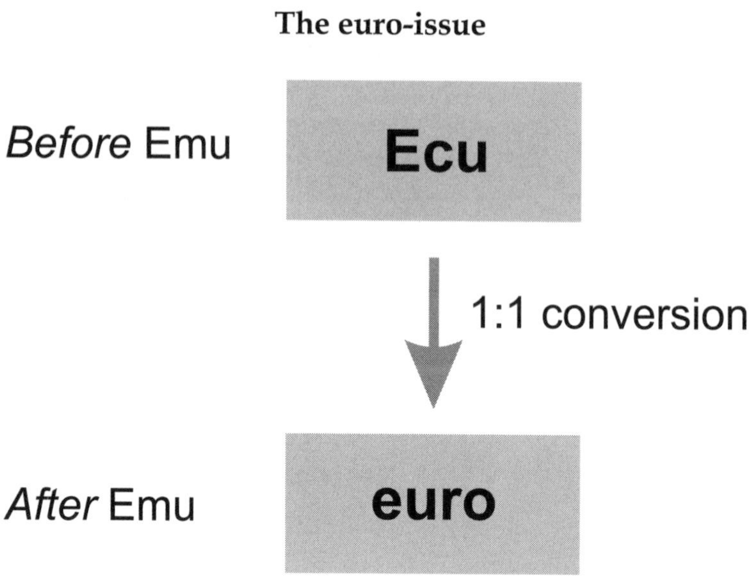

The euro-issue

Before Emu

Ecu

1:1 conversion

After Emu

euro

Figure 15.18   Euro issue

Euro-style issuance: 62 issues in six months

By end-July 1997	Local currency (million)	USD amount (million)	No. of issues	%
FRF	45,250	7921	20	30
DEM	7900	4628	10	18
NLG	5150	2704	6	10
ATS	8500	703	8	3
GBP	650	1067	2	4
PTE	20,000	118	1	0
ITL	4,920,000	2873	8	11
EURO	5250	6335	15	24
TOTAL		*26,349*	*62*	*100*

Figure 15.19   Euro-style issues by currency

one bond. Consolidation occurs without the explicit consent of the bond holder. A schematic representation of an exchangeable issue is shown in Figure 15.17.

There are different variations of the same parallel type structure. A parallel bond is also referred to as a 'twin bond' if there are only two tranches, or as a 'catamaran bond' if the coupon is floating. A 'tributary bond' is when the tranches (two or more) are issued at different dates. The last structure has the added advantage for borrowers in that it enables them to optimize the timing of the launch.

Euro-issue

A euro-issue is a bond in which the payments are in euro. However, until EMU takes place, the borrower guarantees to pay in Ecu at an exchange rate of one Ecu for one euro. A schematic representation of a euro-issue is shown given in Figure 15.18.

Figure 15.19, which lists the 62 euro-style issues by currency, shows that some 24 per cent have been in Ecu/euro and these were clearly all of the straightforward euro-issue type. The remaining issues have been either of the exchangeable or parallel type, with the latter proving the more popular. The French franc is shown to be the most active currency of all for euro-style issues, reflecting not only the currency's prospect of joining the euro-bloc, but also the apparently advantageous relative cost of borrowing in francs and strong domestic demand. The Deutschemark has also enjoyed a certain popularity, with some 10 euro-style issues outstanding. In addition, prompted by Italy's improving prospects of joining EMU in 1999, there has been a recent surge in the issuance of lira euro-style bonds,

To summarize, the euro-style debt market has achieved rapid success since the start of 1997. With many people now convinced that the euro will indeed come into existence on 1 January 1999, this should not come as a great surprise. In fact, for those borrowers who wish to position their credit, and their name, ahead of the creation of what will undoubtedly become a very large market, this sector represents a unique opportunity to do so. As long as investors and borrowers remain convinced that EMU is on track, we expect this new market segment to continue to grow rapidly.

6. Conclusion

The introduction of the euro will have significant implications for European bond markets. In this chapter, we have analysed the impact of this new market in terms of size, notable features, credit aspects and benchmark choice. We have also analysed the implications for both investors and borrowers. In this section, we shall briefly cover our main findings:

The euro will instantly create a bond market of a size in the range of US$3.3bn and US$5bn — a figure which is dependant upon the number of countries which will participate in the euro. On the basis of current figures, the new market would rank third in the world, surpassing even the Japanese market if the relatively larger markets of Italy and Spain also join EMU. The same holds true for the euro swap market.

The market will by no means be a homogenous market, since different characteristics per type of instrument will prevail. However, steps have been taken in an effort to harmonize market conventions and sovereigns have signalled their intention to re-denominate existing debt.

The euro market will be a credit dominated market. With the elimination of currency risk, the valuation of securities will largely be done on the basis of credit aspects.

Rating agencies, to whom EMU represents a unique case, agree that a triple-A sovereign ceiling should apply, but they disagree in their approach towards sovereign ratings — thus providing the potential for pricing differences.

It will be conceptually correct to think of different yield curves within the euro bond market, since sovereigns still have considerable tax raising and spending powers. At the very short end, one money market curve should emerge, as the ECB will operate one key interest for the entire euro zone. The latter is also likely to ensure that there will be one euro swap curve.

Of these difference yield curves, none will represent the true risk-free rate of return. Benchmark status is expected to fall upon either Germany or France, depending on factors such as liquidity, depth and sophistication of their markets upon EMU entry.

The main implication for investors is the change in the composition of their benchmark index. This is likely to induce portfolio shifts into the euro from non-European investors.

Borrowers have also already started to anticipate the single currency, as is evident from the issuance of euro-style debt since the start of 1997. Special structures like the euro-issue and parallel bonds have emerged, thereby allowing issuers to market their credit strength ahead of the establishment of the large euro market.

This chapter is by no means exhaustive and, in the run-up to EMU, further analysis of the impact of the euro on other areas of the bond market will no doubt be carried out. In addition, further in-depth analysis of each section in itself can, and almost certainly will, be furthered. Nevertheless, it is our hope that this chapter has enabled readers to gain a foundation into the principal effects of the euro on the European bond markets.

Of course, while EMU will require rapid and far-reaching changes to the market—some of which will be literally felt overnight in 1999—the wider implication of single currency will only be realized over a longer period, since it will take time to build a liquid and homogenous capital market of this size. Nevertheless, and irrespective of their personal stance on EMU, Europeans should welcome this development.

Mike Young
Goldman Sachs

Chapter
16

The euro and equity markets

In this chapter we review the case for and against particular equity markets in the single currency environment. We argue that the history of Deutschemark appreciation, combined with Germany's continued positive trade balance, suggests that the competitive edge in a single currency environment is likely to fall to Germany-based companies. In an environment in which devaluation against major trading partners is no longer an option, the culture of cost management that steady Deutschemark appreciation has inculcated in industry is likely to give them a competitive advantage until management elsewhere builds experience of the same environment.

In many ways, the question of whether a specific group of companies which we currently call 'the German equity market' or 'the Italian equity market' will do well or badly in the aftermath of monetary union is nonsensical. The defining characteristics of this group of companies historically is that they have their primary listing in a particular geographic area and that they share a base currency for reporting. Time and cross-listing have eroded the importance of the first; and the euro is about to eliminate the latter distinction. The question that is more applicable is whether there is any reason to believe that within the future euro area there is any reason to believe that one region or another will capture a competitive advantage that will benefit companies producing in that region relative to others. To the extent that the listed companies in that market use the local economy as a production base these may be equivalent questions.

Tight fiscal policy still an issue

On the current forecast by the Goldman Sachs Economics group, fiscal deficits in 1998 are expected to be at or below the 3 per cent of GDP target set out in the Maastricht Treaty — with the notable exception of Italy, where

Good bond markets...poor equities

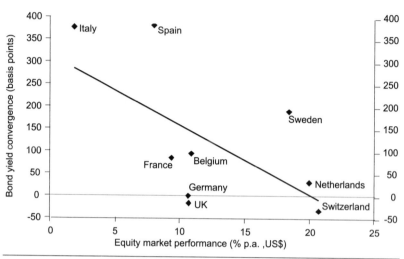

Figure 16.1   **Relationship between bond yield convergence and equity market performance, 1991-1996**

estimates suggest a deficit still near 3.5 per cent. Second, in the context of the Stability Pact agreed in Dublin in December 1996, which provides for penalties if deficits exceed 3 per cent after EMU starts, it seems likely that fiscal policy will remain tight in the first years of EMU. Other things being equal this is likely to affect adversely those businesses most dependent on the economies where further fiscal restraint is needed.

Figure 16.1 illustrates the impact of fiscal austerity on equities by comparing the performance of equity markets and bond markets during the five years to the end of 1996. This period encompasses the most dramatic convergence between the German and peripheral bond markets. In Figure 16.1, we have used the amount of bond market convergence of each local market against Germany as a measure of relative bond market performance measured on the vertical axis. The compound rate of rise of the local equity market in US dollars is measured along the horizontal axis. While the choice of common currency affects the absolute increase, the relative performance is unaffected by a change to a different base currency. As reflected in the figure, on these measures Italy and Spain have managed to produce both the best bond markets, with yields falling relative to Germany by nearly 400 basis points, and the worst equity markets. We believe that the explanation for this is that stringent fiscal policies (necessary to produce these good bond markets) have slowed the growth

Italy and Spain have had to devalue to generate growth...

	GDP	Earnings	Prices	Devaluations vs. US$
Germany	1.4	4	2.9	0.4
France	1.1	-5	2.0	0.5
Italy	1.0	9	4.6	5.9
Spain	1.3	1	4.7	6.3

Figure 16.2   **Economic performance 1991-1996, compound annual growth rates**
Source: OECD and Goldman Sachs

of the local economy and of earnings of the local equity market. Figure 16.2 compares the GDP growth, earnings growth of the listed market, inflation and currency changes against the US dollar for the four largest continental economies. The table demonstrates that to maintain the growth of the economy even at rates near 1 per cent, currencies in both Spain and Italy had to devalue by nearly 6 per cent per year against the Deutschemark. Even this was not sufficient to offset the impact on equity markets of the slow growth of the local economy. In US dollar terms, Spanish earnings fell at a rate of nearly 5 per cent per year through this period (1 per cent less 6.3 per cent).

In Italy and Spain a continuation of a tight fiscal policy without the potential offset of devaluation is likely to be particularly adverse as our estimates suggest that they are more dependent on their local economy for earnings than any other markets in Europe. Whereas Finland or Sweden may do well, despite a weak domestic market, as a result of the high proportion of earnings sourced offshore, this is not an option for Italy and Spain, where 70 per cent plus of earnings are dependent on the domestic economy.

Productivity trends

Productivity trends, however, put Spain in a better light. As reflected in Figure 16.3, among the major continental economies, Spain has had the best productivity trend since 1980: output per employee in the business sector rose by 2.9 per cent per year from 1990 to 1995. Even after allowing for the step down in average productivity after the incorporation of the east,

...but Spain has had strong productivity growth

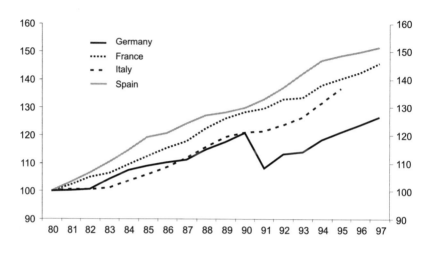

Figure 16.3   Productivity trends
Source: OECD

productivity improved by only 2.2 per cent per year in Germany over the same period. On these trends, it seems likely that Spain could do quite well and that the economy most likely to find itself in competitive difficulty, based on medium-term productivity trends, would be Germany.

Exchange rate trends

However, productivity trends tell only part of the story. An alternative way of assessing potential advantage in an EMU environment is to ask which currencies have had to depreciate historically in order to offset higher domestic costs and prices. The broad trend over the period since 1985 has been for a steady appreciation of the Deutschemark relative to the other major continental currencies.

The combination of a relatively weak productivity trend and a real appreciation of the Deutschemark might of course reflect Germany pricing itself out of goods markets, but even with this steady appreciation of the currency, the broad tendency of Germany's trade balance has been upward with the brief exception of the unification period (see Figure 16.4).

Germany's trade balance is very healthy...

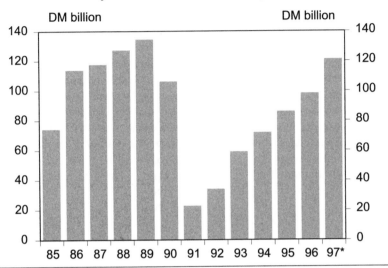

Figure 16.4 **German trade balance (current prices, seasonally adjusted)**
Source: Datastream

...despite a strong Deutschemark

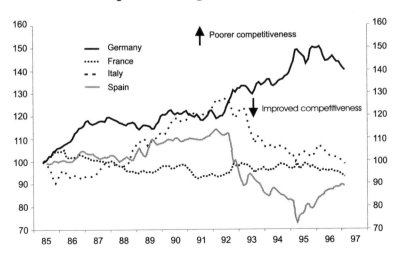

Figure 16.5 **Real effective exchange rates**
Source: IMF

Conclusion

It is difficult to draw conclusions based on trends over the past fifteen years given the distortions created by the advent of the single market, German unification and the sharp changes in the policy environment on the path to EMU, but it appears to us that Germany and the hard core currencies linked to the Deutschemark are more likely than not to win the competitive battle in the initial stages of EMU. In our view, the history of rescuing the economy by devaluation has failed to condition management, in those economies where this pattern has prevailed, to the constant battle to control costs which is a fact of life in a strong currency environment. Given the patterns of trade which prevail in Europe, the advent of the euro is likely to be equivalent to living in a hard currency environment for most European companies regardless of whether the euro is itself a strong currency relative to the US dollar. Deutschemark-based producers have lived with a strong currency for much of the past 40 years. While they have not always been successful in this environment, it has bred a management culture that seems more likely to cope with the euro environment than managements that have not had to live with the cost disciplines of a strong currency.

Section

VI

The euro

The euro:
accounting issues

Chapter 17

John Hegarty
*Secretary General, Fédération des
Experts Comptables Européens (FEE)*

The euro and accounting practices

Introduction

For those who feel that the 18 months remaining until 1 January 1999 provide inadequate time to prepare for the introduction of the euro, the news from the accounting front is likely to be unwelcome: in participating countries, the advent of the single currency should be accounted for in the financial statements for the year ending 31 December 1998, a reporting period less than 6 months away. This is irrespective of whether accounts are drawn up in euro or national currency denominations. Bearing in mind the possible taxation consequences, it is obvious that planning for the impact of the euro must begin now, and the purpose of this chapter is to give an overview of some of the considerations which should be taken into account. As befits a complex subject, however, there are many details and nuances which cannot be covered in a limited number of pages. Information is therefore provided on where more extensive material may be obtained.

Financial reporting - the key issue

In accounting terms, the main impact of the introduction of the euro is to realize all previously unrealized exchange gains and losses between participating currencies. On the assumption, for example, that France and Germany will be among the first wave countries, the French franc and Deutschemark will cease to be foreign currencies with respect to each other on 1 January 1999, when they simply become different expressions of the same currency, the single currency. Traditional rules for foreign currency translation cease to apply, and new treatments for the new euro take effect.

Two questions must be answered, to come up with the appropriate treatment:

- When should exchange gains and losses be considered realized ?

- How should realized exchange differences be accounted for ?

The preponderant view amongst accountancy professionals and regulators is that realization takes place in the period ending 31 December 1998. This reflects the fact that the irrevocable exchange rates will have been fixed by then and that all a company's assets and liabilities as at that date, previously denominated in another participating currency, will be sold or settled at that rate. In the normal course of events, market rates will have converged on the irrevocable rates during the period leading up to 1 January 1999, so that the closing rate on 31 December 1998 will be the same as the opening rate on 1 January 1999. In reality, therefore, the impact on companies already using the closing rate method should be nil. However, for companies not using the closing rate method (for example in Germany, where prudence requires the use of the lower of historical rate or closing rate) or in the event that the irrevocable rates are fixed at a level other than market rates, the choice of 1998 or 1999 is not a neutral one. This is at the origin of the controversy described below.

As regards how the realized differences should be accounted for, the majority opinion is clear-cut: they should be taken direct to the profit and loss account for the period ending 31 December 1998. Again on the assumption that the market rates are the same as the irrevocable rates, this should not have any impact on companies already using the closing rate. This will not be the case, though, if the rates are different or if prudent, German-style treatments have been applied to date. The latter will have ensured that all unrealized losses are taken into account as they arise, but not unrealized gains. There is therefore the potential for a one-off upwards earnings blip for those companies, for example, having outstanding debts in a participating currency which has weakened against the participating currency in which they report (e.g. a German company which borrowed French francs). Since those countries with conservative accounting practices tend also to be those with a very strong link between tax and financial reporting, the introduction of the euro could lead to an additional tax bill.

Given the wish of all concerned that the advent of the single currency should be tax neutral, there are two ways to deal with this problem. The preferable one would be to make the necessary amendments to the taxation legislation in the countries in question, to ensure that there is no tax on good accounting. Unfortunately, it now seems likely that some countries will leave the tax laws unchanged and instead achieve fiscal neutrality by manipulating the accounting treatment. This is explained in greater detail below.

European Commission: 'Accounting for the introduction of the euro'

In June, as part of a series of actions to provide enterprises with some form of certainty as to the regulatory consequences of the advent of the single currency, the European Commission published a non-binding paper on accounting for the introduction of the euro. The document was the result of consultations, undertaken since Summer 1996, between the Commission, the Accounting Directives Contact Committee of Member State officials responsible for the national implementation of EU financial reporting legislation, and the Fédération des Experts Comptables Européens (FEE), which represents the accountancy profession at European level. The paper makes clear that although a majority favoured realization in 1998 and the taking of differences direct to the profit and loss account, a minority did not. Rather than opt for one approach or the other, the document accommodates both, so that:

- Countries may permit the impact of the euro to be accounted for in 1999, instead of 1998.

- Countries may require or allow the deferral of positive exchange differences, instead of taking them immediately to the profit and loss account.

Since the ultimate decision will be made at the level of each individual member state, companies should pay very close attention to the different national dispositions will be adopted, and should assume that divergences in treatment will exist. Given that one of the objectives of the single currency is to strengthen the single market, it is to be regretted that a single accounting approach seems unlikely. Equally, companies that wish to comply simultaneously with national requirements and other standards — such as International Accounting Standards (IASs), or United States generally accepted accounting principles (US GAAP) — will have to cope with the likelihood that not all options included in the Commission paper will be considered compatible with IASs or US GAAP.

Other accounting issues

Exchange differences on consolidation

Only those exchange gains and losses relating to monetary assets and liabilities become realized on the introduction of the euro. No adjustments are required, for example, to fixed assets purchased in another participating currency. Equally, exchange differences on consolidation, which arise because of the impact of fluctuating exchange rates on foreign currency denominated investments in subsidiaries, will not be realized because of the euro, but only when the investment is disposed of.

Comparative information

Because of stock exchange or other requirements, companies may wish to restate in euro financial information relating to dates or periods predating the introduction of the single currency. This is problematical, because no national currency/euro rates exist until 1 January 1999. Two second-best alternatives present themselves: either the national currency/Ecu rate for the date in question, or the irrevocable national currency/euro rate. For purely pragmatic reasons, since neither is theoretically perfect, the balance of opinion has come down in favour of the latter. This has the advantage that year-on-year trends previously expressed in national currency remain intact (e.g. percentage growth in sales or earnings-per-share) and it avoids the counter intuitive phenomenon of exchange gains and losses arising in companies which had no foreign currency transactions or exposure. However, unlike the use of the national currency/Ecu rate, it ignores all previous fluctuations between participating currencies, and therefore distorts any comparisons of prior-period information between companies with accounts previously denominated in different participating currencies.

Conversion costs

The decision whether to capitalize or expense costs associated with the introduction of the euro will be governed by the same tests and rules as apply to other expenditure. In this sense, there is nothing different about the euro, such that costs should be written-off as incurred unless there is some identifiable future benefit. Equally, existing rules will determine whether a company can establish a provision for costs associated with the introduction of the euro, but not yet incurred.

Disclosure

In light of the many issues to which the single currency gives rise, and the likelihood of different treatments in different countries, companies should ensure that sufficient footnote disclosure is made in their accounts to allow users to have a clear understanding of the underlying events and transactions, and of the policies adopted to account for them.

Accounting records and publication of accounts

The realization of exchange gains and losses on monetary assets and liabilities denominated in other participating currencies, as described above, is triggered by the introduction of the euro, irrespective of whether a company prepares its accounts in euro or national currency denominations. In this regard, a company has no choice.

In line with the Madrid scenario, however, and the rule of "No compulsion, no prohibition" during the 3-year period of Phase B, a company should be free to choose when, during that period, it wishes to begin keeping its accounting records in euro and publishing its accounts in euro.

The timing of this switch will, in principle, be driven by a number of factors, including:

- The rate at which the company's transactions will switch to being denominated in euro, which in many cases will depend on decisions made by business partners rather than the company itself.

- The readiness of the company's accounting systems (for both internal and external reporting) to cope with the switch.

These considerations are largely academic, however, unless regulatory requirements permit the company to make a free choice. For example, many countries have stipulations (often enshrined in primary legislation) which oblige companies to maintain their accounting records and publish financial statements in national currency, so that changes are required to make operative the supposed freedom of action underlying the Madrid scenario.

Initially, the outlook was not positive. Public administrations in many countries took the view that "No compulsion, no prohibition" applied equally, if not more so, to them, and that they were not inclined to switch until the latest date possible i.e. 1 January 2002. With the exception of those Member States where companies were already free to use any currency of their choice (e.g. Ireland or the Netherlands), companies were confronted with not being able to switch, even if they wanted to, unless they were willing to incur the costs required to keep records and publish financial statements in both euro and national currency.

Recently, though, the situation has improved. Led by Belgium, a growing number of countries have published comprehensive national changeover plans which commit their public administrations to being able to deal in the euro, at least with companies if not always every citizen, from

1 January 1999. This will allow companies to choose the best course of action for themselves. As at the time of writing, unfortunately, two major exceptions remain outstanding: France and Germany. With respect to France, there is reason to hope that matters will change, but in Germany there is less reason for optimism. There, the administration of the taxation system is devolved to the Länder, which have indicated that they will need until 2002 to prepare themselves. The Federal Government may well introduce relaxations as far as record-keeping and accounts publication are concerned, but if tax authorities still require the use of Deutschemark denominations, the option to switch will remain unattractive.

Taxation - administrative issues

The likelihood of differences of approach in both the accounting and the taxation fields between participating countries reflects the reluctance of the European Commission to propose harmonizing legislation at EU level to facilitate the introduction of the euro and to ensure a consistent approach by all member states. With the exception of the two regulations establishing the legal framework for the use of the euro, no further proposals are likely to be forthcoming. To a certain extent, this is due to the lack of time to steer legislation through the normal decision-making process, but it also reflects a preference for allowing the operation of subsidiarity. In part, though, it is a consequence of an unwillingness of Member States to agree to fresh legislation, especially in the taxation field where, despite the Amsterdam summit, unanimity is still required.

To the problems of filing tax returns and making payments/refunds in euro should be added the issue of penalties for errors and omissions. Based on the experience of introducing the transitional VAT regime, it is inevitable that the changeover to the euro will lead to inadvertent mistakes in the making of declarations and returns. It seems unjust that these should be penalized, yet many countries' legislation leaves no room for discretion in the levying of penalties in such cases. In particular for SMEs, for whom the relative burden will be higher, Member States should introduce the amendments required to ensure a more pragmatic and equitable approach.

Taxation - technical issues

There is universal agreement in principle that the introduction of the euro should be tax neutral, but the earlier comments on accounting indicate how this may not be the case unless changes are made to the law in some Member States. The question of the tax treatment of exchange gains triggered by the single currency has already been explained. Also of concern is the tax treatment of conversion costs. Unless clarification is provided, there is the risk in some countries that, irrespective of the accounting treatment adopted, companies may not be able to deduct such spending for tax purposes as incurred, but may have relief spread over a number of years. This seems inequitable, as does the possibility that tax losses carried forward may be lost if the euro leads to the discontinuation of certain activities e.g. treasury operations involving participating currencies. Companies should not delay in examining their exposure to risks such as these.

In relation to indirect taxes, particularly value added tax, the potential problems are less acute in scale for business as a whole, although individual companies may find themselves at a particular disadvantage. Financial institutions, for example, can recover little or any of their input VAT, because output VAT is not levied on most financial services. As a consequence, VAT on supplies associated with preparing for the euro (e.g. computer hardware and software, consultancy fees) is irrecoverable, adding materially to the cost of conversion.

Helping business prepare for the euro

As the leading advisers to Europe's business community, from the smallest SME to the largest multinational, the accountancy profession has recognized its particular responsibility to help ensure as smooth a transition as possible to the single currency. This has been acknowledged by the European Commission which, as part of its overall communications programme on the euro, has provided very generous financial assistance for work by the Fédération des Experts Comptables Européens (FEE). FEE is the representative organization for the accountancy profession in Europe, grouping together 38 professional bodies in 26 countries with a combined membership of approximately 400,000 individuals. Of these, roughly 45 per cent are in public practice, with the other 55 per cent working in industry, commerce, government or education.

A key element of FEE's euro project is an internet-accessible database of detailed information and guidance on the practical aspects of the introduction of the euro. In addition to coverage of tax and accounting issues, it also deals with legal, IT, general and financial management, personnel and public sector topics, and is regularly updated to take account of new developments and information. Those wishing to explore in greater depth some of the subject s raised in this chapter should therefore visit the FEE euro website at:

www.euro.fee.be.

or turn for advice to their accountants and auditors.

Copies of a regular euro newsletter are also available from FEE at:

rue de la Loi 83
B - 1040 BRUXELLES
Belgium
Tel: + 32 (2) 285 40 85
Fax: + 32 (2) 231 11 12

Section
VII
The euro

The euro and the consumer

Paul Temperton
The Independent Economic Research Company (TIER)

Chapter
18

The euro and the consumer

Euro notes and coin will not be available in 1999...

When the euro is introduced in 1999 euro cash—notes and coin—will not be available immediately. The scenario agreed at the Madrid European Council in 1995 provides for euro notes and coin being introduced on 1 January 2002. A period of dual circulation of national currency and euro cash will then follow but by 1 July 2002 national currencies will no longer be legal tender and will be withdrawn from circulation.

If the euro is to become more generally established in the European economy, it would clearly be desirable for it to be used for retail and consumer transactions as soon as possible after its introduction. The absence of euro notes and coin is not necessarily an impediment to this: after all the many consumer transactions already take place by non-cash means—cheque, credit card, debit card etc. But notes and coin are psychologically important and without them it may well be difficult to encourage a widespread switch to use of the euro for consumer transactions.[1]

...but conversion rates will be fixed from 1 January

Conversion rates between euro area member currencies will be fixed from 1 January 1999. These conversion rates will be more than just 'fixed exchange rates'—'fixed' exchange rates can, after all, be changed. They are intended to be irrevocably-locked conversion rates between national currencies and the euro. Thus national currency amounts will simply be another manifestation of the euro amount.

---

[1] *This point is examined more fully in Chapter 9 (Congdon)*

Almost certainly, the conversion rates that link national currency amounts to the euro will not be round amounts such as 2:1 or 10:1, but rather will be fractions. It has already been agreed that conversion factors between national currencies and the euro will be expressed to six significant figures.

...so 'dual pricing' could occur from that time

Suppose, for example, that Ireland is a member of the euro area and that its conversion rate is set at:[1]

$$1 \ euro = I£0.732393$$

This conversion rate would then be used for converting all Irish £ prices into euro and vice versa. An article priced at I£4.99 would then have an equivalent price of 6.81 euros.

Dual pricing: euro prices rounded

Original price: **I£4.99**   Equivalent to: **€6.81**

Could be changed to: **I£4.39**   Equivalent to: **€5.99**

Or: **I£5.12**   Equivalent to: **€6.99**

Figure 18.1

---

[1] *For the mechanics of the setting of these conversion rates see Chapter 12 (McArdle)*

The question arises as to how the retailer and consumer will react once such conversion rates have been set. Some consumer associations have called for the use of 'dual prices' — i.e. national currency and euro amounts — to be made compulsory in the period from 1 January 1999 until euro notes and coin are introduced. Firms, in contrast, seem unwilling to accept the idea of binding legislation. Dual pricing involves costs — double labelling, modifications of computer systems, staff training and so on — which firms themselves would have to bear.

It is possible that consumers and retailers will continue to operate predominantly in domestic currency right up until the time that euro cash is introduced. The equivalent euro price of the national currency amount would then be little more than a detail of interest to some.

But suppose, on the other hand, the retailer wanted to shift to pricing his goods predominantly in euro. Suppose also that he wanted to preserve a price described in 'units plus 99 cents'. Then to use the earlier example once more, he might round the price up from 6.81 euros to 6.99 euros or down to 5.99 euros (see Figure 18.2).

Dual pricing: how price tags might look

Figure 18.2

But relative prices might be affected...

There would be major implications for the price of the product in question. In the first case, with prices rounded up, the price of the product increases by 2.6 per cent; in the second case, with prices rounded down, the price of the product falls by 12 per cent. Of course, such simple pricing strategies (i.e. using 99 as the subsidiary unit) may already have fallen out of fashion to some extent. And it would be possible (for some goods) to correct for any price change by making compensating changes to quantities (the Mars bar becomes bigger, loaf of bread smaller, etc.).

Even so, there could potentially be quite large changes in the relative prices of different goods, acting to distort the pattern of production and consumption.

...and there is a risk of consumer confusion

There is also a risk of consumer confusion. The situation has been likened to that following decimalization in the UK. There was widespread concern at the time that changing from 'pounds, shillings and pence' to 'pounds and new pence' would push prices up (see Figure 18.3).

It is true that UK inflation rose sharply soon after decimalization but it was not the cause: expansionary government fiscal policies, a rapid expansion of money and credit and the quadrupling of oil prices provide an altogether better explanation.

There are already examples of *multiple pricing*

There are already, well before the start of 1999, examples of retailers using price tags with prices expressed in various European currencies. For example, some UK retailers have used price tags similar to that shown in Figure 18.5. Such multiple pricing, however, uses relationships between prices in different currencies which are not based just on current exchange rates. Clearly, production costs, tax regimes and pricing strategies are different in different countries at the moment.

So this type of multiple pricing is quite different to that envisaged with dual pricing between national currency and euro amounts which would legally have to use the fixed conversion rates for converting national currencies into euro. The implication is that the current types of multiple pricing may be illegal after 1 January 1999.

UK inflation rose sharply...

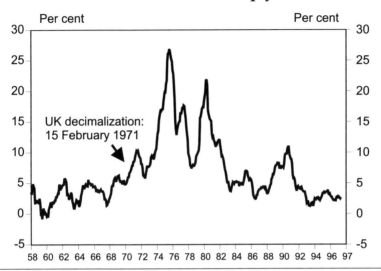

Figure 18.3   UK retail prices, per cent change on a year earlier

...after decimalization in 1971

Figure 18.4

A current example of multiple pricing

Figure 18.5

Costs of dual pricing

Of more practical concern to retailers and consumers, however, are the actual costs involved in switching from prices in national currencies to those — initially — in two currencies (national currency and euro) and then to prices in euro only. Retailers have made various estimates of the costs involved.[1] Marks & Spencer, for example, puts the cost of installing all the new systems and technology at £100 million, which implies a much larger figure (perhaps over £2000m) for the retail sector as a whole. *Eurocommerce*, representing retailers throughout the EU, have recently estimated the costs at 1.8 per cent of turnover. This would suggest that for all EU 15 countries the overall cost of switching to the euro could amount to as much as £25 billion. For comparison, that amounts to a one-off cost of £40 for each of the EU's 372m citizens.

---

[1] *See estimates quoted in Chapter 9 (Congdon)*

European tourism

Costs:
1.5% of turnover, one-off

Savings:
3.0% of turnover, continuing each year

Figure 18.6   Tourism: costs and savings from the euro
Source: Estimates presented to the European Parliament by the European tourist industry

Given the difficulties associated with dual pricing, the fact that it may be difficult to get consumers to switch over to 'thinking in euro' rather than national currencies, that relative prices might change and that the entire process will be quite costly, is it worth it?

The costs need to be set alongside the benefits that will come from the use of a single currency across a wide area. There will be benefits to consumers and retailers alike.

For consumers, there will be much greater transparency in the pricing of goods between countries. No longer will the consumer have to think in terms of which exchange rate to apply and the transaction costs involved in switching between currencies. The price of a good will be will be set in euros in all of the countries in the euro area. This transparency will be coupled with greater freedom of movement of goods and services within the single market and the overall effect should be to encourage competition and drive prices lower.

That will be a disadvantage to retailers who will find it increasingly difficult to differentiate prices between markets. But, offsetting this, retailers will benefit from generally much lower costs in conducting cross border business in the euro area. No longer need they be concerned about currency exchange rates and hedging currency exposure. Furthermore, whereas the costs of switching to the euro are generally 'one-off' — changing cash registers, training of staff, dual pricing for the interim period — the benefits are continuing.

This was recently demonstrated in a submission by the European tourist industry to the European parliament: the costs of moving to euro pricing were a one-off 1.5 per cent of turnover (i.e. a cost similar to those estimated by retailers) whereas the benefits of operating in euro were a continuing three per cent per year.

Conclusion

The transition from national currency to euro prices for the consumer is unlikely to be straightforward. From 1999 to 2002, the absence of euro notes and coin may impede the use of the euro for consumer transactions. And there are problems associated with dual pricing. But these costs to the consumer and the firm — which are essentially one-off costs — are likely to be easily offset by the longer terms benefits of greater price transparency, lower transactions costs and greater competition.

Section

VIII

The *euro*

Regulations & Provisions

Article 235 Regulation

COUNCIL REGULATION (EC) No 1103/97

of 17 June 1997

on certain provisions relating to the introduction of the euro

THE COUNCIL OF THE EUROPEAN UNION,

Having regard to the Treaty establishing the European Community, and in particular Article 235 thereof,

Having regard to the proposal of the Commission [(1), 1]

Having regard to the opinion of the European Parliament [(2), 2]

Having regard to the opinion of the European Monetary Institute [(3), 3]

(1)   Whereas, at its meeting held in Madrid on 15 and 16 December 1995, the European Council confirmed that the third stage of Economic and Monetary Union will start on 1 January 1999 as laid down in Article 109j (4) of the Treaty; whereas the Member States which will adopt the euro as the single currency in accordance with the Treaty will be defined for the purposes of this Regulation as the 'participating Member States';

(2)   Whereas, at the meeting of the European Council in Madrid, the decision was taken that the term 'ECU' used by the Treaty to refer to

---

1
  OJ No C 369, 7. 12. 1996, p. 8
2
  OJ No C 380, 16. 12. 1996, p. 49
3
  Opinion delivered on 29 November 1996

the European currency unit is a generic term; whereas the Governments of the fifteen Member States have achieved the common agreement that this decision is the agreed and definitive interpretation of the relevant Treaty provisions; whereas the name given to the European currency shall be the 'euro'; whereas the euro as the currency of the participating Member States will be divided into one hundred sub-units with the name 'cent'; whereas the European Council furthermore considered that the name of the single currency must be the same in all the official languages of the European Union, taking into account the existence of different alphabets;

(3)   Whereas a Regulation on the introduction of the euro will be adopted by the Council on the basis of the third sentence of Article 109l (4) of the Treaty as soon as the participating Member States are known in order to define the legal framework of the euro; whereas the Council, when acting at the starting date of the third stage in accordance with the first sentence of Article 109l (4) of the Treaty, shall adopt the irrevocably-fixed conversion rates;

(4)   Whereas it is necessary, in the course of the operation of the common market and for the changeover to the single currency, to provide legal certainty for citizens and firms in all Member States on certain provisions relating to the introduction of the euro well before the entry into the third stage; whereas this legal certainty at an early stage will allow preparations by citizens and firms to proceed under good conditions.

(5)   Whereas the third sentence of Article 109l (4) of the Treaty, which allows the Council, acting with the unanimity of participating Member States, to take other measures necessary for the rapid introduction of the single currency is available as a legal basis only when it has been confirmed, in accordance with Article 109j (4) of the Treaty, which Member States fulfil the necessary conditions for the adoption of a single currency; whereas it is therefore necessary to have recourse to Article 235 of the Treaty as a legal basis for those provisions where there is an urgent need for legal certainty; whereas therefore this Regulation and the aforesaid Regulation on the introduction of the euro will together provide the legal framework for the euro, the principles of which legal framework were agreed by the European Council in Madrid; whereas the introduction of the euro concerns day-to-day operations of the whole population in participating Member States; whereas measures other than those in this Regulation and in the Regulation which will be adopted under

the third sentence of Article 109l (4) of the Treaty should be examined to ensure a balanced changeover, in particular for consumers;

(6) Whereas the ECU as referred to in Article 109g of the Treaty and as defined in Council Regulation (EC) No 3320/94 of 22 December 1994 on the consolidation of the existing Community legislation on the definition of the ECU following the entry into force of the Treaty on European Union[1] will cease to be defined as a basket of component currencies on 1 January 1999 and the euro will become a currency in its own right; whereas the decision of the Council regarding the adoption of the conversion rates shall not in itself modify the external value of the ECU; whereas this means that one ECU in its composition as a basket of component currencies will become one euro; whereas Regulation (EC) No 3320/94 therefore becomes obsolete and should be repealed; whereas for references in legal instruments to the ECU, parties shall be presumed to have agreed to refer to the ECU as referred to in Article 109g of the Treaty and as defined in the aforesaid Regulation; whereas such a presumption should be rebuttable taking into account the intentions of the parties;

(7) Whereas it is a generally accepted principle of law that the continuity of contracts and other legal instruments is not affected by the introduction of a new currency; whereas the principle of freedom of contract has to be respected; whereas the principle of continuity should be compatible with anything which parties might have agreed with reference to the introduction of the euro; whereas, in order to reinforce legal certainty and clarity, it is appropriate explicitly to confirm that the principle of continuity of contracts and other legal instruments shall apply between the former national currencies and the euro and between the ECU as referred to in Article 109g of the Treaty and as defined in Regulation (EC) No 3320/94 and the euro; whereas this implies, in particular, that in the case of fixed interest rate instruments the introduction of the euro does not alter the nominal interest rate payable by the debtor; whereas the provisions on continuity can fulfil their objective to provide legal certainty and transparency to economic agents, in particular for consumers, only if they enter into force as soon as possible;

---

[1] *OJ No L 350. 31. 12. 1994, p. 27.*

(8)   Whereas the introduction of the euro constitutes a change in the monetary law of each participating Member State; whereas the recognition of the monetary law of a State is a universally accepted principle; whereas the explicit confirmation of the principle of continuity should lead to the recognition of continuity of contracts and other legal instruments in the jurisdictions of third countries;

(9)   Whereas the term 'contract' used for the definition of legal instruments is meant to include all types of contracts, irrespective of the way in which they are concluded;

(10)   Whereas the Council, when acting in accordance with the first sentence of Article 109l (4) of the Treaty, shall define the conversion rates of the euro in terms of each of the national currencies of the participating Member States; whereas these conversion rates should be used for any conversion between the euro and the national currency units or between the national currency units; whereas for any conversion between national currency units, a fixed algorithm should define the result; whereas the use of inverse rates for conversion would imply rounding of rates and could result in significant inaccuracies, notably if large amounts are involved;

(11)   Whereas the introduction of the euro requires the rounding of monetary amounts; whereas an early indication of rules for rounding is necessary in the course of the operation of the common market and to allow a timely preparation and a smooth transition to Economic and Monetary Union; whereas these rules do not affect any rounding practice, convention or national provisions providing a higher degree of accuracy for intermediate computations;

(12)   Whereas, in order to achieve a high degree of accuracy in conversion operations, the conversion rates should be defined with six significant figures; whereas a rate with six significant figures means a rate which, counted from the left and starting by the first non-zero figure, has six figures,

HAS ADOPTED THIS REGULATION:

Article 1

For the purpose of this Regulation:

–   'legal instruments' shall mean legislative and statutory provisions, acts of administration, judicial decisions, contracts, unilateral legal acts, payment instruments other than banknotes and coins, and other instruments with legal effect,

- 'participating Member States' shall mean those Member States which adopt the single currency in accordance with the Treaty,

- 'conversion rates' shall mean the irrevocably-fixed conversion rates which the Council adopts in accordance with the first sentence of Article 109l (4) of the Treaty,

- 'national currency units' shall mean the units of the currencies of participating Member States, as those units are defined on the day before the start of the third stage of Economic and Monetary Union,

- 'euro unit' shall mean the unit of the single currency as defined in the Regulation on the introduction of the euro which will enter into force at the starting date of the third stage of Economic and Monetary Union.

Article 2

1. Every reference in a legal instrument to the ECU, as referred to in Article 109g of the Treaty and as defined in Regulation (EC) No 3320/94, shall be replaced by a reference to the euro at a rate of one euro to one ECU. References in a legal instrument to the ECU without such a definition shall be presumed, such presumption being rebuttable taking into account the intentions of the parties to be references to the ECU as referred to in Article 109g of the Treaty and as defined in Regulation (EC) No 3320/94.

2. Regulation (EC) No 3320/94 is hereby repealed.

3. This Article shall apply as from 1 January 1999 in accordance with the decision pursuant to Article 109j (4) of the Treaty.

Article 3

The introduction of the euro shall not have the effect of altering any term of a legal instrument or of discharging or excusing performance under any legal instrument, nor give a party the right unilaterally to alter or terminate such an instrument. This provision is subject to anything which parties may have agreed.

Article 4

1. The conversion rates shall be adopted as one euro expressed in terms of each of the national currencies of the participating Member States. They shall be adopted with six significant figures.

2.   The conversion rates shall not be rounded or truncated when making conversions.

3.   The conversion rates shall be used for conversions either way between the euro unit and the national currency units. Inverse rates derived from the conversion rates shall not be used.

4.   Monetary amounts to be converted from one national currency unit into another shall first be converted into a monetary amount expressed in the euro unit, which amount may be rounded to not less than three decimals and shall then be converted into the other national currency unit. No alternative method of calculation may be used unless it produces the same results.

Article 5

Monetary amounts to be paid or accounted for when a rounding takes place after a conversion into the euro unit pursuant to Article 4 shall be rounded up or down to the nearest cent. Monetary amounts to be paid or accounted for which are converted into a national currency unit shall be rounded up or down to the nearest sub-unit or in the absence of a sub-unit to the nearest unit, or according to national law or practice to a multiple or fraction of the sub-unit or unit of the national currency unit. If the application of the conversion rate gives a result which is exactly half-way, the sum shall be rounded up.

Article 6

This regulation shall enter into force on the day following that of its publication in the *Official Journal of the European Communities*.

This regulation shall be binding in its entirety and directly applicable in all Member States.

Appendix 2

Article 109l(4) Regulation

Proposal for a Council Regulation [ ]
on the introduction of the euro

THE COUNCIL OF THE EUROPEAN UNION,

Having regard to the Treaty establishing the European Community, and in particular Article 109 1 (4) third sentence thereof,

Having regard to the proposal from the Commission,

Having regard to the opinion of the European Central Bank,

Having regard to the opinion of the European Parliament,

(1) Whereas this regulation defines monetary law provisions of the Members States which have adopted the euro; whereas provisions on continuity of contracts, the replacement of references to the ECU in legal instruments by references to the euro and rounding have already been laid down in Council Regulation [...]; whereas the introduction of the euro concerns day-to-day operations of the whole population in participating Member States; whereas measures other than those in this regulation and in the regulation on some provisions relating to the introduction of the euro should be examined to ensure a balanced changeover, in particular for consumers;

(2) Whereas, on the occasion of the meeting of the European Council, held at Madrid on 15/16 December 1995, it was decided that the term "ECU" used by the Treaty to refer to the European currency unit as a generic term; whereas "the Governments of the fifteen Member States have achieved the common agreement that this decision is the agreed and definitive interpretation of the relevant Treaty provisions"; whereas the name given to the European currency shall be the "euro"; whereas the euro as the currency of the participating Member States shall be divided into one hundred sub-units with the

name "cent"; whereas the definition of the name "cent" does not prevent the use of variants of this term in common usage in the Member States; whereas the European Council furthermore considered that the name of the single currency must be the same in all the official languages of the European Union, taking in account the existence of different alphabets;

(3)   Whereas the Council when acting according to Article 109 1 (4), third sentence of the Treaty shall take the measures necessary for the rapid introduction of the euro other than the adoption of the conversion rates;

(4)   Whereas whenever under Article 109 k (2) of the Treaty a Member State becomes a participating Member State, the Council shall according to Article 109 1 (5) of the Treaty take the other measures necessary for the rapid introduction of the euro as the single currency of this Member State;

(5)   Whereas according to Article 109 1 (4) of the Treaty the Council shall at the starting date of the third stage adopt the conversion rates at which the currencies of the participating Member States will be irrevocably fixed and at which irrevocably-fixed rate the euro will be substituted for these currencies;

(6)   Whereas given the absence of exchange rate risk either between the euro unit and the national currency units or between these nation currency units, legislative provisions should be interpreted accordingly;

(7)   Whereas the term "contract" used for the definition of legal instruments is meant to include all types of contracts, irrespective of the way in which they are concluded;

(8)   Whereas in order to prepare a smooth changeover to the euro a transitional period is needed between the substitution of the euro for the currencies of the participating Member States and the introduction of the euro banknotes and coins; whereas during this period the national currency units will be defined as sub-divisions of the euro; whereas thereby a legal equivalence is established between the euro unit and the national currency units;

(9)   Whereas in accordance with Article 109 g of the Treaty and with Council Regulation [...] on some provisions relating to the introduction of the euro, the euro will replace the ECU as from 1 January 1999 as the unit of account of the institutions of the European

Communities; whereas the euro should also be the unit of account of the European Central Bank (ECB) and of the central banks of the participating Member States; whereas, in line with the Madrid conclusions, monetary policy operations will be carried out in the euro unit by the ESCB; where as this does not prevent national central banks from keeping accounts in their national currency unit during the transitional period, in particular for their staff and for public administrations;

(10) Whereas each participating Member State may allow the full use of the euro unit in its territory during the transitional period;

(11) Whereas during the transitional period contracts, nation laws and other legal instruments can be drawn up validly in the euro unit or in the national currency unit; whereas during this period, nothing in this regulation should affect the validity of any reference to a national currency unit in any legal instrument;

(12) Whereas, unless agreed otherwise, economic agents have to respect the denomination of a legal instrument in the performance of all acts to be carried out under that instrument;

(13) Whereas the euro unit and the national currency units are units of the same currency; whereas it should be ensured that payments inside a participating Member State by crediting an account can be made either in the euro unit or the respective national currency unit; whereas the provisions on payments by crediting an account should also apply to those cross-border payments, which are denominated in the euro unit or the national currency unit of the account of the creditor; whereas it is necessary to ensure the smooth functioning of payment systems by making provision dealing with the crediting of accounts by payment instruments credited through those systems; whereas the provisions on payments by crediting an account should not imply that financial intermediaries are obliged to make available either other payment facilities or products denominated in any particular unit of the euro; whereas the provisions on payments by crediting an account do not prohibit financial intermediaries from co-ordinating the introduction of payment facilities denominated in the euro unit which rely on a common technical infrastructure during the transitional period;

(14) Whereas in accordance with the conclusions reached by the European Council at its meeting held in Madrid, new tradable public debt will be issued in the euro unit by the participating Member States as from 1 January 1999; whereas in order to allow issuers of

debt to redenominate outstanding debt in the euro unit; whereas the provisions on redenomination should be such that they can also be applied in the jurisdictions of third countries; whereas issuers should be enabled to redenominate outstanding debt if the debt is denominated in a national currency unit of a Member State which has redenominated part or all of the outstanding debt of its general government; whereas these provisions do not address the introduction of additional measures to amend the terms of outstanding debt to alter, among other things, the nominal amount of outstanding debt, these being matters subject to relevant national law; whereas in order to allow Member States to take appropriate measures for changing the unit of account of the operating procedures of organised markets;

(15) Whereas further action at the Community level may also be necessary to clarify the effect of the introduction of the euro on the application of existing provisions of Community law, in particular concerning netting, set off and techniques of similar effect;

(16) Whereas any obligation to use the euro can only be imposed on the basis of Community legislation; whereas in transactions with the public sector participating Member States may allow the use of the euro unit; whereas in accordance with the reference scenario decided by the European Council at its meeting held in Madrid, the Community legislation laying down the time frame for the generalisation of the use of the euro unit might leave some freedom to individual Member States;

(17) Whereas according to Article 105a of the Treaty the Council may adopt measures to harmonise the denominations and technical specifications of all coins;

(18) Whereas banknotes and coins need adequate protection against counterfeiting;

(19) Whereas banknotes and coins denominated in the national currency units lose their status of legal tender at the latest six months after the end of the transitional period; whereas limitations on payments in notes and coins, established by Members States for public reasons, are not compatible with the status of legal tender of euro banknotes and coins, provided that other lawful means for the settlement of monetary debts are available;

(20) Whereas as from the end of the transitional period references in legal instruments existing at the end of the transitional period will have to

be read as references to the euro according to the respective conversion rates; whereas a physical redenomination of existing legal instruments is therefore not necessary to achieve this result; whereas the rounding rules defined in Council Regulation [...] shall also apply to the conversions to be made at the end of the transitional period or after the transitional period; whereas for reasons of clarity it may be desirable that the physical redenomination will take place as soon as appropriate;

(21) Whereas point 2 of the protocol n°11 on certain provisions relating to the United Kingdom of Great Britain and Northern Ireland stipulates that, inter alia, point 5 of that protocol shall have effect if the United Kingdom notifies the Council that it does not intend to move to the third stage; whereas the United Kingdom gave notice to the Council on 16 October 1996 that it does not intend to move to the third stage; whereas point 5 stipulates that, inter alia, Article 109 1 (4) shall not apply to the United Kingdom;

(22) Whereas Denmark, referring to point 1 of the protocol no°12 on certain provisions relating to Denmark has notified, in the context of the Edinburgh decision of 12 December 1992, that it will not participate in the third stage; whereas. therefore, according to point 2 of this protocol, all Articles and provisions of the Treaty and the Statute of the ESCB referring to a derogation shall be applicable to Denmark;

(23) Whereas, according to Article 109 1 (4), the single currency will be introduced only in the Member States without a derogation;

(24) Whereas this regulation, therefore, shall be applicable pursuant to Article 189 of the Treaty, subject to Protocols n°11 and 12 and Article 109 k l.

HAS ADOPTED THIS REGULATION:

PART I

DEFINITIONS

Article 1

For the purpose of this regulation:

–   "participating Member States" shall mean [Countries A, B......]
–   "legal instruments" shall mean legislative and statutory provisions, acts of administration, judicial decisions, contracts, unilateral legal acts, payment instruments other than banknotes and coins, and other instruments with legal effect.

–   "conversion rate" shall mean the irrevocably-fixed conversion rate adopted for the currency of each participating Member State by the Council according to Article 109 1 (4) first sentence of the Treaty.

–   "euro unit" shall mean the currency unit as referred to in the second sentence of Article 2.

–   "national currency units" shall mean the units of the currencies of participating Member States as those units are defined on the day before the start of the third stage of Economic and Monetary Union.

–   "transitional period" shall mean the period beginning on 1.1.1999 and ending on 31.12.2001.

–   "redenominate" shall mean changing the unit in which the amount of outstanding debt is stated from a national currency unit to the euro unit, as defined in Article 2, but which does not have through the act of redenomination the effect of altering any other term of the debt, this being a matter subject to relevant national law.

Part II

SUBSTITUTION OF THE EURO FOR THE CURRENCIES OF THE PARTICIPATING MEMBERS STATES

Article 2

As from 1.1.1999 the currency of the participating Member States shall be the euro. The currency unit shall be one euro. One euro shall be divided into one hundred cent.

Article 3

The euro shall be substituted for the currency of each participating Member State at the conversion rate.

Article 4

The euro shall be the unit of account of the European Central Bank (ECB) and of the central banks of the participating Member States.

Part III

TRANSITIONAL PROVISIONS

Article 5

Article 6-9 apply during the transitional period.

Article 6

(1) The euro shall also be divided into the national currency units according to the conversion rates. Any sub-division thereof shall be maintained. Subject to the provisions of this Regulation the monetary law of the participating Member States shall continue to apply.

(2)

Where in a legal instrument reference is made to a national currency unit, this reference shall be as valid as if reference were made to the euro unit according to the conversion rates.

Article 7

The substitution of the euro for the currency of each participating Member State shall not in itself have the effect of altering the denomination of legal instruments in existence on the date of substitution.

Article 8

(1) Acts to be performed under legal instruments stipulating the use of or denominated in a national currency unit shall be performed in that national currency unit. acts to be performed under legal instruments stipulating the use of or denominated in the euro unit shall be performed in this unit.

(2)

The provisions of paragraph 1 are subject to anything which parties may have agreed.

(3) Notwithstanding the provisions of paragraph 1, any amount denominated either in the euro unit or in the national currency unit of a given participating Member State and payable within that Member State by crediting an account of the creditor, can be paid by the debtor either in the euro unit or in that national currency unit. The amount shall be credited to the account of the creditor in the denomination of his account, with any conversion being effected at the conversion rates.

(4) Notwithstanding the provisions of paragraph 1, each participating Member State may take measures which may be necessary in order to:

– redenominate in the euro unit outstanding debt issued by that Member State's general government, as defined in the European System of Integrated Accounts, denominated in its national currency unit and issued under its own law. If a Member State has taken such a measure, issuers may redenominate in the euro unit debt denominated in that Member State's national currency unit unless redenomination is expressly excluded by the terms of the contract, this provision shall apply to debt issued by the general government of a Member State as well as to bonds and other forms of securitised debt negotiable in the capital markets, and to money market instruments, issued by other debtors;

– enable the change of the unit of account of their operating procedures from a national currency unit to the euro unit by:

a) markets for the regular exchange, clearing and settlement of any instrument listed in section B of the annex of Directive 93/22/EEC on investment services in the securities field and of commodities; and

b) systems for the regular exchange, clearing and settlement of payments.

(5) Other provisions than those of paragraph 4 imposing the use of the euro unit may only be adopted by the participating Member States according to any time-frame laid down by the Community legislation.

(6) National legal provisions of participating Member States which permit or impose netting, set-off or techniques with similar effects shall apply to monetary obligations, irrespective of their currency

denomination, if that denomination is in euro or in a national currency unit, with any conversion being effected at the conversion rates.

Article 9

Banknotes and coins denominated in a national currency unit shall retain their status as legal tender within their territorial limited as of the day before the entry into force of this regulation.

Part IV

EURO BANK NOTES AND COINS

Article 10

At a date to be decided, in accordance with the Madrid scenario, when the present regulation is adopted, the ECB and the central banks of the participating Member States shall put into circulation banknotes denominated in euro. Notwithstanding Article 15, these banknotes denominated in euro shall be the only banknotes which have the status of legal tender in all these Member States.

Article 11

At a date to be decided, in accordance with the Madrid scenario, when the present regulation is adopted, the participating Member States shall issue coins denominated in euro or in cent and complying with the denominations and technical specifications which the Council may lay down in accordance with Article 105 a (2) second sentence of the Treaty. Notwithstanding Article 15, these coins shall be the only coins which have the status of legal tender in all these Member States. Except of the issuing authority and for those persons specifically designated by the national legislation of the issuing Member State, no party shall be obliged to accept more than fifty coins in any single payment.

Article 12

Participating Member States shall ensure adequate sanctions against counterfeiting and falsification of euro banknotes and coins.

Part V

FINAL PROVISIONS

Article 13

Articles 14-16 apply as from the end of the transitional period.

Article 14

Where in legal instruments existing at the end of the transitional period reference is made to the national currency units, these references shall be read as references to the euro unit according to the respective conversion rates. The rounding rules laid down in Council Regulation [...] shall apply.

Article 15

(1)   Banknotes and coins denominated in a national currency unit as referred to in Article 6 (1) shall remain legal tender within their territorial limits until six months after the end of the transitional period at the latest; this period may be shortened by national law.

(2)   Each participating Member State may, for a period of up to 6 months after the end of the transitional period, lay down rules for the use of the banknotes and coins denominated in its national currency unit as referred to in Article 6(1) and take any measures necessary to facilitate their withdrawal.

Article 16

In accordance with the laws or practices of participating Member States, the respective issuers of banknotes and coins shall continue to accept, against euro at the conversion rate, the banknotes and coins previously issued by them.

Part VI

ENTRY INTO FORCE

Article 17

This Regulation shall enter into force on 1st January 1999.

This Regulation shall be binding in its entirety and directly applicable in all Member States, in accordance with the Treaty, subject to Protocols n° 11 and 12 and Article 109 k 1.

Continuity of contract:
State of New York legislation

STATE OF NEW YORK

5049–A

Section 1. Article 5 of the General Obligations Law is amended by adding a New Title 16 to read as follows:

Title 16

Continuity of Contract

5-1601. Definitions. As used in this Title the following terms shall have the following meanings:

1. "Euro" shall mean the currency of participating member states of the European Union that adopt a single currency in accordance with the Treaty on European Union signed February Seventh, Nineteen Hundred Ninety Two.

2. "Introduction of the Euro" shall mean and include the implementation from time to time of economic and monetary union in member states of the European Union in accordance with the Treaty on European Union signed February Seventh, Nineteen Hundred Ninety-Two.

3.   "ECU" or "European Currency Unit" shall mean the currency basket that is from time to time used as the unit of account of the European Community as defined in European Council Regulation No. 3320/94. When the euro first becomes the monetary unit of participating member states of the European Union, references to the ECU in a contract, securitys or instrument that also refers to such definition of the ECU shall be replaced by references to the euro at a rate of one euro to one ECU. References to the ECU in a contract, security or instrument without such a definition of the ECU shall be presumed, unless either demonstrated or proven to the contrary by the intention of the parties, to be references to the currency basket that is from time to time used as the unit of account of the European Community.

5-1602. Continuity of Contract

1.   (A) If a subject or medium of payment of a contact, security or instrument is a currency that has been substituted or replaced by the euro, the euro will be a commercially reasonable substitute and substantial equivalent that may be either: (I) used in determining the value of such currency; or (ii) tendered, in each case at the conversion rate specified in, and otherwise calculated in accordance with, the regulations adopted by the Council of the European Union.

(B) If a subject or medium of payment of a contract, security or instrument is the ECU, the euro will be a commercially reasonable substitute and substantial equivalent that may be either: (I) used in determining the value of the ECU; or (ii) tendered, in each case at the conversion rate specified in, and otherwise calculated in accordance with, the regulations adopted by the Council or the European Union.

(C) Performance of any of the obligations described in paragraph (A) or (B) of this subdivision may be made in the currency or currencies originally designated in such contract, security or instrument (so long as such currency or currencies remain legal tender) or in euro, but not in any other currency, whether or not such other currency (i) has been substituted or replaced by the euro or (ii) is a currency that is considered a denomination of the euro and has a fixed conversion rate with respect to the euro.

2.   None of: (A) the introduction of the Euro; (B) the tendering of euros in connection with any obligation in compliance with paragraph (A) or (B) of subdivision one of this section ; (C) the determining of the value of any obligation in compliance with paragraph (A) or (B) of

subdivision one of this section ; or (D) the calculating or determining of the subject or medium of payment of a contract, security or instrument with reference to interest rate or other basis has been substituted or replaced due to the introduction of the euro and that is a commercially reasonable substitute and substantial equivalent, shall either have the effect of discharging or excusing performance under any contract, security or instrument, or give a party the right to unilaterally alter or terminate any contract, security or instrument.

5-1603. Effect of Agreements.

The provisions of this Title shall not alter or impair and shall be subject to any agreements between parties with specific reference to or agreement regarding the introduction of the euro.

5-1604. Application.

1.   Notwithstanding the uniform commercial code or any other law of this State, this title shall apply to all contracts, securities and instruments, including contracts with respect to commercial transactions, and shall not be deemed to be displaced by any other law of this State.

2.   In circumstances of currency alteration, other than the introduction of the euro, the provisions of this Title shall not be interpreted as creating any negative inference or negative presumption regarding the validity or enforceability of contracts, securities or instruments denominated in whole or in part in a currency affected by such alteration.

Section 2. This act shall take effect immediately.

Continuity of contract: ISDA Provision

International Swaps and Derivatives Association, Inc. (ISDA)

EMU Continuity Provision

[16]. EMU; Continuity of Contract.[1]

(a) The parties confirm that, except as provided in subsection (b) below, the occurrence or non-occurrence of an event associated with economic and monetary union in the European Community will not have the effect of altering any term of, or discharging or excusing performance under, the Agreement or any Transaction, give a party the right unilaterally to alter or terminate the Agreement or any Transaction or, in and of itself, give rise to an Event of Default, Termination Event or otherwise be the basis for the effective designation of an Early Termination Date.

---

[1] *This clause on European monetary union may be (i) included in Part 5 of the Schedule to a 1992 Multicurrency-Cross Border ISDA Master Agreement or in Part 4 of the Schedule to a 1992 Local Currency-Single Jurisdiction ISDA Master Agreement, in each case as an additional section in the Master Agreement, or (ii) added as an amendment to an existing 1987 or 1992 Master Agreement. If the parties would also like to confirm in their Agreement the allocation of responsibility for assessing and understanding the risks associated with EMU, they may consider adding the Representation Regarding Relationship Between Parties released by ISDA on March 6, 1996, where that representation accurately reflects how the parties are acting, their capabilities and the nature of their relationship. Different language should be used, for example, if one of the parties has agreed to act as an adviser to the other party*

"An event associated with economic and monetary union in the European Community" includes without limitation, each (and any combination) of the following:

(i)   the introduction of, changeover to or operation of a single or unified European currency (whether known as the euro or otherwise);

(ii)   the fixing of conversion rates between a member state's currency and the new currency or between the currencies of Member States;

(iii)   the substitution of that new currency for the ECU as the unit of account of the European Community;

(iv)   the introduction of that new currency as lawful currency in a member state;

(v)   the withdrawal from legal tender of any currency that, before the introduction of the new currency, was lawful currency in one of the Member States; or

(vi)   the disappearance or replacement of a relevant rate option or other price source for the ECU or the national currency of any member state, or the failure of the agreed sponsor (or a successor sponsor) to publish or display a relevant rate, index, price, page or screen.

(b)   Any agreement between the parties that amends or overrides the provisions of this Section in respect of any Transaction will be effective if it is in writing and expressly refers to this Section or to European monetary union or to an event associated with economic and monetary union in the European Community and would otherwise be effective in accordance with Section 9(b).

Index